The Development of the Personality

D1253494

The Development of the Personality

SEMINARS IN PSYCHOLOGICAL ASTROLOGY

Volume 1

Liz Greene and Howard Sasportas

SAMUEL WEISER, INC.

York Beach, Maine

First published in 1987 by
Samuel Weiser, Inc.
P. O. Box 612
York Beach, Maine 03910-0612
www.weiserbooks.com

08 07 06 05 04 03 02 01 00
13 12 11 10 9 8 7 6 5

Library of Congress Cataloging-in-Publication Data
Greene, Liz.
     Seminars in psychological astrology.   .
     Bbibliography: v. 1, p.
     Contents: v. 1. The development of the personality.
     1. Astrology and psychology. I. Sasportas, Howard. II. Title.
   BF1729.P8G735   1987
   133.5'815   86-33977

ISBN 0-87728-673-6 (v. 1)
BJ

Cover illustration copyright © 1987 Liz Greene

Typeset in 10 Point Palatino

Printed in the United States of America

The paper used in this publication meets the minimum requirements of
the American National Standard for Information Sciences—Permanence
of Paper for Printed Library Materials Z39.48-1992(R1997).

To our students

CONTENTS

Life has always seemed to me like a plant that lives on its rhizome. Its true life is invisible, hidden in the rhizome. The part that appears above the ground lasts only a single summer. Then it withers away—an ephemeral apparition....I have never lost a sense of something that lives and endures underneath the eternal flux. What we see is the blossom, which passes. The rhizome remains.

—C. G. Jung

INTRODUCTION

There was a time, not so very long ago, when an astrological consultation was something people sought because they wanted predictions about the future—money, love, health—and, if there was any "character analysis" involved at all, it consisted primarily of the astrological "cookbook" kind: You are a Gemini and therefore you are clever, versatile and articulate. This listing of static personality traits was either already well known to the client, in which case there was not a great deal of value to be gained from such a reading; or the client could not immediately identify with the character traits described, in which case the validity of astrology itself was consequently held in question.

Naturally there are still many people who go to an astrologer for these reasons—predictions and a pat on the back about one's apparently fixed and unalterable behaviour—and there are still many astrologers who will happily oblige such clients by providing the information requested. But over the years, particularly the last five years, there has been a gradual change not only in the reasons why people seek out astrologers, but also in the kind of people who seek them out; and the astrological community has in turn met this challenge and has begun to formulate a different and much more creative kind of astrology, built firmly upon tradition but adapted to the changing and more sophisticated needs of the client. There was a time, not so very long ago, when an astrologer's clientele was fairly predictable—a fair number of show business people, notoriously "superstitious" anyway, and a smattering of upwardly spiritually mobile aspirants hoping for a formula for enlightenment without mess. This, too, has been changing. Now the astrologer's client may be anybody at all, from a government minister to a secretary, from a doctor to an artist, from a computer programmer to a fashion model. Having one's horoscope interpreted is no longer an obscure sort of entertainment or a replacement for making choices in life.

The reasons for this shift lie in part in the increasing interest in—and investigation of—serious astrology, which has helped break down the barriers which often spring from the ignorant lay-man's assumptions about what astrology can and cannot do. But this increasing interest is itself a symptom of something. There may be some quite profound underlying reasons why we, as astrologers, are beginning to be taken more seriously; and why we, as astrologers, are increasingly being challenged to take ourselves more seriously, and more professionally, as well. For one thing, the astrological consultant has, willingly or not, been usurping what was once the role of the priest, the physician, and the psychiatrist. The client is no longer merely a gullible soul seeking fortune-telling, nor an esoterically inclined aspirant wondering what he or she was up to in the last incarnation. The client may be depressed without external cause; anxious or fearful; in the throes of an emotional crisis, or the breakup of a relationship; seeking serious insight into potential vocational opportunities; or troubled by apathy and an inability to make anything of his or her talents. In short, the client may have psychological problems and questions, and may be intelligently seeking insight into these problems in order to have a greater range of choices and responses—a situation which can apply to just about anybody at a certain crossroads in life. And with due respect to those readers who might be members of the clergy or of psychiatry, this client with psychological problems may often fail to find the tolerance or depth of understanding that the clergy might justifiably be expected to provide, receiving meaningless aphorisms instead; or may fail to obtain the insight into symptoms and the openness to discuss them without clinical labelling which the orthodox medical establishment sometimes finds rather difficult to offer. So, willingly or not, consciously or not, the consultant astrologer has arrived as a counsellor. And those astrologers who heatedly deny this psychological aspect of their work are at best naive and at worst destructive through their ignorance of what they are really dealing with. But for the most part, astrology has responded to this new role by accepting the psychological dimension of the study, and whatever term we wish to use—psychological astrology, astrological psychology, or simply good and insightful astrological counselling—astrology is coming of age and taking its place among the helping professions.

There is another thread to this fabric which is being woven out of the marriage of astrology and psychology, and that is the thread of meaning. Meaning is essential for life, and human beings seem to require it. Without meaning, there is often the feeling that we have nothing to live for, nothing to hope for, no reason to struggle for anything and no direction in life. Whether it is ultimately up to us to create our own meaning, or whether it is our task to discover some grand cosmic scheme or divine intention, the search for guidelines, goals, and a sense of purpose is an innate drive in all of us. And the problem of meaning has, in the last few decades, become an urgent one. Disillusionment with traditional religious structures accounts for some of this crisis of meaning which is upon us; and the increasing complexity of our lives in a world beset by new and daunting problems and challenges for which there are no existent guidelines or methods of approach accounts for even more of it. Loss of meaning is often the root from which spring the myriad psychological problems which masquerade as clinical symptoms, and loss of meaning is often the crisis which drives the client to seek an astrologer.

The astrologer who uses the chart as a counselling tool is in the unique position of helping others in this all-important search to find meaning in their lives. It is a task to be taken humbly, yet seriously. The man experiencing a difficult marriage with natal Venus square Pluto can be helped if he can find some meaning or relevance in his relationship troubles. What can he learn about himself through these issues? Why has he landed himself in this situation? What are the connections to earlier events in his life? Questions such as these may reveal a theme or pattern which he is unconsciously attracting and living out. A woman with Saturn conjunct Neptune in the tenth house, struggling to forge a career while facing debilitating anxieties, insecurities, and fears of failure, can be helped if these problems are appreciated and given significance within the larger context of her whole life and development. With the astrologer, she can explore the deeper archetypal conflict underlying her career problems, and what the struggle is asking her to learn about, face up to, and deal with in herself. Because of her dilemma, she may be pushed into developing certain qualities, resources or strengths which she might never have bothered to develop if the issue were not there in the first place; and this glimpse of an intelligible "reason" why we suffer is often the magical ingredient which can distill confidence and clarity out of a painful and confusing situation. Sign and house placements, aspects, transits, and progressions, not to mention life itself, all become more meaningful when understood in this way.

Psychological astrology has, like the old Roman god Janus, a double face. It can provide a surgical scalpel which cuts through to the underlying motives, complexes, and family inheritance which lie behind the manifest problems and difficulties which the individual faces; and it can also provide a lens through which can be viewed the teleology and purpose of our conflicts in context of the overall meaning of the individual's journey. Both faces ultimately turn toward a central mystery, the mystery of the human psyche of which astrology is both our oldest and our newest map.

The seminars in this book deal with the experiences of childhood and the development, dynamics, and structure of the personality. They are part of the training programme of the Centre for Psychological Astrology, founded and co-directed by the authors, with branches in both London and Zürich. The Centre was established to promote, explore, and encourage the use of astrology— both as a vehicle to self-knowledge and as an effective approach to counselling. These seminars—and transcriptions of others which will follow in further volumes of this series—are components in the three-year course of seminars, supervision groups, and classes which comprise the in-depth training in psychological astrology which the Centre provides.

In editing these transcripts, we have made every attempt to preserve a sense of the flavour and feeling of each of these one-day events. The reader is invited to fully experience and participate in them. It is hoped that the serious student of astrology will gain not only enriching insights into how to interpret the chart psychologically, but also will grow in the kind of personal self-understanding and self-knowledge which are such necessary ingredients for productive counselling of any kind.

Liz Greene
Howard Sasportas
November, 1986

PART ONE

THE STAGES OF CHILDHOOD

The childhood shows the man,
As morning shows the day.

—John Milton

It's never too late to have a happy childhood.

—Anonymous

YOUR INBORN IMAGES

In today's seminar we are going to explore what the chart reveals about our childhood experiences, traumas and adjustments and how these relate to our current lives. We are going to explore childhood and the past for a reason—in order to unclutter the present. It's no use just wallowing around in what you think your mother or your father did to you; but you can go back and examine your early experiences in order to understand the present better and move forward in your lives right now. We deal with the past when it's standing in the way of the future.

Right from the beginning, I want to draw a basic distinction between the way in which many schools of traditional psychology view childhood experiences and the way psychological astrology looks at early life events. Certain branches of traditional psychology uphold the idea that the child is born a blank slate upon which different things are subsequently written. This is called the *tabula rasa* theory—the notion that how other people treated you in early life gives rise to certain patterns or "scripts" which then determine your self-image and your expectations of what will happen to you later in life.

Let me explain this further. Around different experiences in childhood, certain decisions or attitudes are formed or made about ourselves or about life in general. These might be called "existential life-statements." For instance, if Mother isn't very adept at looking after you, then a pattern or expectation or statement about life is formed such as, "the world is not such a safe place to survive in," or, "those I need most will let me down." Or if Father storms out, disappears and abandons the family when you are three years old, it may give rise to a belief or expectation or statement about life, such as "men are unreliable," or, "I'm so bad I drive people away." Early experiences cut very deeply—you've heard me use the analogy before that if you take a young tree or sapling and make a small cut in its bark, when it grows into a mature tree, it will have a large cut in it.

What happens early in life forms a very deep impression on us. Very often these impressions are embedded in the unconscious; we don't even remember them. But we carry those expectations and beliefs around with us and we continue to perceive and organise experience according to them. In other words, how we see and evaluate the present is conditioned by what has happened in the past. Sometimes this is referred to as "psychic determinism." Any particular mental event or phenomenon is connected to chronologically preceding events. Even a fantasy about what happened in the past can determine how we interpret the present; it doesn't have to be something that actually happened. So, if you imagined that *you* drove Father away, when in actual fact he left for entirely different reasons, the earlier fantasy will still influence your later expectations. Later in life, we selectively perceive or pick out of any circumstance those things which support our assumptions and beliefs, and we fail to see what doesn't fit into these expectations. Someone once said that "life obliges our expectations." In short, our beliefs and expectations give rise to our experience of reality which in turn reinforces the original beliefs.

Now psychological astrology views all this slightly differently. Rather than just being born a blank slate and having things done to you which then lead you to form opinions about life and yourself, psychological astrology believes that you are *already* born with an innate predisposition which expects certain things to happen. It is not just the childhood conditioning which is of primary importance—*it is your own inner nature as seen through placements in the birth chart which predisposes you to perceive experience in a certain way.* Certain inborn archetypal expectations structure what you filter out of experience as a child. I'll explain this more precisely.

An archetype can be defined as a mental representation of an instinct. Because human beings have been around for so long, eons of time and the evolutionary processes have built up and structured into our psyches certain expectations which are passed down generation after generation—a kind of "cell wisdom." One of our built-in expectations is that there is going to be a mother, or to get even more basic, that there is going to be a nipple. Even in the womb we have an expectation of a nipple—it is carried in our cell memory. In our cell memory is also the expectation of a father, and the expectation of growth and death. All these images are there latent in us even before we have an actual experience of such things.

We are already born with an image of mother, an image of that archetype; and we are already born with an image of father, an image of birth, an image of growth, an image of death, etc. But different people have slightly different images of these archetypal phenomena. There are different varieties and brands of these images. For instance, the Moon has to do with mother and all of you have the Moon in your chart, so you all have an expectation of mother already there from birth, even before you actually encounter her. But the nature of your image of mother, the more exact kind of mother *you* are anticipating, is shown by your sign placement of the Moon and what sort of aspects are made to it. Similarly, you have right from the beginning, a sense that there will be a Father. Everyone has this—you all have the Sun in your charts and you can take the Sun to mean father. But the sign placement and aspects of the Sun will more exactly color and describe your own particular inborn image of what father is going to be like for you. Remember that perception is a function of expectation and that content is a function of context. What you are expecting to see will influence how you perceive what is actually there.

Inborn images and archetypes organize and structure what we experience. So, if you are born with Moon trine Jupiter then you have an inborn expectation of abundance and expansion coming through mother. Because this is what you expect to see, your perception will be selective; and you will tend to register more readily the times when she is being generous, expansive and Jupiterian, rather than other times when she may be cold and restricting. But, if you are born with Moon conjunct Saturn, then you already expect some difficulty or coldness around the mother and you are innately attuned to notice the times she fits that picture more than when she acts in other ways.

We will get into a fuller discussion of aspects later, but the point I wish to make now is the distinction between many branches of traditional psychology and psychological astrology. Traditional psychology often blames the parents for what they do to us; but psychological astrology says that we are partly responsible for how we experience our parents—because of our tendency to interpret the mother's and father's actions on the basis of inborn assumptions and beliefs about what we are likely to meet. What the parents are actually like will serve to drive these innate impressions in deeper or perhaps serve to mediate or mollify some of our basic expectations of them. If we expect a very bad mother and she turns out to be loving and an extremely safe container, some of our negative expectations may be toned down. If we are born with an inner image of a Terrible Mother, we will expect to find a terrible mother. So, if it turns out that our actual mother, for whatever reason, cannot cope with us, then that archetypal expectation is driven home deeper. It is given flesh and bone based on our actual experience of her.

For example, let's say that a boy child is born with Moon square Pluto. A possible inborn image of mother based on this aspect could be that she is potentially dangerous or life-threatening (the archetype of the Moon, mother, is connected to that of Pluto, a destructive force). Mother may not actually be all that much of a Plutonic type person, but the child is particularly sensitive to when she has those moods and phases, so notices this in her more. One day she gives him a particularly good feed and puts him down, expecting that he should be happy and content. But for some reason, his Moon square Pluto is activated that day (maybe a fast transit to it by the Moon or Venus) and even after his good feed and after he is gently put down into his cot, for no obvious reason, the negative image of mother is activated in his psyche. So he starts screaming and crying. Now, Mother has just fed him well—what has he got to cry about? If the mother reacts by shaking him and being frustrated and angry, then he thinks, "see, I knew all along she was a witch." In this way, the inborn negative image of mother is driven home deeper. If the mother doesn't react to his frustration in that manner, but picks him up, holds him and contains his screaming fit without responding negatively to it, the image of the bad mother he was born with is mediated and mollified. "Well, maybe she is not so bad after all." Perhaps it would be good for mothers to study the charts of their babies to derive a sense of what the child could be projecting onto them, and learn how to do a dance with these projections so they can attempt to help mollify the more negative ones.

To sum up: what we are talking about is what is known as the "nature versus nurture" conflict in psychology. Those who believe in the *nurture* side believe that it is how we are treated as children that determines who we are. Those who believe in the *nature* side believe that we are born with a certain nature which then determines how we experience life. Psychological astrology obviously has a bias towards the idea that we are born with a certain innate nature, that our archetypal conditioning pre-dates our childhood conditioning. It's undoubtedly a mixture of both, but psychological astrology would put inborn nature first and actual childhood conditioning second, because we have a tendency to perceive the events and people surrounding us in childhood through the spectacles of our own nature. If we are wearing blue glasses, life looks blue. If we are wearing red glasses, life looks red. Most importantly, it is the birthchart which depicts our archetypal conditioning and expectations.

ARCHETYPAL PATTERNS AS SHOWN IN THE BIRTHCHART

Let's do a little work with the chart. A very clear way to see the basic patterns and expectations you are born with is to take certain key aspects and placements in the chart and get a sense of what statements about life or archetypal expectations these might describe. This is what I want you to be thinking about throughout the day—that every aspect or placement in your chart describes some kind of pattern in you. These patterns give rise to statements, beliefs, or assumptions about yourself or about life. For instance, what do you think might be the belief or expectation of someone born with Moon square Saturn? What might this person's statement be about the archetype of mother, even before the mother is actually experienced?

Audience: Some sense of rejection or coldness.

Howard: Make that into a statement.

Audience: Mother is cold.

Howard: Okay, one statement might be "Mother is cold." What other statements can come from this aspect?

Audience: Mother is rigid and unloving or inadequate.

Howard: Yes, but what kind of statements might come up about a person's own emotions?

Audience: There might be a statement like, "I have trouble with my emotions."

Howard: Right. What else is the Moon? The Moon has to do with getting one's needs fulfilled, so what kind of statement is there about having one's basic needs met?

Audience: My basic needs don't get met.

Howard: Yes, this is often the experience of those with Moon square Saturn—some difficulty in having their emotional and even physical needs satisfied. Okay, forget the Moon for now. What if you have Venus square Saturn? Venus is the archetype that has to do with union, with the image of the beloved. What kind of statement might come from that aspect?

Audience: I will be rejected in relationship.

Howard: Something like that, or even something more basic like, "in relationship (Venus) I am going to meet trouble (Saturn)." But don't forget that Saturn also implies hard work. So on another level, there may be a belief or expectation that, "I'm going to have to work hard at making a relationship." What if you have Venus trine Jupiter? What kind of life statement or assumption about relationship might you have with that aspect?

Audience: My beloved is going to be expansive and open me up.

Howard: Yes, and even something like, "I have so much to give in relationship." The archetype of union (Venus) is brought together in some way with the archetype of expansion (Jupiter). These are the kinds of expectations people with this aspect are born with. It exists even before they have a relationship, before they date anyone. This is their image of what they are going to experience through Venus. If that is what they are expecting to meet, that is what they will notice, look for, or help set up, consciously or unconsciously.

Obviously life is more complicated than this. Someone may have Venus both square Saturn and trine Jupiter, as well as Moon conjunct Uranus. What I want you to do today is to look at your chart and reflect on what some of the statements you have about life might be which fit with the aspects and placements in your chart. We'll be examining childhood experiences, because in childhood we can often see these patterns and life-statements operating the most clearly. They come sharply into focus in childhood. We are born with skeletal expectations—a framework of what we will experience—and then our actual experiences as children add layers to these expectations, giving them flesh and substance.

Different archetypes are brought out at different stages of life.[1] For instance, at birth the part of the chart which is foreground is the ascendant. So, issues around your ascendant will be brought up at the birth experience. For the first two years of life the main drive is survival and getting your needs fulfilled; and the principle in the chart which is most important then is the Moon. Therefore, your innate patterning around the Moon will be fleshed out between birth and two years old. Archetypes come through drives and drives come through foreground issues. Between the ages of two and four, the drive is to assert yourself, to be more autonomous: you start to walk, learn to talk, you want to assert your individuality more and flex your muscles. At this time the foreground issue is greater autonomy. The archetypes that are coming through this issue are those of power, self-assertion, self-control, mastery of environment and potency. The *main* planets activated in connection to these principles are the Sun and Mars. So between two and four issues around the Sun and Mars will be more clearly brought to focus in your life. After four, when we become more aware of mother and father as a unit, issues around relationship come out and the archetype of Venus comes to the fore. Your patterns around Venus can be seen during that Oedipal phase.

WORKING WITH PATTERNS

Our purpose today is not just discovering our patterns but also to begin to do something about working with them if we wish to do

---

[1]For many of the psychological concepts presented here, I am indebted to Diana Whitmore, founder of the Psychosynthesis and Education Trust in London, whose workshop on "Childhood and the Unconscious" (October-December, 1980) incited my thinking in this area. Since then, she has written *Psychosynthesis in Education: A Guide to the Joy of Learning* (Wellingborough, England: Turnstone Press, 1986), which examines the psychological and spiritual development of children and adolescents.

so, or if we are not happy with them. And even if it is impossible to change or radically alter some of these patterns, we can at least work on changing our attitudes towards them. I want to talk about patterns in general. There is a poem by an American poetess, Amy Lowell, called *Patterns* and the last line always stuck in my head when I read it in high school: right at the end she says, "Christ, what are patterns for?"

I don't believe that the deeper Self sends you difficult patterns or lots of squares and oppositions just to torture you—I don't think the Self is that wicked. Nonetheless, we are born with certain archetypal beliefs and expectations which we have to work with. Maybe it's related to heredity and genetics—that we inherit unresolved issues or conflicts from our ancestors; that what they have gone through or contended with is passed down to us through some sort of "psychogene," just as physical characteristics are passed down to us. Genes are passed down from generation to generation and we not only inherit physical traits, but we also inherit psychological issues or unfinished emotional business. Maybe an ancestor, or set of ancestors, had trouble with the right use of assertion and power and you are born with Mars conjunct Saturn square Pluto. You inherit something of their unworked-through problems with assertion and it is up to you to redeem this in some way. Or you might inherit a dilemma between one set of traits from certain ancestors and another set of traits from other ancestors. Let's say that certain of your ancestors were Jupiterian swashbuckling pirates while others were Saturnian local magistrates. You might then be born with Jupiter square Saturn. One part of you wants to be free and expansive (Jupiter) and another part is pulled toward conventionality and settling down (Saturn).

Or perhaps we are born with particular patterns, expectations, and beliefs because of something to do with past lives, karma and reincarnation. *Put extremely simply*, if you had certain difficult experiences with mothers in previous lifetimes, you may be born with an expectation of difficulty with a mother in this life—some challenging Moon aspects or hard placements in the 10th (if you take the 10th to mean mother). Or maybe you were an incompetent mother in a previous lifetime, so you are born with an image around the Moon which reflects this.

Once you become aware that you have a bias to see things in a certain context, or that you have certain inborn assumptions or beliefs, then you can start working within that framework to gradually expand the borders of a belief or pattern to allow for other alternatives. Let's take the Moon square Saturn as an example, which we already suggested might be the experience of difficulty with the mother or getting the needs fulfilled. But, on another level, if we stay within the parameters of these two archetypal principles—the Moon and Saturn—then this aspect could also have something to do with learning (Saturn) about the emotions (the Moon). In other words, Moon square Saturn also means learning about and working on emotional issues and working on the relationship with the mother. On one level Saturn is symbolic of difficulty and restriction, but on another level it indicates the mastery of something that comes through hard work and effort. The poet Goethe, who had Saturn rising in Scorpio, once said, "It is in limitation that the master first shows himself." Saturn points out what is weak, lacking or inadequate, but also where, through effort and work, we become strong. Although we are stuck with the archetype of the Moon being influenced by the archetype of Saturn, we can try to find more creative ways of bringing together these two principles rather than getting stuck on a level where we are aware *only* of the pain. Once we discover the underlying pattern and archetypal principals involved—what they mean and the different levels they can manifest on—we can try to bring them together in other ways. We still may need the pain and difficulty, but other things become possible as well.

Audience: That's interesting. I have Moon conjunct Saturn and I lead ante-natal classes for mothers. I always felt that by working with mothers, I was working through something myself.

Howard: It is possible that if you use the aspect up on one level or dimension, you are less likely to have to experience it on other levels. Of course, you may still need the challenge of Moon-Saturn on a personal level to trigger a certain kind of growth.

Nonetheless, as much as possible, I would encourage people to *consciously* create structures in their lives through which aspects can express themselves. Take the Sun square Neptune for example. The Sun represents a masculine principle—assertion, expression and spirit. Neptune touching it brings in the qualities of sensitivity and creativity as well as weakness, dissolution, dissipation and elusiveness. If we take the Sun to represent the image of father, the person's experience of father (the Sun) will be coloured by Neptune. The father will receive the Neptunian projection and the child with this aspect will be sensitive to the father's Neptunian side. Sometimes certain fathers act this out rather well—they drink too much, become dependent on drugs, are ill or ailing, psychologically absent or simply disapper off to sea. (Even if the father's chart isn't all that Neptunian, the child with Sun in aspect to Neptune will register the times he is that way.) In some way the father cannot be relied upon or isn't tangibly present. Or the father is creative, artistic and very sensitive. I once saw the chart of the daughter of a well-known actor in America. She had the Sun square Neptune. The Neptune came not just through his acting talent, but also because of his fame—he was in great demand and often away from home. In her case, she had to sacrifice (Neptune) the father; she had to give him up to the world. She had a lot of pain around that and in some ways she was still trying to attract his attention and make herself special to him. This also can happen to the children of clergymen—the father belongs as much to the congregation as to the family. Consequently, children with this aspect may grow up with a wounded sense of their worth, specialness and identity which is related to a loose connection to the father. There may be a statement about life such as, "I don't know who I am," or, "I have to give up what I want."

Now, if you are born with Sun square Neptune, you are stuck with having Neptune affecting the Sun—there is really no way you can avoid that. You can't even blame others for it because it's your own archetypal pre-conditioning. But you could think about ways you might bring the Sun and Neptune together more constructively or more positively than just wandering around with a weak or nebulous sense of identity or power. Can you think of any way people with this aspect could consciously connect their identity with Neptune in a more constructive way than feeling dissolved or confused?

Audience: What about through doing something artistic or creative?

Howard: Yes, they might work on opening themselves up as a channel through which artistic expression could flow. They could take up dance or poetry as a way of expressing themselves—give themselves to the muse. Or, they could try something like meditation; twice a day sitting to meditate, dissolving and letting go of the ego-boundaries and merging with something greater than the self. Doing this, they are using up some of the way this aspect might manifest. They are taking responsibility for bringing the archetypes of the Sun and Neptune together in different ways than just being confused or vague. They are creating alternatives for the use of these energies. Of course, if they meditated too much, they would end up spaced out and back to "go."

An archetype can express itself on many different levels, and if it isn't working well on one level, you can start experimenting with others. This also applies to house placements. The 5th house has to do with children as well as personal creativity, such as painting, drawing, writing and music. If you are having trouble with your children (something like Saturn conjunct Uranus in the 5th square Mars in the 8th), a good suggestion is to go out and become involved in other levels of the 5th house—other things besides being with or having children. Take a course in art, join an amateur dramatic society or dance group and then you are using up some of what is in the 5th house. Other spheres besides children will appropriate the placements there and it takes the pressure off the relationship with your children to carry the burden of it. I have Mars conjunct Saturn and Pluto in my 7th house, the house of partnership. When Zip Dobyns looked at my chart many years ago, she advised me to form a business partnership with someone. She suggested that the business relationship would use up some of the energy of Mars-Saturn-Pluto so that it wouldn't have to all come through more intimate or personal relationships. I tried it and it worked. I started a meditation center with a Capricorn friend of mine and simultaneously my more personal relationships became less tense and complex. The business partnership carried some of what the conjunction in my 7th indicated.

But, as usual, I am diverting. I want to discuss how we can work with some of our patterns, life-statements, scripts and chart placements in order to experience them more fully, understand them more fully, and then transform and transmute them if possible. As I've already said, patterns or existential life-statements are principles by which we live. Patterns give rise to the kinds of dreams we have, to the kinds of traumas we have, and to the kinds of illnesses we have. Our patterns and beliefs set the parameters of what we are going to experience in life. *Paradigm* is the Greek word for pattern; a paradigm is a conceptual framework through which we view experience. For example, before the 16th century, there was the widely held paradigm that the Sun moved around the Earth—this was a belief upon which the perception of reality was based.

Another word for paradigm or pattern is something called a "mental set." For instance, a very depressed person may have a mental set that the world is out to "get" him and he will organize his experience of the world according to this mental set: he'll see or interpret experiences as threatening and he won't even see the ones which are life-supporting because he can only view the world through his particular framework. Related to this is the idea of self-image or self-model. Some people call the self-image a meta-paradigm or meta-set, because psychologically speaking, our self-image determines so much of what happens to us and so much of the way in which we perceive the world. For instance, a man who is fat may have a self-image of being a fat man. Let's say he goes on a diet and really slims down. However, if he is still walking around with a self-image of himself as fat, he will probably just get fat again.

EXPERIENCING AND UNDERSTANDING PATTERNS

The first step in working with our patterns and beliefs is to fully *experience* them. Different patterns or beliefs related to various aspects in the chart might be statements like, "I have to struggle to survive," or something like, "all men are bastards," or, "those I love, leave me." Experiencing a pattern means fully getting in touch with it. There's an exercise which is designed to help you do this. I am not going to do it with you today, but you can try it sometime. Look at your chart and pick out an aspect in it—let's say Venus square Saturn—and find what your statement about life is which relates to this placement. The statement may be, "I'm not good enough to be loved." Then give a lecture to another person based on your statement. Really exaggerate it; really dramatize it. "I'm so awful and ugly and disgusting, how could anyone love me?" "I'm a crawling insect with nothing to give, pure yuk. . . . etc." Feel the impact of your life-statement and this aspect on your body and feelings. Or if you have Sun square Pluto and your statement is, "men are deceitful or out to undermine me," then give a lecture to someone on that—fully bring this belief out into the open and play it up. There may be other parts of you which think differently, but during this exercise just focus on that pattern or belief. You have to fully experience something before you can begin to dis-identify from it or transmute it. You can't transform something you haven't "owned" or acknowledged in yourself.

Therapy can help bring out patterns; a chart reading can help bring out patterns. Once we have experienced what the pattern is, the next step is *understanding* it. Take a closer look at it, think about it and reflect on it. Examine the archetypal principles involved in the pattern and how it relates to your childhood experiences. Astrology gives us a language and a framework through which these things can be examined and explored. Looking at the chart not only puts you in touch with your basic archetypal patterning but enables you to step back and reflect on it.

WAYS OF POSSIBLY TRANSFORMING PATTERNS

After experiencing a pattern and gaining some understanding of it, the next step is *transmutation*: finding some way to change that statement about life—to change that belief, assumption or expectation. The task is to redirect the archetypes involved into some new life statement, to re-choose how to use the energies involved. I don't think it's easy to get rid of an old pattern because it has quite a hold on us. And if you try to fight a belief or assumption you have about life, you are actually giving a message to yourself about how important that belief is and you may drive it in more. Rather than trying to fight it, I think it's better to create a new belief and pay a little more attention to the new one. In this way, you are not trying to destroy the old pattern, but rather you are starving it of attention by creating an alternative belief or expectation. You create a shift in dominance from the old one to the new one.

I'll give you an example from a chart I did the other day. A twenty year old woman came for a reading. She had Uranus conjunct Pluto in Virgo in the 10th house in opposition to the Sun conjunct Mars in Pisces in the 4th. One of her basic statements about life was that she was weak and ineffective compared to other people. She was very scared of the world. As the opposition from the 10th to the 4th suggests, her early home life had been disruptive. Her father left home when she was still young and part of her sense of weakness might stem from her inability as a child to do anything to stop the parents' splitting up. For a young child, the breaking up of the parental marriage is akin to the whole world falling apart and splitting into two and she couldn't do anything about this. It is as if she felt her will (Sun and Mars in Pisces) was over-ruled by an impersonal force of destruction and change (Uranus and Pluto opposing the Sun and Mars). In addition, she saw her mother as very strong, powerful and slightly threatening, all of which added to her own sense of inferiority. In this case the Uranus-Pluto conjunction in Virgo in the 10th fitted well with the mother. The girl projected her image of the dominant and powerful mother onto the world—for her it was dangerous and more powerful than she was, full of people bigger and stronger than her.

Now, it would be hard for her to rid herself entirely of the belief that the world out there was a threatening place beyond her control—her early environment had brought out such a belief; but we talked about the possibility that the world also had some okay aspects to it and that it was possible for her to be effective and have some influence. We worked on forming a new-life statement which included the old one but added another possibility on to it. "Yes, the world at times can seem overwhelming, threatening and unsafe, but sometimes people are all right and it's also possible to have some influence in it." After all, she did have an angular Sun conjunct Mars and two powerful planets in the house of career. We expanded her life-statement into an "and . . . and" structure: it is sometimes dangerous *and* it also can be on your side. Then we discussed ways she could be more effective in the world, and I mentioned the possibility of her training as a make-up artist. Somehow the Virgo-Pisces opposition had made me think of that. It turned out that she had been discussing that possibility with someone just the other day. It would be a field where she could use her Piscean imagination and sensitivity along with her potential Virgo technical ability. I just know she would be good at it; you could see by looking at her, by the way she presented herself, that she would have a sense of what looked right or didn't look right. In short, a good portion of our session together centered on the idea that she could be effective—that she could have some power and ability—and that such traits didn't just belong to other people as her original life statement insinuated. We didn't deny her original life statement; we just tagged other possibilities onto it. The least she could do would be to try the expanded life-statement out and see what happens.

THE ELEMENT OF CHOICE

There is a question you can ask yourself now: "Are the beliefs I am currently holding—the beliefs I have about myself, about men, about women, about the world in general—are these beliefs consistent with what I want in my life and with what I want in my future?" What we are doing is adding the element of choice, the element of consciousness, the element of being a creative force in your own life rather than just taking what's given and living it out in any old way.

I find this very helpful to bear in mind when I am working on my own patterns. For instance, I am just about to begin work on a second book and I am already intensely agitated about it. I'm already thinking, "Oh my God, I'm contracting to do this book next year and I'm not going to have the time and it's going to be a failure and I'm just going to die because of it." I have three planets in Leo, so I'm allowed to be somewhat over-dramatic. As I revealed earlier, Mars in my chart is conjunct Saturn and Pluto and Mars has a lot to do with how we start things. So my pattern around starting things (Mars) has something to do with dread and fear (Saturn) and when it gets mixed up with Pluto, it becomes a life-death issue. Because this conjunction is in Leo, these issues are particularly activated when it comes to expressing myself creatively. But it helps if I can catch myself mid-stream and say, "Wait a minute Howard, are these thoughts and fears in line with what you want to have happen in your life?" Now, I don't want to die next year necessarily; I don't want to be tortured and not have enough time to do the book, so these thoughts are not congruent with what I want to make happen. I experienced and lived out all these fears and misgivings fully when I worked on the first book last year and I don't see any value in going through that nightmare again. So now when I start having these negative thoughts, I acknowledge they are not consistent with what I want to have happen. I would like to have the time to work on my book, to enjoy being creative and to enjoy the writing. I'm not denying that my fears and apprehensions are there, but I am shifting my attention from them to what I actually want to make happen. Robert Fritz[2], who is the founder of DMA (a useful course designed to help you create your life more the way you want it) stresses the point that the key to your future is right now—not the past, but right now. I hear so many people lament, "Well, such and such happened to me when I was young and therefore I'm stuck with being a certain way now." If you believe that the past determines your future, then you energize that happening. But if you believe that the key to your future is right now, you have a different premise on which to base your life. How you are going to work with things *now* becomes more important than what happened to you in the past.

Robert Fritz points out that it helps to think of your beliefs and statements about life not as hard and cold facts, but as *opinions*. So if you have a belief that you are unlovable (Venus square Saturn), try seeing that as an opinion rather than as an absolute truth about yourself. Then ask yourself, "Is this opinion in tune with or going against what I would like to have happen?" Does the belief or opinion that you are unlovable support what you would like to have happen? Do you really want that to happen? Do you really want to be unlovable? This is what you can start doing today. Create some other beliefs that you would like to see happen and focus on these. When the original belief comes up, you are not denying it, but you are creating some alternative things which you would like to see happen. Speaking astrologically, when you re-choose your statements you have to stick within the archetypes of the planets involved in the aspect or placement you are working with. I do think we are, in a sense, fated to this degree.

---

[2]Robert Fritz's ideas mentioned here form the basis of just some of the many techniques and exercises offered in the DMA curriculum, which has recently been renamed "DMA's Technologies for Creating™." For more information about these courses and where they are taught throughout the world, write to DMA Inc., 27 Congress Street, Salem, Massachusetts 01970. Also recommended is Robert Fritz's book, *The Path of Least Resistance* (DMA Inc, Salem, Massachusetts, 1984) which explains in depth the basic principles behind the "Technologies for Creating™" courses.

Audience: Take something like a Mars-Saturn square. Instead of focusing in on negative manifestation of those energies, you would envision other more positive ways those energies can be brought together and made use of?

Howard: Yes. With Mars square Saturn there may be a statement that "my will is ineffective." But staying within the meaning of Mars and Saturn, that statement could be changed into something like, "if I go slow and am cautious and persistent, then I can get there." That still fits with Mars and Saturn together. Or you could try thinking about what somebody with Mars *trine* Saturn might be like and that may inspire you to come up with a new statement about those same planets in square. In the end, I'm more concerned about creative and constructive ways you can bring the two energies connected by an aspect together, rather than the nature of the aspect itself—be it a square, inconjunct, trine or sextile. If you have Venus square Saturn, think about what an interpretation of Venus sextile or trine Saturn might be and that could be your alternative belief that you focus on. As long as you stickwithin the two archetypes involved, then you are playing within the rules—it's *kosher*. If you have Venus in aspect to Saturn and you try to make a statement about love and union which is Jupiterian, it's simply not in line with what the core Self has in mind for you and it probably won't work. So what is an alternative statement for Venus square Saturn besides, "I am unlovable," or "I don't get what I want in relationship"? Think about someone with Venus trine or sextile Saturn and that might help you reformulate your statement. Keep within the confines of the principles of Venus brought together with Saturn.

Audience: How about, "if I work on a relationship, I can grow stronger, more loving and more loyal."

Howard: Fine. But before you can get there you will have to fully experience and understand your original statement, and *then* you can try to shift your awareness to an alternative one.

Let me take you through this in another way. Let's say a woman comes to me for a chart reading and she has the Sun conjunct Saturn in the 10th house. During the session, it comes up that she is frightened of her boss. I'm looking at her Sun conjunct Saturn in the 10th and I'm wondering if there is a deeper issue behind her fear of her boss. So I enquire, "Who else have you felt frightened with?" And she replies, "Authority figures in general." We are beginning to broaden out. Then I can ask that very handy question: "Is this feeling of fear a familiar feeling in your life?" And she answers, "Yes, as a child I was frightened of my mother." Then I ask her, "What were you afraid of with your mother?" She says, "I was afraid that my mother wouldn't like me." Then I could explore further: "What would have happened if she didn't like you?" (These kinds of questions are useful when you are working with placements in the chart psychologically.) And she says, "I guess I was afraid that if she didn't like me, she wouldn't look after me and then she would leave me." So, we have moved from feeling frightened of the boss to a fear that if mother didn't like her she would be abandoned. I could take it even further and ask, "What would have happened if she left you?" And she might answer, "I would have died."

On some deep level, her fear of the boss could be linked to unfinished business with the mother and a fear about her own survival. You see, if she came to me and told me she was frightened of her boss and I said, "Okay, let me do a synastry between the charts and we'll sort this out." I might do a comparison and say something like, "Don't be silly—you don't have to be frightened of him, you have more planets in fire than he does." And then she goes off happy and more confident about dealing with her boss. But later when she has a new job, the same problem comes up again or she finds herself frightened with other people. In other words, unless she perceives and deals with the underlying issues behind her present problem, she will just find someone else to live the pattern out with. Unless she goes deeper and starts to do something to change the basic pattern, it will just reappear in different manifestations.

In a single astrology session you may only be able to start this process going, but if you are doing ongoing work with the person, you have something clear to work on. Or you can refer the person to somebody who does ongoing work. But at least we have discovered something important—her fear of not pleasing the boss is related to a fear of her mother not liking her. Everyone still has a child inside, and the child in this person is frightened that if she doesn't act the way authority figures want her to act, then she will die.

Audience: It's a bit hard to make the transition correlating the *male* boss figure with her mother.

Howard: It doesn't make any difference. The stuff around mother can be put onto anyone—husbands, bosses, or the prime minister. In any case, she is afraid of being who she is because she is afraid that if people don't like her she is going to die. But, wait a minute. She is an adult now and she can look after herself. She doesn't need to kowtow to others in order to survive. Yet, the little girl in her is still feeling that way, The priority in her case is a choice between being what other people want because that makes the child in her feel more secure, or acting in a way which is true to herself, honouring what she thinks or feels. She has Sun conjunct Saturn in the 10th and her statement is, "I am afraid to be who I am." But this can easily be changed to, "I must work hard to develop my identity." This is ultimately what Sun conjunct Saturn can mean—the building (Saturn) of an identity, the building of a sense of influence, power and self-sufficiency.

Here is another example. Recently a woman came to see me who had Pluto in the 9th house and talked about her fear of airplanes, a fear of flying—not Erica Jong by the way. With Pluto in the 9th, what might be the deeper issue behind the fear of the airplane crashing?

Audience: A fear of getting destroyed if you venture too far abroad.

Howard: Can you take it deeper than that?

Audience: A fear that if you let go, if you venture or explore, you might be destroyed.

Howard: Yes, and I think on even a deeper level it is a fear of God: a mistrust of God, a belief that God is out to destroy her. Pluto has to do with destructive energy and it's in the 9th house of religion as well as travel. Now, this woman could go to a behavioral therapist and he could deal very well with her fear of airplanes. You know, he could take her a little bit each day on an airplane, first on the ground and then make her feel better that way. But the deeper pattern is still there; and ultimately it's more effective to get at the deeper issue of the mistrust of God and what that is all about.

One more thing about working with patterns, and this is from Jean Houston's book *The Possible Human*[3]. She gives a short case history of a woman she worked with called Meredith. Meredith had a very traumatic early life. Her mother put her up for adoption at birth. Then every time the mother had a new boyfriend and began to settle into some sort of home life, she would take Meredith back with her. By the age of nine, Meredith had been abused by a succession of her mother's boyfriends. She grew into an attractive woman who was terribly frightened of the world; she would shake with trauma at the thought of going out and doing things. When Meredith was twenty-six, Jean Houston worked with her in this way. She instructed Meredith to picture herself being born—to be present at her own birth. Meredith would imagine herself being born and then visualize holding herself aged zero. So Meredith, aged twenty-six, was imagining herself nurturing and holding Meredith, aged zero. Then Ms. Houston would ask, "Do you feel loved?" And Meredith said, "Yes, I feel loved"; and then they would work on another age. Meredith would think of another time in her childhood that she needed to be held and loved. And Jean Houston would say, "Okay, have Meredith aged twenty-six give to the younger Meredith what she needed then." Meredith would do this in her mind until at each stage she could say, "Yes, I feel loved." Meredith and Jean Houston worked a number of hours in this manner until the twenty-six year old Meredith embraced the twenty-six year old Meredith. Many years of trauma were eased in this way. Follow up studies showed that Meredith was freer from the negative feelings of the past years.

Now, you don't erase the old trauma completely in this way, but what you do is create an alternative track in the mind-brain system; you create an alternative experience to what you actually had. You keep the pathos from the past but you have created a new kind of physiology in addition to what was previously there. This new physiology can support new experiences besides the old ones you were limited to. Ms. Houston calls it creating an alternative track in the mind. She says that if you do this, you also become present to the continuum of your life.

Audience: And you become the possible human.

---

[3]Jean Houston, *The Possible Human* (Los Angeles: Jeremy Tarcher, 1982), 85-7.

Howard: Well, you are more on the way there. But for Meredith it was a healing experience. Someone once said that "therapy is getting things out, but healing is getting things in."

Audience: Did she do things through visualisation?

Howard: Yes. Through visualisation techniques, it's possible to enter from the present time into an earlier time and enrich the reality of the earlier self in a new way. It's never too late to have a happy childhood. The three year old child is as alive in us right now as it was then and there is no reason why we, as we are now, can't connect to the child in us and give it the love it needs.

Audience: It's funny that this all happened to Meredith at age twenty-six during her Moon return.

Howard: Yes, it did, didn't it? The work was done when the progressed Moon was coming back to Meredith's natal Moon—when we have a chance to gather in and examine earlier events and then start off in a new direction.

The Phases of Childhood

Let's look more closely at the stages of childhood, examining how your experience of each of these phases is shown by the chart. Earlier I explained that different archetypes are brought out at different stages of life. We'll begin right at the beginning with the pre-natal experience. The central archetype of this phase is that of Unity. We'll look at the placements in the chart which shed light on our relationship to this archetype and to the womb experience in general. Then we'll move on to birth and the archetype of initiation and "getting things started," and a discussion of the relationship of the ascendant to birth. From there, we'll explore what is known as the oral phase, in which the predominant drive is survival and getting our needs fulfilled. This has a lot to do with the Moon. During the next phase—what is known as the anal phase—the main drive or motivation is the urge to assert the self and become more autonomous. The archetype of Power is foreground during this stage, and placements involving the Sun and Mars come quite clearly into play. As psychologists have traditionally understood it (and there is quite a bit of controversy about the timing of these stages), the anal phase leads on to the Oedipal stage, which is characterized by the child's desire to win the love of the opposite sex parent. The archetype activated at this time is that of Union, and various placements in the chart will be brought to the fore accordingly. From there, we'll look at what is known as "The School Age" or "The Play Age" (ages six to ten) and wind up with a brief overview of adolescence.

As we examine these various stages and their relation to the chart, please join in the discussion with any material or information you wish to add, either from a psychological or astrological angle. After all, we're talking about things we've all been through—not to mention the fact that most all of us are still trying to sort out issues leftover from these early experiences.

THE PRE-NATAL EXPERIENCE

"A child's neurosis begins in the mind of the parents." This is a quote from Dr. Arthur Janov's book *The Feeling Child*.[4] The reasons why a woman decides she is going to have a baby will actually influence the future psychology of the child. Does she want a child because this is what society expects of her and, in actual fact, she isn't that inclined to mothering? Does she want a child because she desperately wants someone to really need her?

Life experience begins in the womb. By the age of two months after conception, there is a rudimentary brain forming in the embryo—a rudimentary brain that is able to register experience. Therefore, even in the womb some of our inborn patterns and archetypal expectations are already being activated, fleshed out and set into motion as we register certain things that our mothers are going through. It's curious, but very often we do end up with a mother whose chart fits pretty closely the kind of mother we are expecting to get. A child with Moon conjunct Pluto, for instance, may wind up with a mother who has Scorpio rising or Sun or Moon conjunct Pluto. Or the child with Moon conjunct Pluto may

---

[4]Dr. Arthur Janov, *The Feeling Child* (New York: Simon & Schuster, 1975; and London: Abacus, 1973), 13.

be born to a mother who is going through a significant Pluto transit at the time, so the child's early, formative experience of her is coloured by that planet. But, I'm diverting and we must get back to the womb. Some of you in the group may have more knowledge of fœtal development than I have, so please feel free to make comments and additions.

What can the chart reveal about our pre-natal experience? I said earlier that archetypes express themselves through drives, and different drives are foreground at various stages of life. The archetype which is activated during the intra-uterine phase is that of *Unity*. The drive is the desire to be one with everything. Arthur Koestler talks about life in the womb—he says that "The universe is focused on the Self and the Self is the universe."[5] Ideally in the womb we have a sense of oceanic totality, a sense of oneness with the rest of life. Many of you have heard me speak about this before. It's something I talk about a great deal as you will know very well after studying with me. I think it's because my major drive in life is to get back there!

Audience: You're not alone.

Howard: Yes, the thing is—the trick is—trying to find wholesome ways of getting back there. . . .

Now, if we are examining the chart to assess how we experienced life in the womb, then I would look at what is going on in the 12th house. What is in the 12th (any planets there, the sign on the cusp, the ruling planet of the sign on the cusp and its aspects) gives clues about what our tiny, little rudimentary brain is registering via the umbilical connection to the mother. I'd also examine Neptune in the chart. How is Neptune aspected? Jupiter trine Neptune will associate the experience of unity (Neptune) with ease and expansion (Jupiter). Saturn square Neptune may associate pain, difficulty and restriction (Saturn) with the archetype of unity (Neptune). Issues later in life to do with various forms of mystical experiences (the sense of being at one with the rest of creation) will also resonate with these kinds of placements.

Audience: What books do you recommend about life in the womb?

Howard: There is a book by Stan Grof called *The Realms of the Human*

---

[5]Arthur Koestler cited in Ken Wilber, *The Atman Project* (Wheaton, IL: Theosophical Publishing, 1980), 8.

Unconscious.[6] He researched using LSD and putting people back into the pre-natal and birth experience. Also Janov's book *The Feeling Child* has a chapter on this. However, his books tend to be a hard sell on Primal Therapy, which he sees as an answer to everything. He is very adamant about this—he has Uranus in the 12th.

Audience: There is a very good book about the umbilical effect by Francis Mott called *The Nature of the Self.*[7]

Howard: Yes, I haven't read that one yet, but Mott is well known for this work. The main thing to note about the womb experience is that we are more or less immersed in a primal paradise. What the Jungians call "uroboric wholeness"—there is no separation—it's pre-time and pre-boundaries. This is why we can associate it with boundless and formless Neptune.

The womb is a kind of Eden. However, it appears that some wombs are five star wombs, while others are four star, three star, two star, etc. In the womb we register things via the mother. This is called "the umbilical effect" and the nature of what passes through the umbilical to the child is probably shown by what is in the 12th house. For instance, if Saturn is in the 12th, then Saturnian feelings pass from mother to developing embryo via the umbilical effect; if Jupiter is in the 12th, then Jupiterian feelings pass through the umbilical. It's as if the 12th house is an indication of what the mother is going through while she is pregnant. I've seen this theory work over and over again. I've never really read other astrologers on this—at least I can't remember if I ever read it or just discovered it or made it up.[8] I don't know, but it's worth bearing in mind because it seems to fit. People tell me stories about what their mothers were going through while they were in the womb and it correlates uncannily with 12th house placements. For instance, I did the chart of a woman with Saturn influencing the 12th who had access to her mother's diaries after the mother had died. In the diary, her mother wrote that she didn't want to have

---

[6]Stanislav Grof, *Realms of the Human Unconscious* (New York: Dutton, 1976; and London: Souvenir Press, 1979).

[7]Since doing the seminar, I have discovered that Mott's book is unfortunately out of print.

[8]Since giving this seminar, I have come across Tad Mann's interesting and well thought-out book, *Life-Time Astrology* (London: Allen & Unwin, 1984), which discusses houses 9-12 in relation to gestation.

the child (my client) she was carrying. The mother was an artist and just didn't want a child to interfere with her creative work.

Audience: Have you noticed any correlation with Uranus in the 12th?

Howard: Yes. Very often something unexpected or disruptive happens to the mother or the family while the child with that placement is the womb: the parental marriage breaks up, the family is forced to change homes—something significant happens which brings change. Thus, the child with Uranus in the 12th is already born with the idea in the back of his or her mind that life is unpredictable or that anything can change at a moment's notice. From then on it becomes difficult to easily settle into anything because of this vague but all-pervasive feeling that disruption is around the corner.

Anything in the 12th house is very deeply buried and free-floating. It seeps into all the various areas of our life, not just what the 12th house represents. A man with Saturn in the 12th, for example, may have had a difficult time in the womb and then is born with the belief in the back of his mind that life is not on his side, although nothing externally has happened to him yet to substantiate this. Also, remember that most natal placements in the 12th will transit over the ascendant and into the 1st house relatively early in life, and therefore are bound to have an important influence in shaping the person's outlook.

Another way to track back pre-natal experience is to analyse separating aspects of the Moon. Again, this is not something I've ever read in a book, so please feel free to experiment with it yourself. By using a form of *converse progressions* on separating aspects of the Moon, I believe that you can pinpoint what month during pregnancy that certain archetypes were constellated in the foetus' rudimentary awareness. Let's take an example: the Moon in 9 degrees of Scorpio square Pluto in 3 degrees of Leo. This is a separating aspect because the Moon moves faster than Pluto and it's moving away from the square. The Moon moves roughly one degree a month by secondary progression and normally we count it forward. So at the age of one month after birth, the Moon has progressed to 10 Scorpio, at 2 months after birth the Moon is in 11 degrees of Scorpio, etc. But we can also do converse progressions and move the Moon backward one degree for each month previous to the birth. In this case, moving the Moon backward 6 degrees will make it 3 degrees and exactly square Pluto in 3 Leo— and this would have occurred 6 months before birth or 3 months after conception. In other words, using this system, the converse Moon ran up against Pluto in the 3rd month after conception. Therefore, at the time, the developing embryo would have encountered something Plutonic through the Moon/mother. Later in life, whenever a transit comes along and touches off the natal Moon-Pluto square, it may re-activate the same pattern that was first brought out the third month after conception.

Again, the important question to ask is, "How is this pattern operating in your life now?" And if it is there now, is it in a form which is consistent with what you want in your life? If it isn't in accord with what you want, then what are some alternative statements that could be derived from this kind of aspect?

Janov reported a few experiments which were done on pregnant rats who were exposed to loud noises: these rats produced smaller offspring than the ones who weren't. This suggests that stress or fear in the pregnant mother has an effect on the offspring. A loud noise and the accompanying reaction of fear produced hormonal changes in the rat mothers which then affected the embryo's development. Stress increases the mother's heart rate and thereby increases the foetus' heart rate. The mother's heartbeat has a profound effect on the foetus. The foetus can actually hear the mother's heartbeat. It has been proven that the foetus can hear noises and if the mother's heartbeat is irregular it is not very reassuring for the embryo. So, already in the womb, the person doesn't feel very assured about life. I wonder if someone with Uranus in the 12th had a mother with an irregular heartbeat?

Audience: When you are lying in the bath—and I do this sometimes—and you put your head down under the water and your ears are underwater, you hear your heartbeat. I should think it's very much the same as being in the womb and hearing your mother's heartbeat.

Audience: There is a fantastic recording made by the Japanese of what the foetus hears in the uterus. It's the most moving thing because the heartbeat is tremendously powerful, and you also have the swishing of the blood through the aorta. It's so beautiful.

Howard: Yes, rhythm is so important.

Audience: It's very soothing for a baby too. I mean you play this recording to them and they shut up.

Howard: Yes, I read of an experiment in a ward in Thailand where there were 400 women and their babies. They played this type of recording and the ward was ever so silent—just the sound of this music playing.

We might ask what kinds of rhythms the developing foetus responded to in the womb, and there could be a connection between the plant or sign in the 12th and the nature of the mother's heartbeat and her rhythms. Aspects the converse Moon makes to natal planets could also shed some light here.

Audience: What about Jupiter in the 12th?

Howard: I've always imagined that those with Jupiter in the 12th must have felt pretty good in the womb, except that you will have to take into account any aspects to Jupiter. On the whole, later in life these people have an underlying faith in life, a kind of basic optimism. They may even find themselves in very tricky or dangerous situations and yet manage to escape in the nick of time—like Indiana Jones in *Raiders of the Lost Ark*.

Audience: What about Neptune there?

Howard: If Neptune was well-aspected, then it would be a five star womb—the Ritz of wombs. That's why so many people with Neptune in the 12th give me the feeling that they never really wanted to be born in the first place. Why leave that paradise to come into the harsh world of form and separateness?

Audience: I've got Uranus in the 12th and I find it very interesting in light of what you say. While my mother was pregnant with me, it was wartime and we had to be evacuated. My mother was very disoriented. I'm sure I picked up on that.

Howard: Yes, in the womb and right through very early childhood, mother is the whole world to us. What she goes through is what we go through. At some point we may need to separate or squeeze out just how much of what we are carrying is our stuff and how much is what we have taken on through the mother.

Audience: What about the South Node of the Moon in the 12th?

Howard: Many believe that the South Node indicates the path of least resistance. In the 12th, the person may exhibit a strong regressive tendency—wanting to stay blended and merged with others rather than coming out and developing the self as a unique and separate individual. The North Node would be in the 6th and the conflict is between the 12th house urge to stay in the embrace of the Great Mother—the urge to be swallowed up and identified with something greater than the self—as opposed to the 6th house concern of finding those particular characteristics which make you distinct from everything else. In my book *The Twelve Houses*[9] I discuss in depth the significance of all the different planets and signs in the 12th house.

Audience: While we are still on the 12th house stuff, I read about another experiment with pregnant rats. Pregnant rats who were stroked during pregnancy produced a greater number of surviving offspring than those rats mother who were not touched.

Howard: So, there is the idea that the mother who is stroked and loved during pregnancy produces a baby with a greater chance of survival. A nicely aspected Venus in the 12th maybe? Have you noticed we are all getting stuck in this womb phase right now? Let's move on to birth.

THE ARCHETYPE OF BIRTH

The archetype constellated at birth is that of *Initiation*: how we get things started. We are already born with an image of what it is going to be like whenever we have to get something started. The actual birth serves to activate that innate image. The actual physical birth adds a layer of substance to the inborn image of the birth archetype. Later on in life, anytime we have to begin something new or move into a new phase of life, our original pattern around birth along with all its subsequent layering will come up again.

The sign on the ascendant reflects our inborn image of the birth archetype. I would also examine the ruler of the ascendant

[9]Howard Sasportas, *The Twelve Houses* (Wellingborough, England: The Aquarian Press, 1985).

and what that planet is up to by sign, house and aspect. Any planets closely aspecting the ascendant are also activated at birth. These all give you clues about the person's birth experience as well as how one approaches any new phase of life or major new undertaking. The placement of Mars, by sign and aspect, should also shed some light in this respect.

Birth really means taking on a body and it heralds the beginning of life as a separate individual. The body is a boundary which distinguishes us from others. Actually, even for the first six to nine months of life after birth, we still don't really "twig" that we are a separate entity. This phase is called "primary narcissism"—the feeling that everything around us is just an extension of who we are. According to the most recent psychological thought, an infant needs to have this experience of being the center of everything. In other words, the baby shouldn't be jolted out of the non-differentiated environment of the womb into a sense of separateness too quickly or suddenly. The first six to nine months of life should be a gradual adjustment to the idea that we are separate and distinct. During those early months of life, the child can't be loved or nurtured enough. Then, gradually, the child begins to acknowledge and recognize its separateness and can tolerate more frustration and greater independence. Many books about raising children written in the 1940's and 1950's didn't advocate this. Rather, it was advised that the baby should be made to adjust to the mother's routine. It was believed that the baby should be fed only according to a strict schedule and not just because it was screaming. The advice was to let the baby scream. The result is that we have a whole generation of people who grew up and are still running around trying to find ways to reconnect to that sense of unity from which they were too quickly jolted. This is the pathology that arises from having to experience separateness too early in life: you are left craving for that unity which you were forced to relinquish too soon. Later in life, you are constantly looking for that person or thing which will fit perfectly with you and make you whole again. As a general rule, if you don't get what you need at any stage of early life, there is always the tendency to want to go back there again in order to finish it up properly.

Conversely, a pathology arises if this phase of primary narcis-. sism goes on too long—if the mother is *over-adapted* to the child's needs beyond the first year and a half of life or so. In this case, you don't learn to acknowledge your separateness and then later on don't have the mechanisms to cope with life not being exactly as you want it just when you want it. You expect instant fulfillment of your desires because your mother always made sure of that. You expect everyone to adjust to you. You can't cope with the "other-ness" of other people. This is why the English pediatrician, Winnicott, talked about "the good enough mother."[10] If the mother tries to be too perfect and overly adapted to the child for too long, the child doesn't learn how to deal with frustration and is not well equipped for the realities of everyday life. But more about this latter. Let's go back to the birth experience itself.

It's worth enquiring into what your actual birth was like. This will reveal a great deal about your patterning around the archetype of Initiation and getting things started. Remember, it is not necessarily what happens at your birth which causes you to have certain patterns—it's more the other way around: your innate patterning and *a priori* expectation around the archetype of birth influences what your actual birth experience is like.

The Ascendant

An idea I had recently, and which I'm finding very useful in chart readings, is considering the ascendant as the way we hatch—the different ways a bird might peck itself out of an egg. How would an Aries rising bird peck itself out? How would a Taurus rising bird peck itself out? This will not only describe something about how you are born, but also what happens whenever you are getting something new going or entering a new phase of life.

An Aries rising bird will rush headlong into hatching; it just goes for it and in one fell swoop cracks the egg and appears onto the scene—bang, like that. Of course, if Mars (the ruler of Aries) is square Pluto, then it may go through some degree of torture and strain before marching out. What about the Taurus rising bird?

Audience: I think it will spend a lot of time looking out the window first to see if it is safe to make a move.

---

[10]D.W. Winnicott, *Playing and Reality* (New York: Methuen, 1982; and Harmondsworth, England: Penguin Books, 1985), 11.

Howard: Yes, it will wait as long as it can before making the change; but when it senses it has to be done, it will be very determined—no stopping it. What about a Gemini rising bird?

Audience: It pecks here and there all over the egg, or it starts to peck and then gets diverted into something else. Or it begins to think about whether it should do it at all and explores all the reasons why it should or shouldn't.

Howard: Yes, the Gemini rising bird may want to read up on the nature of pecking out before it does it—or maybe discuss the prospect with other birds in the neighborhood first. I've noticed that people with air signs on the ascendant like to find out as much as they can about something before going into it. People with Aquarius rising, for instance, require some sort of conceptual understanding of the "whys and wherefores" of something before they take action. Taurus rising, on the other hand, responds to a physical pressure—an organic, biological urge to make a move.

Cancer rising birds *feel* the need to peck themselves out or make a move. The Cancer rising bird is another one that starts to peck and then hesitates, thinking, "I actually prefer the space I already know," and goes back in. But it doesn't feel comfortable staying there and starts to peck itself out again. Leo rising birds often wait until the moment is best to make a dramatic entrance and then burst proudly onto the scene. A Virgo rising bird will want to hatch into a new phase neatly, pecking a little then tidying up, pecking a bit more and then tidying up again. Virgo rising has a fear that it is not going to do it well enough—that's why it tries to do it so right. A Libra rising bird will want to approach birth or any new phase of experience in a beautiful way—to do it with style and taste. Being an air sign, it will want to make sure there are sound justifications for why this has to happen and then proceeds in a way that's fair—at least fair from its own perspective. Or the Libra rising bird may provoke other people into forcing it to change or act—in that way it can abnegate personal responsibility for the action. As you move into the second half of the zodiac, there's more of a tendency to create situations which require you to change rather than just directly changing because that is what suits you.

Audience: Next time you do some of the signs will you pick some from the second half?

Howard: All right, I don't want to be a bad mother. Let's finish them off. What about a Scorpio rising birth?

Audience: The birth may entail a life and death struggle.

Howard: Yes, many people with Scorpio rising or Pluto near the ascendant have reported to me that they or their mothers nearly died at birth. Scorpio rising birds seem to set up dramatic situations which require that they grow and change or else they might die or at least remain very miserable. Sagittarius rising is usually keen to get on with any new phase or venture: "Oh boy, what's waiting around the corner!" Usually Sagittarius rising will justify the change from some sort of philosophical basis. Or, having taken an overview of the situation, they deem it the right action to make. Capricorn rising usually resists change: "Oh God, do I really have to go through with this—it's such an effort, but I know I should." Capricorn may balk at the whole prospect right up until the last moment still wondering if it's the right thing to do, until it finally gives in. I've already mentioned Aquarius. A Pisces rising bird will probably prefer to stay in the egg, unless someone else entices it out or asks it to move. Pisces rising people are coerced into new phases or coerced into action if they feel that someone or something *needs* them to do it.

Audience: What about the early or late births or Caesarians?

Howard: From the charts I have seen, Uranus on or aspecting the ascendant may describe something unusual about the birth. Uranus or Jupiter near the ascendant could also mean someone who is in a hurry to get out. In a few cases I have seen with Mercury on the ascendant, the person was born while the mother was still in transit to the hospital. Some Caesarians appear to have a correlation with Mars or Pluto around the ascendant or aspecting it— these planets have to do with surgery. But, honestly, I haven't undertaken any legitimate research into these things. What I am telling you is what I have observed in my fifteen years of doing charts.

It is worth thinking about these kinds of births from a purely psychological point of view. In one study about early births, it was shown that these people grew up with a longing for permanence and a panic at change, because change had come too soon to them. Some of those who had delayed births may have had the feeling that the mother was holding them back from being born. Very often, the child has projected his or her reluctance to be born onto the mother. The mother is felt to be the one who is holding back or trapping the child, but more often than not these people later exhibit a pattern of holding themselves back or trapping themselves in tight corners.

Regarding Caesarian births, Janov felt that these people were deprived of something important. During a natural birth there are contractions, but the Caesarian doesn't have this experience. Contractions are important because these movements stimulate the skin of the baby. You know how animals lick the skin of their newborn. They lick their offspring in order to stimulate the skin, which in turn activates the bowels and bladder into action. This is why touch is so important to us in the beginning of life—being touched literally stimulates organs into action. It's like being massaged. You might be constipated and then you have a good massage and you are off in an instant. Caesarians may also go though life with the sense that something big is just about to happen, because they were deprived of the full birth experience and they are still expecting it.

Audience: You know how you were talking about Pluto on the ascendant as possibly signifying a traumatic birth. I know a man who is an Aries with Pluto on the ascendant in Leo opposing the Moon and Mars in Aquarius. His mother was Polish and they were escaping from the advancing Russians when she gave birth.

Audience: Could you say something about induced births?

Howard: This is a big issue in astrology. I tend to think that we come out when we are meant to come out. If we are induced, then for some reason it has been computed by the Self to get you out then.

Audience: I did a synastry for a mother and her three children and I found that she had a particularly strong link with her first born who was a boy. When I mentioned this she said, "That's strange. He was the only one who was induced, because I didn't know any better." And yet, he was the one whose chart had the closest links to hers.

Howard: That reminds me of a case I came across not long ago. It was the chart of a baby girl whose mother was diagnosed as having a brain tumour while she was pregnant with this child. The doctors decided to induce the birth because they were really very worried whether the mother was going to live for very long. They brought the birth forward. It turned out that the time they chose to induce the child happened to be the exact hour in which the nearly total eclipse of the Sun happened in Gemini this year (1984). Can you imagine—picking out a time to induce a child and just happening to arrange it at the hour of an eclipse! What happened is that they were wheeling the mother into the operating theater in order to carry out the induction when suddenly the child popped out of its own accord before they even got to the operating room. It just came out right there and then anyway. Sadly, the mother died three days later. The baby girl has Pluto in the 12th in 29 degrees of Libra and Scorpio rising. Pluto in the 12th fits with what we have been saying about the child's experience of what the mother was going through during the pregnancy—I mean, the mother found out she was going to die. And the Scorpio ascendant with Pluto in the 12th nearby would suggest the dramatic and rather disturbing situation surrounding the birth itself—not to mention the eclipse. I tend to think that there is some great computer in the sky which takes all these things into account, even induced births.

We must push on. Now that we are born, the next phase is the oral phase. I'd like to finish the oral phase in time for lunch. Then we can do the anal phase while we are digesting our food.

THE ORAL PHASE

Archetypes come through drives and drives express themselves through various organs in the body. Different organs are activated at different times in the early stages of childhood. In the oral phase (from birth until age two), we relate to the world primarily through the mouth and the activity of sucking. I also think that the skin is important in the oral stage—being touched, stroked and held is crucial in this early period. Harlow's experiments with monkeys showed this.[11] Some monkeys were kept in a cage with a wire mother while others were put in a cage with a cloth mother. Both the wire and the cloth mothers were equipped to feed the monkeys, so feeding wasn't the issue: *touch* was the critical factor. The monkeys with the cloth mother grew up less frightened of the world and new experience than the monkeys reared by the wire mother. The fact that they could snuggle up close to the cloth mother fostered better relationships later in life. Then Harlow used "sock mothers." The experimenters worked out some way to heat the sock. They found that the heated sock mothers produced better adjusted offspring than the unheated sock mothers. The mothers that provided both a soft touch and warmth were the best of all.

The archetypal principles which are important in the oral phase are love, nurturance and survival. According to the psychologist Erik Erikson,[12] the main issue of this phase is the development of *Basic Trust* versus *Mistrust*. The big question is, "Am I going to make it?" The Moon is the main astrological principle which is activated during this state, although placements in the 1st, 4th and 10th houses as well as any Taurus or Cancer emphasis also come into consideration. Placements and aspects in the chart which relate to love and nurturance will be activated.

During the first two years of life, we form opinions about how safe the world is for us—how good a place it is. Mother is really the whole world to the child during this time. If mother is a safe container and can provide the baby with what it needs, then the baby will form an opinion that "life will provide me with what I need; the world is a safe place for me." This forms the basis of what Erikson calls *abiding hope* or *trust*. But if mother neglects the baby or isn't sensitive to the baby's needs, if she is too depriving, or if she is a "stuffing" type mother, then the baby may form the opinion that life is not so conducive to its survival. Erikson calls this *basic mistrust*.[13] Furthermore, if the baby is hungry and mother doesn't come, or if it needs to be held in a certain way and moth-

[11]For a discussion of Harlow's experiments with monkeys, see Bowlby, *Attachment and Loss: Volume 1* (Harmondsworth, England: Penguin Books, 1984), 213-16.

[12]Erik Erikson, *Childhood and Society* (New York: W.W. Norton, 1964; and St. Albans, England: Triad Paladin, 1977).

[13]Erikson, *Childhood and Society*, 222-25.

er's hold is too tight or too loose, then the baby begins to think, "What's wrong with me? I must be bad—I can't even get my needs fulfilled." Melanie Klein[14] referred to this as introjecting the bad mother or the bad breast. Obviously, such a situation doesn't do much for the infant's self-image later in life.

Another big question that arises during this period is: "What do I have to do to get nourishment and love?" "Do I have to keep still to get fed or held?" "Do I have to assert to get fed?" "Do I have to scream my head off to get love?" "Do I have to be good and well-behaved to win what I need?" These kinds of life-statements are brought to the surface in the oral phase.

Let's focus in on the Moon and see what kinds of life-statements and what kinds of experience correlate with different aspects to the Moon. Remember that the planet that aspects the Moon will indicate something about our experience of the mother—those things she does which register with us.

Audience: I had to stop breast feeding at seven weeks because I had blocked milk ducts. My daughter has the Moon in 7 Libra opposite Saturn in 9 Aries. We were living in the middle of the African bush then and I only had one bottle.

Howard: You see, around the age of two months, your daughter's Moon progressed from 7 to 9 Libra and exactly opposed her Saturn. So her experience of you (her mother) was coloured by the principle of Saturn. In this case you were the perfect reflection of this. Your milk—her source of sustenance (the Moon)—was blocked (Saturn). Even if your milk hadn't been blocked she probably would have experienced something of a Saturnian nature via you during that time. Later on, based on that experience and possible other things, your daughter may not feel that the world is a very safe place for her.

Audience: Well, she is a raging punk now, shocking coloured hair and all. For a while she tried to dress conventionally in order to find a job. She didn't get a job so she went back to being punk. She really does believe that the world is against her.

Howard: Patterns from childhood often re-emerge full-fledged at adolescence. I'll be talking more about this later. Sometimes, we

---

[14]Melanie Klein, *Love, Guilt and Reparation and Other Works 1921-1945* (New York: Free Press, 1984, and London: Hogarth Press, 1985), 291.

have a chance to redeem negative childhood patterns during adolescence. For instance, if your daughter finds a close female friend who positively satisfies some of her emotional needs, this may heal some of the early wounds.

Audience: What about Moon-Uranus aspects?

Howard: Let's look at the hard aspects first. The child is born with an inner image of mother as erratic, inconsistent, or unpredictable. The mother may actually be like that, or the child with this aspect is predisposed to notice when she is acting that way rather than in other ways. When I put the archetype of the Moon together with the principle of Uranus, I think of a mother who might not be that comfortable with the maternal role. The traditional Moon-Mother is the Earth-Mother. However, if Uranus touches something then it will bring out the less conventional sides of the archetype or principle it aspects. Therefore, the mother may not have been experienced as a traditional maternal type mother. Perhaps she was someone more like Athene, the goddess of cool wisdom. Or more like Artemis, the huntress, who was a virgin. Many people with Moon-Uranus aspects have reported to me that they felt their mothers would have liked to be doing something else rather than being at home changing nappies and washing dishes. The picture I have of a Moon-Uranus mother is someone holding and feeding the child but her mind is off somewhere else. She is thinking about the future, or other things she might be doing, or of something she saw on television. The child is being held and fed and yet the mother is not really totally tangible and present. The child will sense the mother's lack of presence. It confuses the child who is left unsure if it can rely on the mother. If the mother is an unknown quantity, then the whole world feels very uncertain. The child feels that the mother is not in tune with its needs, and then later on the child grows up feeling out of tune with the world. Think about it. Think about what an inconsistent mother is like for the child. For instance, let's say that one day the child smiles and puts out his hand and his mother picks him up. So he thinks, "Okay, when I smile and put out my hand, then mother will pick me up." The next day he smiles and puts out his hand and his mother doesn't pick him up. So he thinks, "Well maybe it's every other time I smile and put out my hand that she picks me up." Children with the Moon in aspect to Uranus become very inventive in an attempt to fit the unpredictable mother into some sort of logical equation. They are good at organising diverse information into systems. Perhaps Moon-Uranus people grow up highly original, inventive and independent because they never really felt they could totally rely on their mothers to do things for them. Some with this aspect will grow up restless and unpredictable themselves, and a step ahead of everyone else. Later in life, men with this aspect are often attracted to women who are not maternal types. Now if these men have something like Venus conjunct Saturn, Capricorn on the 7th house cusp and Moon square Uranus, there is a lot of confusion. The Saturnian and Capricorn side is looking for a partner who is conventional, while the Moon square Uranus indicates an attraction for women of an Uranian nature, who reflect a side of the man's nature which is not that suited to conventional forms of domesticity.

Often I have seen Moon-Uranus aspects corresponding to a change of home in the early environment. For instance, if the Moon is 2 degrees Cancer and Uranus is 6 degrees Libra, then by secondary progression the progressed Moon squares Uranus at the age of four months. And you find out that at age 4 months the family moved or something disruptive occurred in the home environment. The newly born infant is just settling into the home and it is all disrupted. The statement that arises from this is, "I can't settle into anything." The Moon wants to settle and is seeking security and containment, while Uranus is saying, "Just you try and get comfortable and I'll change it all on you." Later, the person has trouble settling into one thing for very long because the archetype of containment (the Moon) is connected to the archetype of change and disruption (Uranus).

A woman with Moon in aspect to Uranus who has children often relates to them better as the children grow older. She can detach herself from strictly maternal feelings and talk objectively with a child. Taking objectively to a six month old infant who is wet or hungry doesn't mean much.

Audience: How can Moon-Uranus aspects express positively?

Howard: A child with Moon sextile or trine Uranus may have a mother who models originality and individualistic thinking and behaviour to the child. If it is a girl child, she grows up thinking, "I can be a woman but I don't have to be conventional—I can still do my own thing." If it is a boy-child, he grows up liking women who are individuals in their own right and there may be no problems for him about this. Also, remember that if a mother totally represses her Uranian side, then a child with a Moon-Uranus aspect is likely to grow up and live-out the mother's unexpressed urges to be different and unconventional.

Audience: What about the Moon in aspect to Pluto?

Howard: Moon-Pluto aspects may be similar to Pluto in the 10th house (if you take the 10th to correspond to mother), Moon in Scorpio or even the Moon in the 8th. Astrology is a language in which things can be expressed in many different ways. In this case, we have to connect up the principle of the Moon with that of Pluto. I'm sure you have heard Liz talk about this one, but let me recapitulate it.

The image of Mother may be dark or negative (not always, but we'll talk about the positive Moon-Pluto image in a minute). There could be a sense that your mother is not conducive or attuned to your needs and even a feeling that she is out to destroy you. She is seen as suffocating, devouring and threatening. Not that she actually beats you or feeds you nails but she feels dangerous. She may be suffocating and overly clinging, holding you too tight. Or you will be especially receptive to her dark moods and her depressions, or something unpleasant seething inside her. The Moon is what we take in, what we drink in from the early environment. Moon in aspect to Pluto will be receptive to what is Plutonic in the environment. This is usually mediated via the mother, but it can come through anyone in the house, such as an aunt, nanny, or a sister.

Recently I did a chart for a woman with the Moon at 1 degree Scorpio and Pluto 2 degrees Leo. At the age of one month, the progressed Moon came into an exact square to Pluto. Therefore, there is the suggestion that at this time the child would have picked up on something Plutonic in the atmosphere. In this case, it turned out the mother suffered a severe post-natal depression and wanted to reject the new baby. And remember, any time later in life when a transit comes to the first few degrees of a fixed sign, it will trigger that natal aspect and may re-activate some of the feelings that were there in her when she was just one month old: that same sense of anger, fear, frustration, and terror which she must have experienced when the mother was so depressed and rejecting. In addition, this woman would also have been left with a feeling that she was "bad"—otherwise why would Mother reject her? You can see why this aspect suggests that there is a great deal of emotional house cleaning to do.

This reminds me of one woman I worked with over a few years who had Moon square Pluto. I took her through a re-birthing exercise in which she relived her birth and then had her imagine she was being put onto her mother's breast. She screamed out how disgusting it was and that she wanted to vomit. Any aspects of the Moon can be projected onto the breast. In this case, she envisioned the breast as full of poison—a Plutonic breast. This woman grew up very concerned with matters of diet and health and ways of improving the body. In a woman's chart, the Moon may also indicate the way in which she relates to her own body. The mother is the first role model of the feminine. What she saw in the mother or projected onto the mother) is something she must look for and do something about in herself.

Audience: What is a positive Moon-Pluto image?

Howard: I'm thinking of a few cases in which the person had Moon in aspect to Pluto (the trine, sextile and even a square) and the mother had cancer or some life-threatening illness while the child was still small. What happened in these cases is that the mother survived the crisis and beat the cancer. So the image of the mother is someone who can be transformed in a positive way through a crisis—an image of being able to endure something negative and yet rise out of the ashes to new life again. The mother was seen to fall apart and yet put herself back together again, and this modelled to the child the ability to do this for him or herself later in life—like in the movie *Alive Doesn't Live Here Anymore*. Life is disrupted and the mother does rebuild.

Audience: Can you do Moon-Neptune?

Howard: That's another juicy one, isn't it? The mother gets caught up with Neptune; the child is sensitive to what is Neptunian about the mother. The image of mother as a victim or a martyr comes to mind. This might also be seen by Neptune in the 10th (if you take the 10th to mean mother), Pisces on the cusp of the 10th or the Moon in the 12th house. In certain cases I have seen, the mother has given up an artistic or creative career to become a parent. Or the mother was afraid to commit herself to the challenges of a career as a singer or dancer, and having children opened up another avenue. But still the mother emanates that "look what I have sacrificed for you" feeling.

All children are sensitive to their mothers, but those with Moon in aspect to Neptune are uncannily attuned to her. They don't even have to be in the same room and yet they feel what the mother is going through. If the mother has pain, the Moon-Neptune child experiences that pain as if it were his or her own. Sometimes, they may even feel responsible for the mother's pain—as if they had caused it. In short, Moon-Neptune aspects give a problem with boundaries. Those with these placements don't know where they end and others begin. They take on the feelings and needs of others and grow into adults who suffer a lot, or they become people who repeatedly rescue others.

The tendency for those with Moon-Neptune aspects is to feel that everything is somehow related or connected to them. Because in the womb we all had (to some degree) a sense of oneness with the rest of life, we retain a memory that on some deep level we are connected to everything. Mystics speak about reconnecting to this universal Self. Children have a memory of the interconnectivity of all life: if something happens "out there," they feel they have something to do with that, and perhaps even that they caused it. This happened in the movie *Kramer versus Kramer*, where the little boy believed that his mother left because he had been bad. Once a little girl told me that her daddy left home because she wasn't pretty enough.

As children, we also believe that *thinking* or *wishing* something is the same as actually *doing* the deed. If, as children, we have a negative thought about mother and then the next day she falls ill, we think we have caused that to happen to her. Those with Moon-Neptune aspects will especially feel guilty in this way, thinking that somehow they are responsible for everything bad that happens around them. It's a kind of magical thinking. As a result, they feel guilty and bad about themselves and don't grow up with a very positive self-image. Or else they have a confused self-image because they are like vacuum cleaners, absorbing so much from the environment they don't know who they are in themselves.

Audience: Howard, I have Moon in aspect to Neptune and I tend to feel hurt when I should actually feel angry.

Howard: Do you feel guilty about getting angry?

Audience: Right, that's true.

Howard: As I was saying, Moon-Neptune has problems with boundaries, and the difficulty with not having clear boundaries is that it's hard to stand up for yourself. Because *who* are you anyway? You can be so sensitive to why another person is being a certain way that you wind up actually commiserating with the person who is making you angry. Moon-Neptune indicates the burden of being an extra-sensitive person. Of course, that can be rather fun in a theatrical kind of way—everything becomes so meaningful and "too, too much." In certain cases, people with Moon-Neptune contacts can be a bit too precious. At the same time, they are often hurt and disappointed because life fails to live up to their dreams. The Moon is what we take in, what we drink in from what is around us. If you want to drink Neptune from the environment, you are looking for angels and birds singing and heavenly trumpets, or Julie Andrews on some mountain in Austria, or Richard Gere to sweep you away to a desert island. You don't want fragmentation, pain, and disharmony—you want to merge and blend and be whole again. It's called "divine homesickness." When the world is harsh, cruel, and nasty, Moon-Neptune is truly disappointed. It's interesting that many people with these aspects often end up working in hospitals and institutions to help those who are limited or afflicted in some way. It is as if part of them is trying to make the world a little bit more ideal, or part of them can truly identify with those society calls the underdog. Meanwhile, all the time there is this yearning to be back in that place where everything is celestial, ideal and fits perfectly.

Audience: I get to the point where I feel I must arouse my anger, and then I'm worried about hurting the other person.

Howard: Yes, this is what I mean about the burden of being an extra-sensitive person. Moon-Neptune people may be so understanding and accepting of another person that any angry part is shoved under the carpet. At some point they may have to contact and release that anger or sense of injustice, but usually they come back to trying to be understanding and accepting again. Often, this can facilitate a kind of healing for the other person involved, who thinks, "I've really hurt her and yet she still accepts me." Sometimes, that kind of acceptance helps to melt another person's hardness and rigidity. At other times, however, it might drive the other person crazy because he can't get a straightforward, dynamic, gutsy response from you. Or you end up being their doormat.

The Moon in aspect to Neptune may also ask that we sacrifice the personal mother in some way. Maybe she has to work during the day to make ends meet, so we are forced at a young age to sacrifice her—to give her back to the world. I've seen this aspect in the charts of a few people whose parents ran pubs. The pub is the child's home and yet even within the home they have to watch the mother serving and paying attention to others.

Audience: I have Moon in aspect to Neptune and my mother was a Sagittarius with Moon in Pisces. It was a difficult marriage and she sacrificed going to University and getting a degree in order to be a mother.

Howard: In this case she came from her Moon in Pisces and didn't live out the Sun in Sagittarius—the sign of higher learning. And here *you* are today studying astrology and psychology. Okay—we have to break for lunch. We are not done with the oral phase yet, but lunch can be a practical experience of it. Notice what you have to do to get fed.

Need, Love and Hate

We'll continue with further developments in the oral phase. Basically, the inner world of the child consists of three factors—*need*, *love* and *hate*. As children, we are incredibly needy. If Mother is good enough and feeds us and holds us in the way we need, then we feel tremendous love for her. Invariably, it will happen that even the best mother will mess up or frustrate us and then we feel fear and rage—after all, our life depends on her doing her job right.

Look at it this way. In the womb, everything was more or less there as you needed it. After birth and as you grow a little older, you begin to realise that mother is actually not the same person as you—she is different and separate from you. This is very scary: if she is different from you, she may not always be in tune with you. She has feelings and moods of her own and these may not always gel with what you want and need. Because you are so dependent on her for your survival, you become frightened and enraged when she isn't there in the way you need her, and you hate her. You want to kill her. This is your primordial, instinctive, infantile rage—the stuff that Pluto and nightmares are made of. I'll be speaking more about this in the Aggression Seminar, but we are touching on what Melanie Klein referred to as "splitting."[15] The child actually "splits" the mother into two different people: the good mother (or good breast) and the bad mother (or bad breast). You love and adore the good mother—the one who is there when you need her; and you hate and despise and want to destroy the bad mother—the one who doesn't respond as you require. Splitting the mother into two makes it safe to do this, because if you fantasize destroying the bad mother, then you still have the good one left. You can express hostility and rage at the bad mother because she is not the same person as the good mother. You can destroy the bad mother in your mind and yet still keep the good mother intact. Do you recognise this from fairy tales? The wicked step-mother *and* the real mother who is actually a princess?

According to many psychologists, splitting occurs up to the age of eighteen months. Ideally, by that time you are meant to realise that the mother who is the good mother and who comes when you need her is the same as the mother who sometimes messes up. Therefore, you come to see that mother contains both good and bad. Then you begin to think, "Well, I should temper some of my hatred towards the bad mother because she is also the same as the good one I need." This is how you learn to accept that another person can be both good and bad. If you don't succeed in resolving the split, it can be quite pathological later in life. In this case, if you are with somebody and he or she is not fitting with you properly or giving you what you want—be it your boyfriend, girlfriend, husband, wife, boss or teacher—then you may start to see this person as *all bad*. And if he or she is all bad, then you have every justification to unleash *all* your hatred, destructiveness

---

[15]Melanie Klein, *The Psycho-Analysis of Children* (New York: Free Press, 1984; and London: Hogarth Press, 1980), 153.

and anger and you don't feel as if you are destroying anything good. You might notice some regression to the splitting stage when you have a fight with your lover and suddenly you have an image of this person as wicked and out to destroy you because he or she is not being what you want. You lose sight of anything good in your lover, or anything good in the relationship. I wonder if the psychopathology of someone like Peter Sutcliffe, the Yorkshire Ripper who murdered all those women, isn't mixed up with something unresolved around splitting. When he was killing his female victims, he was seeing them as all bad; and in his twisted mind he wasn't killing anything with any good in it.

Resolving splitting means finding that place in yourself where you can accept another person as being both good and bad, and accepting that any relationship will also be a mixture of both good and bad factors. I am finding that people with a strong emphasis of mutability in their charts may have some difficulty resolving splitting, especially if the Moon has variable aspects to it. For instance, the Moon in Gemini already has a tendency to have a dual image of the mother. I'm thinking of a chart I did recently for a woman with the Moon conjunct Uranus in Gemini trine Jupiter in Libra, but square Mars in Virgo. During the reading, she was receptive, open, and appreciative of what we were discussing. Then a few days later, I received a letter from her and she was in a rage: "The reading was a lot of bunk, astrology was a lot of bunk and I was a lot of bunk." Words to those effect. So during the reading, everything was *all* good and then later on it was *all* bad. When I spoke to her later on the phone, there was nothing I could say which was acceptable, not even "hello," absolutely nothing.

Problems with splitting can also occur if the Moon has mixed aspects. For instance, I know a woman with Moon conjunct Jupiter square Pluto. When her lover is being good, she sees him as the most magnificent man to ever grace the earth (the Moon-Jupiter feelings). When he doesn't fit her exactly, he then becomes totally and completely vile in her eyes (Moon square Pluto). Or a person may have Moon trine Neptune but also square Mars. Then there is a tendency to shift from being all-appreciative (Moon trine Neptune) to all angry (Moon square Mars).

Persecutory and Depressive Anxiety

Melanie Klein also talked about two different kinds of anxiety which the young infant suffers which are related to the splitting phase.[16] First there is "persecutory anxiety," which is the feeling that there is something out there which is going to destroy you. However, in most cases the child is actually projecting his or her own badness and destructiveness onto the environment.

Eventually there is a shift from persecutory anxiety to what is called "depressive anxiety," the fear that *you* might destroy that which you love. Depressive anxiety is actually very healthy, because it inhibits us from blindly acting out all our negative impulses. When children are at the point of experiencing depressive anxiety, it is a signal that they are beginning to see that mother is both good and bad. Then they start to make reparations. That is, if they feel negative and hostile to the mother one day, they will try to make up for it by being extra nice the next day. In this way they reduce the anxiety that they might destroy the one they love and need.

How many of us still operate in this way in our adult life? I've noticed it often in myself as well as in my therapy clients. In the process of therapy, clients may project something onto me because I'm not giving them everything they need. I'm thinking of one woman in particular who started to see me in a bad light. In one session she verbally attacked me for being no good and for not making everything better for her right away. She was angry with me for not telling her exactly what she should do with her life. The next session after that she brought me a bunch of flowers, as if to make reparations because she was afraid I might have been destroyed by what she said, or that I might want to stop working with her. It was important for her that I was still there even after she had been angry at me. Through this she was learning that she could have negative feelings and it was still alright. Similarly, it is important for mothers to be able to let their children experiment with the whole range of feelings which are coming up in them during the splitting phase and the time of persecutory and depressive anxiety. This means giving the child an invitation to experiment with emotions rather than being a mother who reacts to the child's feelings in an overly subjective way.

I've definitely observed some astrological correlations here. People with the Moon in hard aspect to Mars, Saturn, Uranus, Neptune or Pluto may still harbour a deep fear that they will

---

[16]Klein, *Love, Guilt and Reparation and Other Works 1921-1945*, 263-76.

destroy or lose those they love. They may have—way in the back of their minds—the idea that if they love something they will destroy it. It could be that as children they felt angry towards the mother and then the next day she fell ill or had to go away for some reason, and the children are left thinking that they have caused that. Or sometimes this pattern is there for children who have been breast fed and then for some reason they lose the breast—the milk dries up or the mother becomes ill. These children may be left feeling that their greed exhausted the breast. Later in life, they still have a nebulous fear that those they love will die, or leave them, or be driven away. If we have a statement or pattern like that, then very often we unconsciously make it come true. The nature of a complex is to try to prove itself true. Becoming aware of these complexes helps us to change them. We are dominated by anything we are unconscious of in ourselves. The chart can make us more aware of some of these issues and then we can begin to explore them and work with them, and allow for other alternatives as I've explained earlier in the seminar.

The Issue of Survival

Survival is really the key issue during this oral phase. The early bonding relationship with the Mother is very much based on the belief that, "I need you to love me to survive." In infancy this is true. We are all born potential victims; unless there is someone bigger and more mature to look after us, there is a good chance we will die. What happens, though, is that the infant in us (the child-in-the-adult) often still feels this way in later adult relationships when the issue really isn't survival at all. A close intimate relationship in adult life will reawaken unfinished business and patterns from the first all-important bonding situation with the mother or caretaker. Later in life you are in a relationship with someone and that person threatens to leave you or plays around with somebody else and you think, "I'll die if you leave me," or, "I can't live without you." This isn't true—you are an adult now and you don't need someone else to love you or to be there in order to survive. But the child inside you is still thinking this, still feeling this on a deep primal level. Therefore, it's very hard for us to be really cool, detached, and objective in our most intimate relationships: too many anxieties, ghosts and fears from our earlier life as a helpless infant are stirred up. Astrologically, what I am talking about now can be clearly seen if there are squares from the 4th or 10th houses to the 7th or 8th houses. With such squares, parental issues (the meridian axis) are obviously interfering with partnership issues (the 7th and 8th). However, projecting unfinished parental stuff onto close partners is so universal it can hardly be pinned down to one placement or aspect. The closer we become to someone, the more likely we will start "seeing" them as "Mother."

In this respect, it is also worth considering the theory of Dr. Bowlby, another English psychiatrist.[17] Bowlby wrote about our pressing need to feel *special* to Mother. Centuries of evolution have ingrained into our species the belief that if Mother finds you very special, she will want to keep you alive. Smiling alluringly at her, enchanting her, and captivating her are ways of making sure she likes you. If she likes you, then she will stay by you and protect you in case any hairy predators come along to eat you up. So, later in life you are in a relationship but the child-in-you is still thinking that in order to survive you must be the most special thing to this person. If the person you are involved with starts flirting with someone else or has a job, hobby, or preoccupation which diverts him or her, the primitive part of your brain becomes agitated and starts to ruminate: "I'm going to die if I'm not the most special thing to this person." This is deeply embedded primal jealousy originally associated with the fear of losing Mother.

I've noticed this pattern operating strongly in people who have squares to Leo from either Taurus or Scorpio. In fact, I think the whole generation with Pluto in Leo (the sign of specialness) is trying to work through some of these issues. But it is ultimately a universal human dilemma. One part of us which is more mature and which is governed by the self-reflective and more recently evolved cerebral cortex area of the brain can reason that "my lover's individuation demands that he or she has other needs and interests besides me which fulfil them." Very well, this is undoubtedly true. However, the more primitive parts of our brain and the frightened infant in us are meanwhile plunged into a state of terror at such a prospect.

---

[17]A clear, brief summary of Bowlby's work can be found in Maggie Scarf, *Unfinished Business: Pressure Points in the Lives of Women* (New York: Doubleday, 1980), 70-77.

Audience: I think that we have to learn to become our own mothers and fathers and stop projecting those things onto other people.

Howard: Yes, I would agree, although this is not always so easy because of these "older parts" of our brain. But much in the same way as Jean Houston worked with Meredith, if we find our own inner mother and learn to nurture and look after ourselves, then we take the burden off someone else to have to do it for us. We take the onus off someone else to make up for what we were deprived of as children.

Now, a few more things about the oral stage. It's during this phase of life that we start to develop teeth. With the advent of teeth, a crisis occurs. When the teeth come in there is the natural urge to want to bite. So we are happily feeding at the breast, let's say, and then we have this urge to bite. We bite—Mother is startled and taken aback, and the breast is quickly withdrawn. Should weaning come at the stage you are developing teeth, this gives rise to an association that being aggressive (biting, in this case) means losing love. We are left with a deeply ingrained belief that if we are assertive or aggressive we risk losing love, wholeness, and a sense of unity with life and Mother.

In one sense, growing teeth is analogous to developing autonomy and individuality. Time is marching on and we are beginning to further differentiate ourselves from a uroboric wholeness with the mother. Before growing teeth, we have to swallow everything whole; now we have the ability to chew things over, breaking things down into component parts and making whatever we take in more digestible. Bear in mind that the advent of teeth and starting to bite (which is an aggressive act) means we are becoming more of a separate individual. It's comparable to a shift from the 12th house to a 6th house kind of experience, or a shift from the Moon and Neptune to the Sun, Mars and Mercury. You see what is happening—other archetypes besides Neptune (pre-natal phase) and the Moon (oral phase) are beginning to be activated and take precedence.

THE ANAL PHASE

The next phase is the anal phase. The zone of the body associated with this phase is the sphincter and the concern is our ability to control the sphincter muscles. This phase occurs roughly between the ages of two and four, and some writers have labeled it "the terrible twos." Whereas in the oral phase we formed opinions about what the world is going to be like for us based on how we experienced Mother and the early environment, in the anal phase we are forming opinions about what sort of person we are—about our power, worth, and general capabilities. The issue is no longer trust versus mistrust, but "Autonomy versus Shame and Doubt." The main question is no longer, "What kind of place is this world?" but rather, "How do I feel about myself?" or, "What kind of person am I?" or, "Am I powerful and effective or dirty, nasty, bad and impotent?" The archetypes which are clearly brought to focus during this stage are those of the Sun and Mars. Our own inborn expectations and archetypal patterns (as shown by the Sun and Mars) are brought out and embellished. I have also noted that oppositions between Taurus/Scorpio, Cancer/Capricorn, and Virgo/Pisces may show problems or difficulties with this stage. In other words, keep an eye on the earth-water polarity. I'll explain more about this later.

Another major question that arises during this phase is the one of *who decides? Who decides—you or me? Mother or child?* During the anal phase we are establishing greater separateness, individuality, and autonomy. This is directly related to certain physiological changes. We are becoming better co-ordinated and our range of influence is extending. We learn to walk and we begin to talk; we can explore more. More of the world begins to open up to us. Previously we were mostly in a receptive position, taking things in or gripping onto things. Now we are able to assert ourselves more directly onto the environment. Given that we feel reasonably secure and providing that the environment is not overly repressive, we naturally enjoy our increasing autonomy and independence. Ironically, however, our increasing ability to move about and operate in the world confronts us with a frustrating sense of our own smallness and inadequacy. There are things out there which are much bigger than us, which scare and threaten us. There are limits to what we are allowed to do or say. Mother gets angry and foul with us if we want to extend our autonomy out onto a busy road or if we say certain things she doesn't like. We are made to feel shameful and nasty because of some of the things we take pleasure in doing and trying. This is why Erikson highlighted the dilemma of "Autonomy versus Shame and Doubt" for this stage.[18]

Mother takes on the role of the great "No-sayer," inhibiting us and curtailing certain forms of expression. If, when you express your autonomy and individuality at this stage, you are for some reason chastised or slapped down, then you develop a sense of being bad and impotent against life. Later on, whenever you want to express your will or your independence, it may be accompanied by feelings of insecurity and anxiety. If you are brought up in too repressive or judgemental an environment, then you may grow up thinking that you dare not be yourself or that you need others to tell you what to do. You feel guilty to transgress authority or stand up for your own rights. You are left with a feeling that life is more powerful than you. We'll look at astrological correlates to these kinds of experiences in a minute.

There is no doubt that children are difficult at this stage, but it would help if the parents appreciated the positive implications of the development of the will for a child's growth. Sometimes I watch the way a mother puts down a child and it really hurts me. I see it on the street or in a restaurant and sometimes I feel like reaching for my diary and booking an appointment for the child for the year 2003 when he grows up into an adult with serious personality problems. I saw something like this at the supermarket the other day. A child about four or so was helping his mother push the supermarket trolley. His mother went off to pick up some other things from a different shelf and told him to stand just where he was with the trolley and not to move. So, the mother went further down the aisle and the little boy stood there fixed to the spot with the trolley obeying his mother's instructions perfectly. But the problem was that the child was blocking everybody's way. A few people asked him to move over with the trolley. He was really in the way and finally he did it—he started to walk further down the aisle with the cart and the people passed by. Just at that point, the mother came back and saw him moving the cart. She started screaming at him and slapped him: "I told you not to move that trolley. . . . " I watched this poor kid in this predicament. I must admit, I couldn't keep my mouth shut and I had to inter-vene—right over the tinned peaches counter I started to tell the

[18]Erikson, *Childhood and Society*, 226–229.

mother just what had happened and giving her a little lecture on the development of the will and autonomy versus shame and doubt! She looked back at me with a mixture of horror and blankness. But really, what an experience for the poor boy. I wonder what statement about life and the use of his will he was forming? He was certainly in a double bind—either way he couldn't win.

The Battle of the Chamber Pot

It's almost a cliche to talk about how toilet training affects our development, but this is a major concern of the anal stage. The Battle of the Chamber Pot, as it is sometimes called, is actually symbolic of many other conflicts we go through in the struggle to become socialized. In most cases, the mother is the prime socializing influence on you and your first big act of socialization is sphincter control. Now, what happens here? Issues around authority figures, self-assertion, self-control and power are brought to the fore. Who is going to win? If Mother insists, "You go when I say go," or, "You go only when I tell you to go," then later in life there is an expectation that authority figures will be cruel, harsh and inconsiderate. If Mother's will is over-imposed on your will in this respect, then you may not believe in your own authority, in your own ability to operate as a separate individual.

Then there is the reverse situation. If Mother is too easy and she allows you to go whenever you want, then you form the belief that *only* your will matters—only what you want counts—and you haven't learned to compromise. Then there is the case of Mother being inconsistent. Sometimes she forces toilet training on you and sometimes she lets you do what you want. In this case you may grow up never knowing whether your will is right or not. When to assert and when not to assert, when to take control and when not to take control, become very confusing later on in life.

In a curious way, toilet training resonates with issues around being creative. As children we take a certain pride in producing our feces. It is one of the first things our bodies produce. We feel that feces is something we are creating. Inherently, we don't feel shameful about it, but eventually we learn that it is bad and nasty. One of the patterns brought out during the anal phase is whether we feel what we create is good or bad. This is related to issues later in life around how the world will receive our creations. Now, if you are made to feel that what you are creating is dirty and shameful, then you are left with a feeling that what you assert or give out is undesirable.

In the anal phase, you discover that there are bits of you that Mother doesn't love. This is scary because you still need her love to survive. Creating something she doesn't like makes you feel ashamed and frightened. It's a bit like the feeling you may experience in a classroom when you ask a question or make a comment which just doesn't fit in, or which nobody picks up on; we say "you dropped a clanger." After dropping a clanger, you are left with a sense of shame and you just want to disappear and hide away. These kinds of feelings stem from the anal phase.

Another issue activated during the anal stage is when to hold on and when to let go. This applies not only to feces but also to whether we hold onto and suppress feelings or whether we freely express them. Some people are "anal expulsive." Whatever is inside them explodes all over the place, sometimes leaving a mess wherever they go. Others are "anal retentive." Everything is tight and held in. You don't know what is lurking in there, but something smells.

Astrological Correlations

As I said earlier, the sign placement and aspects of the Sun and Mars in particular are brought out and given flesh during the anal stage. The Sun gives us our sense of being a separate individual and Mars is related to how we assert our will. Right from birth, even before Mother sits you down on the potty and says "go," you have an inborn predisposition to expect certain things to happen when you assert your individuality, or when you are being creative and expressive, or when you are coming up against the world or another person's will.

Let's play around with this for a while. What might you feel if you have the Sun or Mars trine Jupiter? What are you going to feel about what you have to assert, or who you are?

Audience: Pretty good.

Howard: Yes, you are already born thinking, "What I have to give out is expansive and wonderful." What if you have Sun square

Neptune or Mars square Neptune? How do you feel about what you have to assert, give out or create?

Audience: Diffident and unsure.

Howard: Yes, and you may feel guilty about asserting your will as well. I did a chart for a man with an exact Mars square Neptune. When he was quite small, he walked into his Grandmother's room and found her dead. For the next twenty-five or thirty years he walked around believing that something he had done had caused her to die; he mistakenly equated the action of entering her room with causing her death. Neptune obscures whatever it touches, and in the case of Mars it can obscure the true significance of an action. He built up this fantasy that he had made a very bad thing happen; he didn't tell anyone about it and carried his secret sin inside himself. Later in life, he was terrified of asserting himself. He became a civil servant and did his job perfectly. But he kept being rejected for advancement in the service; they told him he wasn't assertive enough or that he didn't have the right kind of drive.

I've seen a similar issue with Mars square Pluto. I did a reading for a woman with the Sun, Mercury, and Mars conjunct in Scorpio, all applying to a square with Pluto in Leo. When her progressed Sun reached the Mercury-Mars conjunction and approached the exact square to Pluto, her younger brother had a serious accident while she was meant to be looking after him. It is not unlikely that at some earlier time she would have had some negative feelings towards him, because he had intruded into her special place as the first child. She might have wished him out of the way entirely. When the accident happened, she might have thought that her negative feelings towards him made the mishap occur. In the reading, it came out that she had great difficulty achieving what she wanted for herself. She was a great boon to all her friends and exceptionally good helping them with their lives and careers, but not so successful in fulfilling her own personal aims and goals. It is as if she is afraid to realise her own desires because in the past when a personal wish was fulfilled (the negative wish towards her younger brother), the consequences were disastrous.

Audience: The Sun or Mars in difficult aspect to Saturn could also bring out a feeling of being blocked in one's assertion.

Howard: Yes, indeed. In my lecture on "Victims and Saviours" I talked about this. Remember the study done by the psychologist Martin Seligman?[19] He was looking into what kinds of people get depressed and what makes them that way. His theory is called "The Learned Helplessness Model of Depression." He found that depression was related to the experience of learning early in life that outcomes were out of your control. He measured something called the "locus of control." If you feel that you have the ability to create your own life, that you have a certain influence or power over what happens to you, then you have an *internal* locus of control. However, if you feel that what happens to you is beyond your control then you have an *external* locus of control. Seligman found that depressed patients tended to be people who have an external locus of control; they have lost the belief that they have the power to act on their own behalf, or to influence their own experiential world. They develop a sense of helplessness and hopelessness.

I've noticed an astrological correlation to his theories. Those with Sun and Mars in difficult aspect to Neptune often tend to develop an *external* locus of control; they feel their own power is somewhat impotent, diffused, or ineffective. They may fantasise about having great power and influence, but underneath is a sense of impotency. Those with the Sun or Mars square or in hard aspect to Saturn also have a feeling that their personal will or expression is restricted or limited or that they will endlessly bump up against brick walls. Both types may try to compensate for such aspects by attempting to be extra tough, hard, or assertive—almost caricaturing the image of a "macho man." Or they continually have to test their will and prove their worth over and over again to allay an underlying insecurity about their ineffectiveness. The anger and frustration at those who appear to be blocking them may erupt into violence from time to time. Or the frustrated will-to-power may turn inward and give rise to various forms of self-destructive behaviour. Or they may look mild and compliant, but underneath they are angry and dangerously explosive.

---

[19]The Seligman study is clearly summarized in Irvin Yalom, *Existential Psychotherapy* (New York: Basic Books, 1980), 262-64.

Audience: What would you correlate with an internal locus of control?

Howard: Can you answer that?

Audience: Maybe something like Mars trine Jupiter, or the Sun or Mars in good aspect to Uranus. That would give the power to direct one's own life.

Howard: More likely than not.

Audience: What if you have some aspects which block the Sun and Mars but also other aspects which suggest you can direct your life and freely express yourself?

Howard: Then in some situations you feel mighty, or in control, or the one who calls the punches, while in other situations you quake in your boots. Check out the houses involved to see in which area of life the one or the other situation is met.

Audience: Don't you think that in our culture this is partly gender related? I find that a lot of women clients are most afraid of expressing their power.

Howard: Cultural conditioning must be taken into consideration. As children, women do receive more messages about not express-ing their anger or assertiveness. You know, things like, "You're not a pretty sight when you get angry." Or, "No man will want you if you are too demanding." So what happens to a woman who has a strong Mars or powerful Sun?

Let's say a woman is born with Mars, Jupiter, and Uranus con-junct in Aries on the Ascendant trine her Sun in Leo. If we under-stand the chart to be a set of celestial instructions about how she can best unfold who she is, then she had better develop some of that stuff on the Ascendant. I believe that more likely than not she will—one way or another—she will interpret the environment as conducive to her being assertive. But let's say she has the Moon in Cancer and her mother told her to be demure and sweet all the time. Then what's going to happen? There are various possibili-ties. She listens to her mother and denies her Mars-Jupiter-Uranus conjunction in Aries on the Ascendant, and is miserably unhappy because we are unhappy if we are not true to ourselves. Or, she finds ways of looking sweet and demure on the outside and subtly she is manipulating everyone around her to get precisely what she wants. Or, she marries a man who lives out her unexpressed power need—what some call the "Hollywood Wife Syndrome." Hopefully, though, she decides not just to live from her Moon: she takes steps to develop her own will and authority but finds ways to do this which are tactful and sensitive. In this way she is both the sensitive Moon and the more self-sufficient Aries conjunction. It will take practice to learn how to be more assertive and yet not overly aggressive.

Earth-Water Polarities

Before the break, I want to say a few more things about the anal phase and looking at it astrologically. Earlier I mentioned that you should consider the earth-water polarities in this respect. Let me explain how this fits. Take Cancer opposite Capricorn. If you see this opposition brought out in the chart, then anal issues could be highlighted. Cancer is instinctive, primitive, and chaotic, whereas Capricorn adjusts to society, and accepts boundaries, rules and limits. This opposition highlights the dilemma between being instinctive and being civilized. You may favour one side of the opposition and see the other part as the enemy or as being forced on you. So you want to be free-flowing and natural (Cancer) but you see the world stopping you (Capricorn) and telling you to act more respectably. Or, you are exceptionally orderly, tidy, and respectful of etiquette (Capricorn), and you experience people who are too emotional or instinctive (Cancer) as threatening or disgusting. The opposition is within you—the battle is between two different ways of being which are inside you.

Or take a Virgo and Pisces opposition. Pisces doesn't want to have to control itself too much—it is a "loose" sign. Virgo, however, wants life to run to a routine. Taurus and Scorpio also bring up issues of appetite indulgence versus appetite mastery, or holding onto things versus letting them go.

Zonal Confusion

Another thing you should be aware of about the anal phase is that power issues can become mixed up with feeding issues. If you are determined to assert your will over the mother, then you might also refuse to eat as a way of exercising autonomy. Some research into anorexia has suggested that the anorexic deems it more important to have power and control over her own body than to survive and eat on demand. Also, be aware that power issues can easily become mixed up with sexuality issues. There could be a connection between sexual dysfunctions like retarded ejaculation or premature ejaculation and the whole conflict of holding on or letting go. For instance, if your mother really wanted you to go to the toilet on demand and you are angry at her for it, your way of getting back is to say no and hold on. This can be displaced from the anal zone to the phallic zone—what is sometimes called "zonal confusion." So, a man who, as a boy, was very angry with his mother because she was so demanding could revenge himself against women later in life. With premature ejaculation, he lets go too soon. In some cases of retarded ejaculation, he is depriving or holding back. Aspects to Mars may shed light on some of these situations.

The Third House

The 3rd house has some relation to the anal phase because of its association with movement and mobility. During the anal phase we gain sufficient physiological co-ordination to move around the environment more easily. Signs and planets in the 3rd reveal our predisposition to selectively perceive certain aspects of the imme-diate environment and neglect or overlook others. For instance, those with Venus in the 3rd would pick up on the more pleasing and welcoming aspects of the environment. Correspondingly, they will feel congenial and hospitable with what is around them. But those with Saturn in the 3rd may perceive the more sinister, restrictive or colder features of the environment. Therefore, in their eyes, it is not a safe place in which to freely move about. How we feel about siblings and our interaction with them will also be shown by the 3rd as well.

For a child, the ability to move about in the environment is very important because *movement is experience*. Both movement and experience stimulate the brain and stimulate thinking. Hence, we associate the 3rd house not only with the immediate environment but also with the mind—with how we think. You notice that when I lecture, I move around a great deal. I finnd that moving around activates my thinking and helps me make connections. You could say that movement actually helps the brain to develop. Mercury is the natural ruler of the 3rd which rules short journeys as well as thinking.

Some researchers experimented with monkeys along these lines. There were two groups: some were reared in a cage with a moving pendulum and another group were brought up in a cage with a stationary pendulum. The little monkeys reared with the stationary pendulum grew up more terrified of humans, less exploratory and generally maladaptive compared to the others. Perhaps we can deduce that if during the anal phase children are kept under too tight a rein, they are not only limited in movement and experience, but their brains may not develop as well compared to children who are allowed more freedom.

Restriction of movement and experience doesn't just mean being kept in a play-pen too long. Parents can put their children into *mental strait jackets*. Some children are only allowed to think or say certain thoughts which are in line with what the parents approve. In this way, the children are conditioned into having to be very careful about what they do, say, or think, and, therefore, they lose the ability to be spontaneous and immediate. If they hate a teacher at school, they can't come home and talk about it. They have to suppress the thoughts and figure out what is acceptable to say. Consequently, certain feelings never get fully dealt with and the whole psyche becomes congested. Examine your 3rd house for issues relating to this—spontaneity versus inhibition of thought, movement, and experience.

If you studied biology at school you probably heard the phrase "ontogeny recapitulates phylogeny." In the womb we evolve from being a fish to being a human. Similarly, in the first thirty-six months of life we recapitulate that evolutionary development again. Jean Houston has a chapter in *The Possible Human* called "Awakening Your Evolutionary History."[20] She worked with Moshe Feldenkrais on these ideas—he was the founder of a technique which helps develop greater awareness through movement. Houston's idea is that if we fail (in the first thirty-six months of life) to have a smooth transition from being a fish to being an

---

[20]Jean Houston, *The Possible Human*, 96-114. Further material on this topic can be found in Moshe Feldenkrais, *Awareness Through Movement* (New York: Harper & Row, 1972).

amphibian to being a reptile to being a monkey until we stand erect as a human, then damage is done to the overall psychology. When we are born we have a "fish brain," we move around like a fish, and there is a part of us which needs to be able to function like a fish. In turn, these movements activate growth of that part of the brain which deals with amphibian and reptilian development. At this stage the infant begins to crawl on his belly and to co-ordinate movement of the arms and legs. (We should really all get on the floor and try these phases.) This movement in turn activates the early mammalian parts of the brain and we begin to crawl on all fours. The crawling movement activates the neo-mammalian parts of the brain and we start to make movements similar to those of a monkey, swinging from side to side. I'll demonstrate it for you—like this. And so on until the more human parts of the brain are developed.

Houston argues that to be physiologically and psychologically healthy we need to fully experience each of these developmental stages. If the child is prevented from fully experiencing the reptilian phase, for instance (when he or she begins to crawl on the belly and co-ordinate movement of the arms and legs as well as learning to co-ordinate the upper and lower axes of the body), then there is a danger of trouble with sexual development. If the child is severely restricted or harnessed during the monkey phase I showed you, then there is a decrease of curiosity and a lessened ability to learn skills and imitate. So movement and some degree of free expression in the early years of life are important if we are to grow into adults who can use more of our full potential. Now, I'd like to move on to the Oedipal phase.

THE OEDIPAL STAGE

Traditionally, the Oedipal stage was thought to have occurred between the ages of four and six, but studies are now putting it earlier, anywhere from age two-and-a-half. Erikson writes that the main issue is that of "Initiative versus Guilt."[21]

The Oedipal phase is known as a three-person area. Previously, in the oral and anal phases there were primarily two peo-

---

[21]Erikson, *Childhood and Society*, 229-32.

ple involved: the child and the mother/caretaker. However, during the Oedipal phase the child becomes much more aware of the father and the parental relationship in general. The archetype which is constellated at this time is that of *Union*. (In the oral phase, *love* was important; in the anal phase the *will* is developed; but in the Oedipal phase love *and* will are seen to be operating together.) The main planet which is activated during this phase is Venus, although this stage of life will constellate certain other parts of the chart which I'll discuss more fully shortly.

Let's say something first about the role of the father. In the very early years of life, the mother is usually much more obvious to the child than the father. As you grow older, you become increasingly aware of "the otherness" of the father. In the beginning you are at one with your mother—that uroboric wholeness we mentioned earlier. Father can be experienced as an intrusion or disruption into the uroboric mother-child cocoon. In normal circumstances, you are with the mother all day and you establish a close bond with her. Then father arrives home from work and he brings something wholly different into the home: he brings the smell of the outside world home with him. Liz once pointed out that someone with Sun square Pluto could experience the father's arrival as a kind of rape or intrusion into the intactness with the mother. Sun in difficult aspect to Mars or Uranus might also give this experience, or an image of the father as violent and unpredictable. Later in life, women with these kinds of aspects may carry an image of the man as a rapist, etc.

More positively, the father provides the needed energy of the masculine principle which helps you separate from the mother. With pretty good aspects to the Sun, the father is often seen as someone who can prepare and advise you about how to go out and do battle with the world outside the home and break away from the protective embrace of the mother. He tells you stories about his adventures as a lad, how he had this or that experience. In this way, you are inspired to go out there and face the world yourself. He equips you to be a hero or heroine.

If the father hasn't done too well with the world himself, then he is not a very good role model for this. The girl-child with a disappointing father may grow up expecting all men to be like that, or else will be looking for the ideal father she didn't have. On the other hand, if the father appears all too wonderful and never shows any of his faults or weaknesses, then the boy-child might worry about ever being as good as his father. The girl-child in this case might spend the rest of her life comparing the men she meets to this idealised image she had as a little girl about her father. I can't go into all the astrological correlations with these kinds of experiences, they are too complex and too varied to do now. But bear these typical patterns in mind when you are looking at a chart and see if any of them fit with aspects to the Sun and placements in the 4th (if you take the 4th to mean the father). For instance, if you are looking at a woman's chart and you see that she has Sun conjunct Jupiter, it is worth exploring if the father was tied up with the Jupiter projection. I've heard many women with this aspect talk about how divine and wonderful the father was or is. It reminds me of Fallon in the soap opera *Dynasty*, who only sees positive things in Blake Carrington. It will be difficult for other men to live up to the little girl's image of a Jupiterian father. Or, with Sun in aspect to Neptune, a girl-child may idealise her father and then as she grows older she sees him in a different light and is disappointed or let down. This, too, can become a pattern for her with men later on.

As you move from the oral phase to the anal phase to the Oedipal stage, the urge to express and assert yourself becomes stronger. Sexuality emerges more clearly. As the sex drive increases, it is usually lived out in a fantasy with the parent of the opposite sex. On a deeper, more symbolic level, what is happening is that the "contrasexual element" of your nature is being activated. Oedipal desires give you the first real introduction to the sex that you are not. The boy-child who has previously separated from the mother during the anal phase is now consciously seeing her as different from himself and making contact with his own "inner femaleness" through desiring her. The girl is making contact with her own "inner maleness" through desiring the father. You project your image of the masculine or feminine onto Father or Mother and you attempt to complete yourself by re-uniting with that image. Symbolically, the incest wish can be understood as an attempt to unite the male and female principal in yourself. It is at this stage that the boy projects the Moon and Venus onto his mother; and the girl projects her Sun and Mars onto her father. When the boy desires his mother, in a sense, he is desiring his Moon and Venus back. When the girl desires the father, she is attempting to reunite with her own Sun and Mars. In the early years, you experience much of your chart as external to yourself—as being "out there." Individuation involves taking back into the Self what you have previously attributed to others in this way.

The Oedipal complex (or the Electra complex as it is called for women) is actually an attack on the parental relationship. I don't believe that the child literally wants the parent sexually; rather the child wants to be *the most special person* to the opposite sex parent and resents the same-sex parent obstructing this. As the boy-child becomes more aware of the father, he also becomes aware that the father is a rival for the mother's attention. The boy sees her paying attention to the father and he feels jealous because he wants her all to himself. The girl child is seeking to unite with the father and sees the mother as the rival. Traditionally, at least, this is how it is. I've noticed that people with strong placements in Leo often have great difficulty with the Oedipal phase—Leo is so concerned with being special and the centre of attention. Aries is another sign that may carry issues related to Oedipal rivalry—it likes to beat others and loathes being rejected. Libra is another sign which is acutely aware of what is happening in relationship, so it is sensitive to Oedipal issues. And I wouldn't put it past Gemini to entangle itself in various triangles. Scorpio likes to undermine the one who has the most power and influence. We are gradually covering all the signs now: the Oedipal dilemma is fairly universal for one reason or another.

Erikson wrote that this phase highlighted the issue of "Initiative versus Guilt." Let's consider this from the point of view of the boy-child first. The initiative is expressed in the desire to win the mother and conquer the father. The sense is, "I want to get rid of Daddy and take over his role with Mummy." Thus, we have a triangle forming. Obviously, on some level the boy will be feeling guilty about his desires. The boy fears his father might find out what he is thinking and then punish him. The situation is similar for the girl-child. She fears her mother will find out that she wants Daddy to herself and then she will be punished. All of us experience a common regression back to the Oedipal phase when we have the feeling that if people *really* knew what we were thinking or wanting, we would be disliked or punished.

Now, in terms of the boy-child, he is competing with the father: "I'm a big boy now and I'd like to have Mummy to myself and get rid of Daddy." But then the boy starts to compare himself to his father and usually he doesn't fare too well by comparison. Daddy is bigger; Daddy is better equipped to take care of Mummy's needs; Daddy works and earns money so he can look after her better; and what's more, Daddy already has her.

Similarly, the little girl starts comparing herself to Mother, "Well, Mother can cook and run the house better than me; she is so much better skilled at keeping Daddy, etc." Both the little boy and girl must face the fact that they are small and inadequate compared to their respective rivals. Another common regression back to the Oedipal stage is the feeling which many of us have of being afraid that other people will find out that we are not as good and able as they think we are. A fear may linger from this phase that other people will discover that underneath it all we are inadequate and inept. Ninety-nine people can applaud you and say you are wonderful; and then one person says you are not really that great and you say, "Aha, now I have been found out." If you are truly stuck in the Oedipal stage, you will remain feeling inadequate and inferior to other people your whole life: the little boy or little girl in you is still comparing yourselves to "Big People."

We have worked ourselves into a tight corner. How do we resolve this dilemma? The resolution of the Oedipal complex comes when the boy-child stops trying to compete with Daddy and decides to emulate or imitate him. "There is no use competing with Daddy—he is obviously way ahead of me, so why don't I try to be like him and then when I grow up I can get a Mummy for myself." And the girl-child decides to be like her mother so she can get a Daddy for herself one day. Rather than competing with and trying to depose the parent of the same sex, we choose to identify with them and model ourselves on being like them.

However, there can be complications in this stage. What if the mother actually finds the little boy more desirable and attractive than the father? If the father is hopeless at providing, lousy in bed, a drunken bastard and the parental relationship unfulfilling, then the mother may actually turn to the little boy for the kind of emotional satisfaction she should be deriving from the father and the marriage. A kind of erotic quality (not necessarily explicitly sexual) begins to creep into her maternal relationship with her son. At first, this may seen wonderful to the boy: "Gee, I won," but underneath there is the feeling he has destroyed the father and that sooner or later he will be punished for this. It also means that the boy's libidinal energy remains so tied up with the mother that it isn't free to flow in other directions or into other relationships. He stays "Mummy's Big Boy" and the father is shut out. A proper relationship is not formed with the same-sex parent. A similar situation can occur for the little girl if her father turns to her for the kind of emotional appreciation and love which he is not getting from the mother. She feels she has won the competition with the mother, fears the mother's reprisal and risks perennially remaining "Daddy's little girl."

A similar difficulty could arise if the opposite sex parent dies or leaves home during the Oedipal years. The father might go off to war or the parents might get divorced. Again, the little boy thinks he has won the mother from the father, but also harbours the fear that he will be punished for having destroyed the father. The same thing would happen to the little girl if her mother leaves or dies during this period.

To make it even more complicated, there is also something known as the "reverse Oedipal complex" or the "homosexual Oedipal dilemma." Normally the child desires the parent of the opposite sex. But what if the opposite sex parent is so undesireable that there is no way that the child would crave that parent? If mother is so ghastly for whatever reason, it might be that the boy will want to win the father and get rid of mother; or if the father is so awful, the little girl may want to marry mother and do away with the father. In these cases, the boy may want to provide for the father what the mother should be providing; and the little girl may want to provide for the mother what the father should be giving. This is the reverse or homosexual Oedipal complex. And, of course, there are further complications to this stage if we consider the growing number of single parent families. In these cases, the parent's lovers may be drawn into the scenario.

Audience: What kind of aspects would you put with the reverse Oedipal complex?

Howard: I can't give you any hard and fast rules here, but there are a few things I've noticed. Consider the case of the boy-child finding the mother so difficult or unappealing that he wants to win father rather than her. I've seen this situation in the charts of men where the Moon has very difficult aspects, but the Sun is well-aspected. If the Moon is in a mess, then the boy may have a lot of problems relating to the mother or he may find her intolerable—therefore the father (as shown by the favorable Sun aspects) is more desirable and attractive. The converse situation could exist for women, when the Sun is weak or difficultly aspected, but the Moon is pretty clear. In this case, the little girl could find the father unattractive or he even might be virtually nonexistent physically, emotionally or mentally—what's called "an absent father." In these cases, the little girl's libidinal drive could stay linked with the mother and doesn't switch over to father.

In general, however, the Oedipal complex is resolved when the urge to emulate and identify with the same-sex parent becomes stronger than the urge to compete. It is very important how lovingly the opposite sex parent rejects the child's advances to "marry" them. The father has to appreciate the daughter's grace and beauty and yet not let her think that she can have him all to herself. The father needs to reject her lovingly. The mother has to make the son feel she is not rejecting him because he is too "weedy" and insufficient.

The Oedipal dilemma resurfaces in adolescence with the rivalry of the boys in the class for the best girls and vice versa. Throughout life you can still see vestiges of this complex with women or men who always seem to fall in love with people who are already married or who are unobtainable for some reason. I am thinking of two clear cases right now. One is a man with Moon conjunct Pluto in Leo in the 7th—he has a history of breaking up other people's marriages. In some way he proves his worth and adequacy via competition with another man for that man's wife. The Moon in the house of relationship immediately equates the area of partnership with mother issues; and Pluto in Leo brings in the idea of rivalry, intrigue, and unconscious complexes. Some women with Sun in aspect to Neptune seem to fall in love with men who are already married or hard to get, and there could be unresolved Oedipal influences creeping in here. A similar situation arises quite often with Venus in aspect to Neptune—wanting that which is elusive or difficult to have, and then the need to sacrifice the relationship in one form or another.

Audience: What about Venus in aspect to Uranus?

Howard: I don't think that necessarily suggests Oedipal issues. In my experience, this is more frequently what is known as a freedom-closeness dilemma. One part of the person wants union (Venus) but another part craves independence and freedom (Uranus), so the person sometimes chooses a lover with whom it is difficult to make a lasting bind, and in that way the Venus-Uranus person stays loose.

Another later manifestation of left-over Oedipal feelings is the desire to be noticed for how wonderful you are without necessarily doing anything to *earn* that recognition. It's the difference between *demanding* attention rather than *gaining* attention. Earlier, I associated the Oedipal complex with the Leo side of our natures and the desire to be appreciated in this way is very Leonine. I know people with strong Leo placements who have a burning desire to be applauded for their abilities and yet they are afraid to seriously develop their talents in case they fail. They think that other people should see how special and wonderful they are before they have proven it. This is similar to feelings in the Oedipal child who wants to be seen as good as Mummy or Daddy—as good as an adult—before they have actually arrived there.

Sometimes exhibitionism is a hangover from the Oedipal phase. Leos are generally known for this, but I believe it is a Sagittarian trait as well. The Oedipal dilemma has a fire and air feeling about it. Fire wants to stand out and be special, while air is learning to adapt itself to being part of a larger system. Leo wants to be special and unique and the most central, but Aquarius sees itself functioning as part of a system, and asks that power be distributed equally among the components.

Aspects to Venus will be constellated during the Oedipal phase. We have already talked about how Venus in aspect to Saturn expects pain and restriction in relationship. Those who have Pluto in aspect to Venus might have a very difficult Oedipal phase because the archetype of union is in aspect to the planet of destructive and secretive energy, which is what is entailed in the Oedipal phase anyway.

Audience: What about Venus in aspect to the Moon?

Howard: This aspect could easily denote Oedipal problems, especially in a man's chart. The image of the Moon/mother becomes entangled with Venus—the image of the beloved and union. There is a mix up of the maternal (Moon) and the erotic (Venus). The feminine principle has many different facets: one is the mother who feeds you and looks after you and the other is the lover or mistress who tantalizes, flirts, stimulates and seduces. The boy with Moon in aspect to Venus has trouble separating these. Often there is a collusion here. The Mother is feeding the child and experiencing something erotic and sensual through it at the same time; the child also gets an erotic stimulation from being fed. If the mother is not fulfilling her sexual and emotional needs through her husband, she may pour all of herself into the relationship with the child. Feelings and sensations of a sensual nature well up as she is performing the mothering role. So these kinds of loving innuendoes pass between the mother and child. Such a situation might keep the boy hooked in the Oedipal phase longer; or there is no room in his life for other kinds of relationships with women because he is so involved with the mother. Some men with Moon and Venus in hard aspect have difficulty in marriage later in life. If a man sees his wife too much as a "Mother" (Moon), he may lose his sexual feelings for her (Venus), because it is such a societal taboo to have sex with the mother.

Audience: Does Venus square Saturn mean that the child felt rejected by the parent he or she wanted to unite with?

Howard: Yes, possibly. The little girl with Venus in difficult aspect to Saturn may be left with the feeling that she lacks something which would make her attractive to the father. Later in life she may unconsciously equate a man she is after with the father she didn't win. Succeeding in attracting the present man's love is tied up with the little girl in her still trying to get Daddy. Instead of falling for people who also fall in love with her, she is attracted to those who are more of a challenge: "If I could only win this person's love, then I've proven I'm not so bad." Or, she tries to avoid the whole conflict altogether and goes for men who feel safe and who don't trigger her insecurity. Some women with Venus in hard aspect to Saturn may look rather self-sufficient and independent, but underneath they are often highly sensitive and vulnerable to rejection. We often try to mask where Saturn is.

THE SCHOOL AGE

This next phase is called "The School Age," or sometimes "The Play Age" and is normally linked to ages six through ten. It is the equivalent to Freud's "latency period," the quiet before the storm of puberty. Erikson writes that the issue is "Industry versus Inferiority."[22] We are coming through the Oedipal dilemma and beginning to think: "Okay, I'm not an adult yet, but I can start working toward being grown-up and start learning how to be a good Mummy or Daddy of the future." This is the time for seriously developing those skills which will enable you to function more independently in the world. We go to school and begin to relate more regularly with other people besides our parents. We begin to get a sense of who we are in relationship to others than just our family. We broaden our awareness of life in general.

We are beginning to explore ourselves as potential adults. The archetypes which come into play during this phase are ones which have to do with productivity and competence. If we do well at this stage it helps us to grow up thinking we are capable and effective people. If this phase is difficult, we feel inadequate and inferior to others. It's obvious that how we fare in this period has much to do with how things went during the earlier anal and oral phases, when we developed an even more basic sense of our worth or goodness.

In the Oedipal stage we measured ourselves against adults and didn't have much of a chance. In the School Age we measure ourselves against our peers. We crave recognition for producing things. We need a certain feeling of pleasure in being productive.

Astrologically, Mercury, Jupiter, and Saturn all relate to issues of this stage. Placements involving these planets will be brought to the fore during this period. Mercury shows the kind of mind we have, how we learn and whether we feel confident or insecure about our mental ability. Mercury also has something to do with how we use our hands and how adept we are with tools. Mercury square Saturn may be a mind that works more slowly than others, and, therefore, those with this placement may feel insecure about their mental capability. Sometimes, they feel they have to work extra hard to prove themselves. Mercury in difficult aspect to Uranus may reason and think in a markedly different way from other children. Those with this placement might feel alienated and uncertain of where they fit in. Mercury in aspect to Neptune could be a spatial, right-brain type mind, and may not be very much at

---

[22]Erikson, *Childhood and Society*, 232-34.

home with traditional education which stresses a more rational, linear, left-brain approach. The 3rd house will also give a sense of how a person experiences school. More often than not, Jupiter in this house has a good time of it and feels alright about the self in this sphere. Saturn in the 3rd brings out feelings of uncertainty or inadequacy and worries about fitting in. For those with Pluto in the 3rd, doing well at school and being considered intelligent may become almost a life-death issue. "If I do well and prove how bright I am, then I will live—if not, I might be destroyed." Naturally, a person with this placement won't feel too comfortable at school for these reasons. How can he or she ever relax if life and death issues are at stake? The 6th house also relates to skill development, and placements there are likely to be brought to the fore during the School Age. Also, the 6th house carries the issue of what it is like to work alongside other people, which is something else we learn more about during this phase.

You may wonder why I associate Jupiter and Saturn with this age. Jupiter applies because it is a time during which we are growing and expanding our possibilities. We aspire to be like certain heroes or heroines we admire. Jupiter is the dangling carrot which pulls us forward, the urge to be something bigger and better. Saturn is around at this stage, however, because we are encouraged to grow *only* within certain restrictions and limits. Through the educational system, society is trying to form us into good citizens—to direct our aspirations (Jupiter) into acceptable Saturnian forms. We are encouraged to grow and to expand our creativity and productivity, but it has to be within the confines of what is normal or collectively validated (Saturn).

Audience: What if somebody has Jupiter in hard aspect to Saturn? Will it make this stage more difficult?

Howard: Yes, it could. The child's desire to explore and expand (Jupiter) may be squeezed by the restraints of Saturn. Or he is so aware of being judged and watched (Saturn) that he is afraid to be free and expressive in a Jupiterian manner. A similar dilemma could arise with Saturn in difficult aspect to Uranus. Highly individualistic and creative Uranian urges may be quashed by a need to conform to the way something is traditionally meant to be done.

Another Jupiter-Saturn type problem is biting off more than you can chew. At this stage, a child is trying to be as good as an adult and may not be respecting the limits of his or her age, experience, and size. This is a form of exaggerated initiative, which can be dangerous because a child is likely to fail at being as good as an adult at that stage. If this occurs, a lingering sense of being a failure can stay with the person for life. Or, the child becomes an adult who keeps making big plans which are unrealistic and almost doomed not to succeed. People with Jupiter or Neptune square Saturn are often painfully aware of the discrepancy between where they actually are and where they would like to be.

ADOLESCENCE

There is not much time left, but I want to introduce the phase of adolescence which occurs anywhere from ages ten, eleven, twelve to nineteen, twenty, or twenty-one. During this phase, you emerge out of the womb of the family into society. It is akin to another birth. Through adolescence, all the earlier stages of growth are recapitulated and brought to the surface again. Unfinished business and unresolved feelings from the oral phase reappear. "Is this a safe world for me to survive in?" Unresolved feelings and patterns from the anal phase are there in adolescence as well. "Am I going to be good enough for the world—will I be potent, effective, good or bad?" And Oedipal issues re-emerge with a vengeance. "How will I fare in relationships? Will I be popular and attract the people I want to attract?"

One of the nicer things I've heard said about the difficult period of adolescence is that it affords the opportunity to redeem what has gone wrong in childhood. The old issues resurface again: if you didn't feel that your mother was a safe container as a child, when you venture out into the world during adolescence you may feel it is not a safe place. But at least you have the opportunity to more consciously work through these feelings and change some of the earlier patterns. A teacher may provide you with something your mother didn't provide, and therefore mediates some of your negative expectations. A close relationship may heal your Oedipal wounds. Being older, you have had a chance to acquire certain skills and abilities, which means you can handle the world more effectively than when you were screaming away helpless in the crib.

The central concern of adolescence is the search for identity. You spend hours in front of the mirror trying to figure out who you are. You experiment playing different roles and being different people. The quest for your sexual identity becomes an urgent, pressing concern.

Adolescents can be broadly classified into four main types or categories.[23] First there are the *conventional* types: these are the people who generally marry young and don't question the values or ideals of their parents or society. They do similar things the parents did. Usually Saturn or Capricorn is strong in their charts. There is no struggle to find a sense of individuality in one's own right—no adolescent rebellion. Later on in life, often during the mid-life crisis (when Uranus opposes Uranus, or Saturn opposes Saturn), these people actively rebel against the constrictions and conventions into which they have previously slotted. In other words, their adolescent rebellion catches up with them at mid-life.

Then there are the *idealistic* types: they are moody, romantic, and dreamy. Some are highly moralistic and obsessed with perfection. Some are revolutionaries absorbed with progressive movements. Usually they have strong Uranian or Neptunian charts, with a dash of Mars and Jupiter thrown in. They discover Transcendental Meditation at eighteen and are going to change the world through it. They become absorbed into a vision of what life can be like, invariably contrary to how their parents lived. If their parents were the sort who were heavily involved with wholefood and the peace movement, sometimes the idealistic adolescent will swing just the other way: "You have to be tough and aggressive to survive in this world," and they become punks or whatever.

A third type of adolescent is *the hedonist*: the beach boy, the surfer, or the drop-out. They could drift into drugs, glue-sniffing or even casual prostitution. They may have strong Jupiter or Neptune tendencies in the chart, or perhaps a Plutonic fascination for what is taboo and decadent.

A fourth type of adolescent might be labelled *the psychopath*. Here you have your neo-Nazis, your National Front youth in England, some skinheads, or the most extreme varieties of Hell's Angels.

---

[23]This information on the four types of adolescents was given to me in a series of lectures I attended at the Westminster Pastoral Foundation in London (1979-80) in Developmental Psychology led by Dr. M. Margalit.

In any of these four broad categories, the issue is the search for an identity. In terms of astrological correlations to the phase of adolescence, I have noticed that people with difficult placements in the 3rd house often have quite traumatic times during this period of life. Traditionally, the 3rd house is associated with ages seven to fourteen, and placements in this house may describe something about one's initiation into young adulthood. I would also scrutinize the 5th house to see how one fares with issues of dating and romance which are so important at this time. The 8th house reveals something about one's attitude toward sexuality. The 11th house will describe involvements with groups, social circles and friends, which are all important during this phase of life.

In assessing the concerns which crop up during adolescence, it is useful to closely examine the significant transits and progressions which took place anywhere from age ten and eleven to seventeen and eighteen.[24] Keep a close eye on Pluto during this period. In itself, Pluto is an archetype closely aligned with adolescence: you *die* as a child and are *reborn* a young adult. The myth of Persephone's abduction by the god Pluto can be read as an analogy for what happens during adolescence. In the beginning, Persephone is the little girl, also known as *Kore*, the maiden. She is playing innocently in the meadow with various virgin goddesses. It's Spring and the ground is moist with flowers. She is under the protective embrace of her mother and then Pluto comes along and abducts her—takes her into the underworld, rapes her and marries her. Something like this happens in adolescence: we are jolted out of childhood innocence. It is often through a passionate crush or sexual encounter that deep underground feelings and emotions are brought to the surface. Adolescence is never an easy transition, but if Pluto is involved in an important transit or progression during this time as well, the wrench out of childhood may be associated with even a greater degree of torment and upheaval.

Just to give you an example of what I mean, let's say a woman has the Sun in one degree Scorpio and Pluto at 13 degrees Leo. By secondary progression the Sun makes an exact square to Pluto at age twelve. Regardless of the progression, this age is Plutonic in any case because of the striking physical changes taking place in

---

[24]For further insight into secondary progressions which occur during this phase, I would recommend Nancy Anne Hastings' book, *Secondary Progressions: Time to Remember* (York Beach, ME: Samuel Weiser, 1984.)

the body at the onset of puberty. Now the girl in question *also* has an important progression involving Pluto at this time. It's like a double hit of Pluto, and the dramatic intensity of the change is enhanced. She is developing her secondary sex characteristics—her breasts are growing and her pubic hair is showing and menstruation might begin. Up to age ten or eleven she might still be taking baths with her father, but now it all changes. Daddy can't be quite as physical with her as he used to: now that she is becoming more womanly it feels awkward and uncomfortable for him. She may then equate her emerging sexual desires with this loss of closeness to the father. She may feel that what is happening to her is bad and causes bad things to occur. A feeling remains even later in life which makes her feel uncertain, guilty or uncomfortable with the sexual side of her nature.

If a parent should die while the child is entering adolescence, the child may feel thrust too quickly into having to assume an adult role. If the father dies, then the adolescent boy might have to take on some of his father's role in the family. If the mother dies, the adolescent girl will take over her position. If Saturn, Uranus, or Pluto make important transits or show up by progression during the onset of adolescence, the person may experience a sense of being thrust out of childhood too suddenly. There hasn't been the chance to gradually change from being a dependent child into a more responsible young adult—this person may feel the need to go back and re-live that transition more gradually or may need the chance to go back and play out some of the unlived childhood or adolescent urges that were missed because he or she was jolted into adult responsibility too soon. Also, if someone never had a happy childhood, there may be a reluctance to let go of that stage and grow into an adult. The person may want to stay a child in order to still have the chance to experience those things he or she has missed.

Another transit to keep an eye on is Saturn coming up to oppose natal Saturn, which happens roughly around age fourteen. The houses and signs involved will reveal a great deal about the kinds of tests and trials that are important at this time. Saturn opposite Saturn suggests that the patterns which have been troublesome in earlier phases of childhood will be met against via the world and society.

Audience: What about those children born in the 1960's who have the Uranus and Pluto conjunction in Virgo?

Howard: You bring up an interesting point—something called generational aspects. There is a whole generation coming of age who were born with Uranus conjunct Pluto in Virgo from late 1962 to 1968 or thereabouts. Historically, this period was a time of acceleration and change. The world was going a bit crazy. America went "crazy" after President Kennedy was assassinated, and then Martin Luther King and Bobby Kennedy. The children born then emerged into a world where old values and mores were being challenged and overthrown, as described by Uranus conjunct Pluto. It was the swinging sixties complete with sexual freedom and the rebellion against the establishment. The children born then are now coming of age with this conjunction in their charts. Virgo is the sign linked to work and the labour force. In England, these kids are finishing school and having to look for work in a country where there is mass unemployment, where the whole work thing is in upheaval. Because of this situation, new schemes are being worked out for youth employment opportunity, and we have such things as job-sharing and the four-day week. One person I heard about was offering to pay someone to give him a job. This is certainly a Uranian reversal of Virgo affairs. While some of the young people with this aspect are being very creative finding work, others are turning their rage, nihilism, and sense of injustice (Uranus conjunct Pluto) towards society. There is a compulsion in the punk movement to shock in the way they dress and adorn their bodies—all Virgo issues. With Uranus and Pluto in earthy Virgo, punks are using their bodies to make a statement to society. On another more positive level, you see a growing interest in alternative health, diet and medicine—Virgo is the sign of health.

Time marches on. We usually finish at 5:30, so there is just enough time to put a chart on the board and look at it in reference to some of the things we have been talking about today. Anybody care to be exposed? Thank you—this is Mandy's chart. Let's look at some of the early progressions of the Moon and see what these correspond to. (See Chart 1 on page 78.)

Howard: At age three months, the progressed Moon conjuncts Jupiter so you are not doing so badly. You are picking up Jupiter via the mother and Jupiter is in the 7th house. My sense is that your

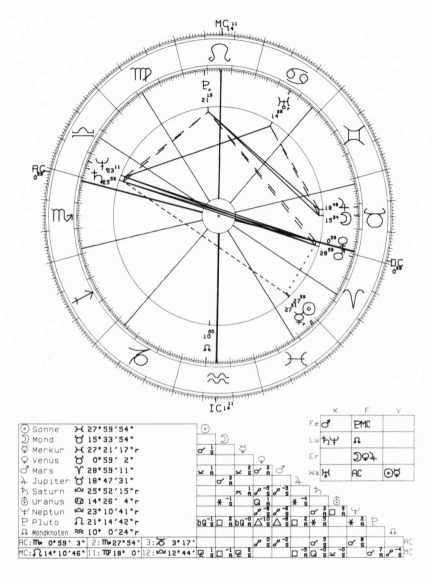

☉ Sonne	♓ 27°59'54"
☽ Mond	♉ 15°33'54"
☿ Merkur	♓ 27°21'17"r
♀ Venus	♉ 0°59' 2"
♂ Mars	♈ 28°59'11"
♃ Jupiter	♉ 18°47'31"
♄ Saturn	♎ 25°52'15"r
♅ Uranus	♋ 14°26' 4"r
♆ Neptun	♎ 23°10'41"r
♇ Pluto	♌ 21°14'42"r
☊ Mondknoten	♒ 10° 0'24"r

AC: ♏ 0°59' 3" | 2: ♏ 27°54' | 3: ♉ 3°17'
MC: ♌ 14°10'46" | 11: ♍ 18° 0' | 12: ♎ 12°44'

	K	F	V
Fe	♂	PMC	
Lu	♄♆	♌	
Er		☽♀♃	
Wa	♅	AC	☉☿

Chart 1. Mandy. The birth data has been withheld for confidentiality. Chart calculated by Astrodienst, Postfach, CH-8033, Zürich, Switzerland, using the Placidus house system.

mother must have been feeling pretty good, and her relationship with your father must seem okay at that time.

Mandy: I know a little about this from what my mother has told me. She was married to my father just a year before I was born and having me was helping to solidify the marriage. She felt good about having me; she felt it was the right thing to do. She was relieved to be in a marriage and doing the conventional stuff.

Howard: So Mother feels good to you then. But at age six months the progressed Moon squares Pluto and begins to make an inconjunct to Neptune. So something is changing. Jupiter is not foreground anymore and you are picking up Pluto and Neptune through your mother. Do you know what happened when you were six months old?—anything which would spell upheaval or change?

Mandy: She got pregnant again. My brother is about a year and three months younger than me.

Howard: So, the progressed Moon is hitting Pluto and Mother gets pregnant. You are only six months, but somehow you are registering her changing. It must have frightened you in some way. Do you think she wanted to be pregnant again so soon?

Mandy: I don't think she was happy about being pregnant again. Not long ago she said to me, "I don't understand why you feel so unwanted when you were the only one that was really planned."

Howard: The Moon is squaring Pluto by progression and she is upset at being pregnant again. She is walking around brooding and maybe seething underneath and you feel it. Your early bonding with the mother starts out fine with Jupiter and then runs into difficulty with Pluto. A relationship starts full of hope and promise but then ends up feeling uncomfortable and threatening. Does this ring a bell for you?

Mandy: Well, actually, it does. When I start a new relationship it usually feels wonderful to open up, but only for a little while. Then I start thinking, "Wait, something will get you."

Howard: Moon conjunct Jupiter square Pluto—the feelings start by being expansive and open (Jupiter) but then the element of fear and danger (Pluto) creeps in. So we find a pattern or expectation suggested by that placement. This is one worth exploring and working on. We have tracked it back historically with what happened in relation to the mother. You can also reflect on how it has appeared in your life in other relationships. This is what I mean by experiencing and understanding a pattern. After that, you can try to work more creatively with the planetary principles involved. There's not enough time to do that now. Let's look at a few more things in the chart though.

The progressed Moon is square Pluto and inconjunct Neptune and Saturn from six to ten months after you are born when your mother is dealing with being pregnant again. She doesn't feel so good to you anymore and her own problems may be obscuring her ability to look after you as well. Then around one year your progressed Moon sextiles your Mercury. What happens?—any moves? Mercury sometimes indicates a move.

Mandy: Yes, we moved when I was one year old.

Howard: You see, just watching the early progressed Moon can reveal so much. The progressed Moon in Taurus sextiles the Mercury in Pisces. The sextile suggests the move was alright.

Mandy: My mother hated where I was born. She liked it better where we moved.

Howard: The progressed Moon moves into Gemini and the 8th house and your brother is born. That's interesting—the Moon changes sign and house and you are seeing your mother in a new light. She is more dual, she is not just there for you now, you have to share her with your brother.

Mandy: I'm just calculating in my head now. Around age four-and-a-half, we moved from England to Australia, and I think the progressed Moon must have been around Uranus in Cancer in my 9th house near that time.

Howard: Yes, that fits nicely. Let's leave the progressed Moon for now. I'm curious about the Mars opposite Saturn and Neptune. Earlier in the day I was talking about this aspect being associated with an external locus of control, with a feeling that life was more powerful than you or you felt a sense of being impotent and ineffective.

Mandy: In 1959, when I was six, my mother was pregnant again and gave birth to "a thing." They still have it in a jar in a university. She came home from hospital ill and for the next several years was very depressed—she was mourning for the dead baby. It was born on her birthday.

Howard: At that time, Saturn had just moved into your 3rd house, the house of brothers and sisters, and you have this death of a sibling and your mother's depression.

Mandy: For the next few years I had to look after my younger brother and sister because my mother was so depressed. I think I felt the Mars opposition to Saturn and Neptune in that way. I was put in charge of my brother and sister and I never felt I could do it very well.

Howard: Yes, transiting Saturn was moving through the 3rd house of siblings at that time, so you meet difficulty there. Also, your natal Saturn rules Capricorn on the cusp of your 3rd so there is another connection between Saturn and your siblings. Your sense of power and capability (Mars) is opposite Saturn, which natally is tied up with your 3rd. It must have felt hard to have such a big responsibility of looking after two young kids when you were only six years old yourself.

Mandy: I've always felt that people think I'm prepared to do things *before* I am really ready to do them.

Howard: That statement reflects a pattern in your life related to Mars opposite Saturn and Neptune and was brought out when you had to look after your little brother and sister.

● ● ●

I'm afraid we have to draw to a close now. But remember that by understanding some of the childhood issues connected to that aspect, you are taking the first step toward working constructively with your feelings of inadequacy and fears of not being ready or good enough for what you have to do. After that you are more free to bring the Mars and Saturn-Neptune principles together in a new way. Remember, the higher Self—or whatever you want to call it—doesn't burden you with any aspect or pattern just for the fun of torturing you.

Hopefully today's seminar has given all of you some guidelines for getting in touch with and better understanding your patterns and life-statements as seen in the chart. Now it's up to you to do what you can to work on, transform, or change any of these. The past may be colouring the way you see life, but your future depends on what you do with it right now.

PART TWO

THE PARENTAL MARRIAGE IN THE HOROSCOPE

Parents are patterns.

—Thomas Fuller

Archetypal Background and Psychological Implications

The theme of today's seminar, the parental marriage as it appears in the horoscope and the implications of this in personal relationship, is not only a situation in actual life. The parental marriage is also an archetypal image, and it is this dimension which I would like to examine first. The power of the parents' marriage over the psyche of the child, and in turn over the child-turned-adult's later relationship patterns, is in part due to this archetypal dimension, because the actual parents are conduits or carriers of the archetypal parents. They are the World Mother and the World Father to a child, and only become real people later in life—if at all. An archetypal image describes a pattern or predisposition toward a particular kind of instinctual expression, a life experience which is common to all human beings. The human psyche experiences these instinctual drives as compulsive and therefore as numinous, because they arise from levels that we cannot understand and cannot control. So the psyche formulates spontaneous images to express the power of the instincts. These are the gods and goddesses of myth, and they are psychic self-portraits of basic developmental patterns.

For example, we all experience puberty, because that is an essential biological and psychological crossroads where the sexual nature of the individual begins to differentiate. Puberty is accompanied by profound changes on many levels, emotional and spiritual as well as physiological. Often, for example, a person becomes very religious at this time of life, and displays a deep and consuming interest in spiritual issues. In myth and in fairy tales, the change from child to sexually differentiated adult may be imaged in many ways, but it is almost always portrayed as a rite of passage, an initiation process. The motif of the "death-marriage," for example, which appears in both the Hades-Persephone myth and the Eros and Psyche story, might be understood as, in part, an image of the passage from childhood and its psychic unity with the mother to adulthood and its state of aloneness and self-consciousness. Persephone is a virgin who lives in union with her mother and is untouched by life, and she is abducted and dragged into the underworld by the god Hades, where she is raped or sexually penetrated by the god and is thus changed in her essential nature. She can never again return to the innocence of her former state. In the tale of Eros and Psyche, Psyche is condemned to death and is carried off by her invisible bridegroom, the god Eros, whom she cannot yet see. Once she looks upon his face, she is changed, and although they are united at the end of the tale as they are at the beginning, it is a different kind of union, and Psyche has transformed.

These initiation images could be said to correspond, on one level, to the physiological and emotional changes which occur at puberty. But the same pattern of change, penetration, transformation and renewal can also describe psychological events that occur at other critical periods in life. In other words, the mythic image is a vivid portrayal of the experience of puberty, but the passage of puberty is also itself an image of other stages in life where a movement into deeper or broader consciousness occurs.

Now, when we consider the parental marriage and its signature in the birth horoscope, we are dealing with the same kind of image—an archetypal one. The coupling of the parents is a symbol of the source of life, the place where one began. If you think about this for a moment, you will see fairly clearly that the parents conjoined are really the World Parents whose coupling in myth represents the beginning of the world. For example, in early Greek myth the universe is created by the mating of Ouranos, the god of heaven, and Gaia, the goddess of earth. Out of this union comes the manifest cosmos, which from a psychological point of view is really the separate individual, incarnated into physical form. Out of the parents' union emerges me, my world, my manifest body. There is both a personal and a universal level to this union of the parents. The source of being is a profound mystery with a numinous core, despite the advances of science on the subject of the development of biological life. Over the millennia, the question, "Where do I come from?" has constellated from the depths of the unconscious the image of the World Parents coupling.

This theme is dressed up differently in different cultures, and the emphasis and details may vary. In the case of the early Mediterranean civilisations, which were primarily agricultural, the original creator, the One, is female. Sometimes she is imaged as the sea, or the earth, or Chaos, or Mother Night, or the Great Abyss. These pictures describe a feminine deity who fertilises herself, so that the coupling of the World Parents is enclosed within a feminine framework. The goddess possesses a phallus so that she can inseminate her own womb. Or she couples with a snake which she has created, which is the same thing but put a little more decorously. In Northern European myth, which arises from nomadic cultures whose resources lay in cattle and horses rather than crops, it is a male deity who begins the process of the creation of the world, and the feminine vessel is enclosed within him. This is also the case with our Judeo-Christian mythology, which also arises from a nomadic culture. In the beginning was God, and the spirit of God moved over the face of the waters. Here the feminine waters which are fertilised by the divine spirit are first created by God, and are thus enclosed within a masculine framework. Out of this fertilisation the work of the creation emerges.

You can see that there is a difference in emphasis, depending upon the particular slant of the culture whose myths one is considering—the force of nature or instinct to which that culture attaches its highest value. But the theme remains essentially the same. The World Parents represent the source of creation, and the thing which is created is "I." Obviously to the rational mind this is ridiculous, because we have enough knowledge now about the processes of fertilisation and birth to have dispensed with the idea that Eurynome mated with a snake. We now possess all kinds of impressive theories about the physical formation of the universe which have nothing at all to do with Father Heaven and Mother Earth. Nevertheless, in the unconscious these primordial images are still alive, unchanged, and very real, as our dreams frequently indicate, and it is on this magical-mythical level that the child experiences the parents before the individual ego or seat of consciousness has formed. A baby cannot intellectually grasp the fact that father puts his penis in mother's vagina and that his sperm fertilises her ovum. To the baby, the parents are all-powerful gods, and they are not yet even separate. They are One, and they are the original source, the male and female aspects of the deity out of which the baby has emerged. The parents are therefore invested with divine powers, for they hold the power of life and death over the infant. I feel this can help us to understand why, when we begin to explore the question of why the parents' marriage should have such an overwhelming and "fated" effect upon the individual, we find that it is not simply a question of a particular person's parents being superhumanly horrible, destructive, or wonderful. The marriage of the parents is the model of creation itself.

If Heaven and Earth are in harmony, then the universe can exist, which means that if the parents are in harmony, then the child can exist. But if the World Parents are not in harmony then creation may be destroyed, and the same anxiety besets the individual. Obviously there is an enormous spectrum between "harmony" and "disharmony," and the perfect image of the World Parents in sublime equilibrium cannot be duplicated by human parents under any circumstances. But it will be obvious to you, if you consider all I have said so far, why disturbances within the parental marriage have such profound ramifications for a young child and for the psyche of the adult later. It is not just that mother and father might divorce and therefore there will be quarrels about who gets the house, the dishwasher and the subscription to *Readers Digest*. It is also that the World Parents, the Ouroboros out of which creation comes, might split in half, and if this container breaks then all life within it will be snuffed out. Naturally no pair of parents can live in complete harmony except in Barbara Cartland novels. Inevitably the experience of every child involves a certain amount of anxiety and separation, because there is no such thing as a home where the parents are at one as the World Parents sometimes are in myth. But in the imagination of the child they are at one, or ought to be, and the first inklings that this might not be so are a natural anxiety-provoking process through which the individual ego of the child begins to emerge, able to cope from its own survival resources. Or at least, one hopes that it emerges, because if the actual parental marriage is really awful, the individual will often cling to the fantasy of the perfect World Parents well into adulthood, and will seek this image in his or her own relationships later.

Between the archetypal image of the World Parents in union, and the mortal actuality of two people who are muddling along trying to make the best of it, there is an inevitable gap. So there is no such thing as a person who has not experienced some degree of difficulty around the issue of the parents' marriage, and there is no parental marriage without cracks and fissures in it. What I think we must consider, especially in the light of astrology's presentation of the pattern already existing at birth, is not whether there are problems, but rather, what is the nature of these problems. It is a bit like Jung's remark about complexes. The question is not whether one has complexes, since everyone has them; but rather, what the individual does with those complexes, and what lies at their core, and how they manifest in the person's life.

The coupling of the World Parents and the creation of the universe are not events which are bound by time and space. "Once upon a time" also means that the World Parents are in perpetual union in the unconscious. This is a little like what theology describes as God creating his creation continuously in the moment. A child doesn't think, "Aha, they had sex nine months before I was born." The World Parents are perpetually making life, making the child's life. The archetypal image precedes the actuality of the physical parents. It is this archetypal perspective which is behind Jung's assertion that a child is not a blank slate upon which the parents can write any script they like. There already exists an image of the parental marriage in the psyche of the newborn child. Now we come to the unique contribution that astrology makes in this area, because the parental marriage is an *a priori* image in everyone but the actual nature of the World Parents is perceived selectively by different individuals in different ways. Varying facets of the masculine and the feminine may appear in a person's psychology as the World Mother and Father, just as they do on a collective level in the myths of different cultures. So the parental marriage is experienced and perceived differently because the birth horoscope is a very individual pattern. The fact that the actual parents really do seem to behave in accord with the *a priori* blueprint, and themselves possess horoscopes which are superb hooks for the child's projections, is one of those mysteries to which we have no answer.

It is these differences within the basic archetypal image of the parental marriage which are so fascinating to explore, because these differences seem to lead us into all our varied relationship patterns later in life. Even more profound than this is the fact that the coupling of the World Parents and the creation of the universe are also images for the creative process within the individual, and they are constellated every time one tries to create anything. So the World Mother and World Father are not only images which we hook onto our parents. They are also the Mother and Father within us, the corporeal container and the spiritual inseminator, whose union results in any expression of one's own individuality. That is what we call "being creative." A person's internal unity is also profoundly affected by the image of the parental marriage, because the opposites within the individual will align themselves along the same axis that the parents did. The inner mother and inner father will treat each other in accordance with the same pattern that surrounds the experience of the parental marriage. Therefore the possibility of beginning to integrate many of the splits within ourselves hinges upon this dilemma of the parental marriage.

I think this is in part why the image of the parents coupling appears so often in dream imagery. When there is any deep work going on around the issue of healing the splits within the psyche, often a dream will arise which portrays the image of the parents in bed, or the parents' bedroom, or some other inference of this kind. Often it is the first time a person is aware of even thinking about the parents in bed. It is very interesting to consider how difficult it is for many of us to deliberately imagine our parents having sex. Usually there is something vaguely embarrassing or funny about it. Did these people really once . . . ? On the surface, this awkwardness is explained by all kinds of defensive excuses. One finds it hard to imagine mother and father without any clothes, or touching each other with passion or lust, or they seem too old, or whatever. The imagination baulks at it. But I think we baulk because we are treading upon taboo ground, upon a holy mystery. The embarrassed laughter masks something else. This is something sacred which we are not permitted to see, because it is the act of creation. That is why the image, when it appears in dreams or fantasies for the first time, often suggests the possibility of some healing process at work within the psyche. If the parents cannot couple then nothing can be created, and then one falls into a depression, cut off from oneself. When the imagination can conceive of the sexual union of the parents, or when the unconscious produces such an image in a dream, then one is connected in some way with the source, and one is no longer creatively barren.

Audience: What do you mean by splits in the psyche? How do these show up in a chart?

Liz: By a split I mean an apparently unsolvable conflict between two aspects of oneself—for example, between the intellect and the feelings. Or the spirit and the body. Or between feelings of love and need for others, and feelings of anger and aggression and destructiveness. We all possess these kinds of conflicts, and they are part of the pattern of every birth chart. But some people seem to be able to contain them and live with both ends of a polarity in consciousness, while others can only live with one half and must dissociate from the other.

I would look at a number of different factors in the chart to see what these conflicts might be about. One immediate representation of them is the balance of elements. If a particular element is over-tenanted, or under-tenanted, then there is likely to be a split. If a person has eight planets in airy signs and nothing at all in water, then one can see fairly quickly that the individual will identify very strongly with the rational side of the psyche and will have great problems accomodating and accepting his or her feelings. Or one might find someone with a group of planets in earthy signs, and only Pluto in Leo to represent the fiery trigon. So there is likely to be a split between the senses and the physical world—the latter being the side of the psyche with which the person identifies—and the realm of the imagination and the intuition. That is one way in which splits can appear in a chart.

One can also see certain themes running through a chart, suggested not only by the balance of elements but also by the aspects and house placements as well. Usually a dominant motif is represented several times in varying ways. For example, a person might have the Sun in Aquarius trine Uranus in Gemini, while Venus might also be in Aquarius but in close opposition to Pluto and square to a Scorpio Moon. That is a split, portrayed in several different ways. If one considers that example, the oppositeness of the two qualities becomes apparent. It is like two characters in a play who are antithetical to each other in motives and modes of behaviour. On the one hand, the airy, thinking side is very strong, and combined with this rationality is also an impersonal vision of life in which the individual's own feeling responses are of less value than the general ethics and precepts of living that should apply to everyone. But on the other hand, the watery, emotional side is equally strong, and contains not only great sensitivity and intensity, but also a highly personal value-system which places the individual's own needs above any collective set of expectations. We know that the Sun, among other things, suggests the masculine pole of the personality, and has a great deal to do with the inheritance from the father, who is the first embodiment of that masculine pole met in outer life. And the Moon suggests the feminine pole, and has a great deal to do with the mother, who is the first experience of that pole met in outer life. We could look at the astrological example I have just given in a number of different ways, but one of them—and perhaps the primary one if we are seeking a deep psychological portrait of the individual—is that such configurations portray a split which is also a split between the parents, and therefore between the World Parents.

No one is exempt from splits. Even if one finds a very smooth chart with virtually no conflicts, its smoothness will imply a split because something will inevitably be missing for it to be so seamless. This is one of the paradoxes of a grand trine, which is traditionally supposed to be so lucky, yet which from a psychological perspective always implies a pronounced emphasis in one element and therefore a lack in another. It seems to be part of human nature that we have these conflicts. The horoscope offers a very concise picture of where they occur. Although the splits in a chart are our own opposites, they are also the parents portrayed as opposites, and we experience them first through the parents because the parents are the male and female beginning of us. If one happens to be the person with eight planets in air and nothing in water, then it is very likely that one of the parents will be experienced as airy and the other as the poor neglected water. These opposing elements of reflection versus passion are archetypal, but we perceive them first in our parents as a collision of human needs. It is a moot point whether the parents really fit the description. How can we step outside ourselves to see? Obviously a mother or father is not composed wholly of air or water, although an outside observer might see that the parents do seem to display many of the characteristic attributes of these two elements. But they are usually good enough hooks in one way or another to provide fertile soil for us to experience what is essentially ourselves.

The parental scenarios which seem to accompany these splits are also very archetypal. I sometimes wonder whether somebody passes around scripts when no one is looking. If I keep developing the example of the airy person with no water, then one of the parents—usually the father if the Sun is in air—gets cast as the cool, detached, unfeeling one who lives in his head and cannot express warmth of feeling. The other parent—usually the mother if the Moon is in a watery sign or aspects Neptune or Pluto strongly—gets cast as the emotional parent who is hungry and frustrated, ignored and overlooked, always hurting, covertly angry but victimised and long-suffering, and generally rejected by the partner. I am exaggerating, of course, but one should listen to a few case histories. We could of course turn this picture around if there are eight planets in water and nothing in air, and suggest that one parent is emotionally domineering, possessive, powerful, and manipulative while the other one is weak, absent, abstracted, and ineffectual. And so it goes.

You can see that this is really an internal dynamic within the person. The airy side beats up the watery side by withholding genuine emotional responses, and the watery side becomes angry and frustrated and strikes back by undermining with negative moods and depression. But it is very hard to catch hold of this dynamic inside. Sometimes the reverse picture appears, where the watery side beats up the airy side by making everything a grand drama and scorning any effort on the part of the intellect to take a fair viewpoint and consider the other's perspective as well as one's own. The airy side then becomes increasingly impotent and ineffectual, and takes revenge through obsessive negative thoughts. Usually we are possessed by one and unconscious of the other, and this is reflected in the way in which we tend to side with one parent against the other. Generally when people talk about their childhoods, unless they are straining desperately to be polite and excessively fair, someone gets to be the good guy and someone the villain. The first arena in which we experience our conflicts is the parents, and the image of the parental marriage is coloured by the conflict. And generally the inner and the outer reflect each other. The parents really do behave that way, because the archetypal split has not yet been integrated, and people with opposite temperaments tend to be naturally drawn to each other and marry. Probably one can trace it back for several generations. Then the individual in whose chart the split appears has the responsibility of trying to make something creative out of this split.

One can often hear people describing their parents in a very archetypal way. Someone will say, "My father was a very cold person, he didn't show much affection to us," and one looks at the chart and sees the Sun conjuncting Saturn or square Uranus, or Uranus in the 4th house. Or the person says, "My mother was very depressed, she always cried a lot, and my father just treated her with contempt." And one can see the Moon conjuncting Neptune, or square Pluto, or in opposition to Jupiter from Pisces, or something like that. To what extent these things are objectively true is difficult to assess. In cases where I have been able to meet the parents of someone with this kind of situation present in the chart, it seems that the parents really do behave in this way, although some do it more exaggeratedly than others and although their own charts may suggest other potentials or possible ways of relating. But I think it would be fair to say that the weaker the ego and sense of self, the more the collective unconscious has a tendency to take over behaviour in archetypal forms; and probably there are not very many real individuals about, especially in older generations where the social demands were more stringent and self-expression more curtailed. It is as though the archetypal image of the parental marriage has not only possessed the child, but the parents as well. There is a very strange synchronicity between a projection and the hook we hang it on. There is almost always something which is truly there in the objective situation, but we give that something an entirely subjective interpretation. But in the end we can all grow old and grey arguing about how objectively "true" the image of the parental marriage in the horoscope really is. What is more creative is the insight this image can give into oneself.

One's subjective image of the parental marriage is terribly important on an inner level, whether it can be corroborated or not with objective proofs. Much of the importance seems to lie in how these opposite sides of oneself treat each other. We also learn examples from the parents, and if a split appears in the individual's horoscope and the parents deal with that split in their marriage in a destructive way, then the person often cannot see a way through, because there is no model. What the parents cannot solve, we often feel we cannot solve either, despite overt rebellion or conscious belief to the contrary. If there is no example of harmony between the World Parents, then we grow up believing that such conflicts are always going to lead to defeat and terrible suffering. There is a feeling of deep despair or hopelessness around the issue, which is often masked by very good defenses. This is why people often avoid relationship, when the parental marriage is a model only of how destructive conflict can be. There is a very creative dimension to our internal conflicts, but a bad parental marriage gets us off to a bad start in being able to appreciate that creative dimension. Then a person will do absolutely anything to avoid falling into the same trap that destroyed the parents. The pain which one fears one will experience seems overpowering and unbearable because no solution seems possible, and the individual can dissociate or fly off into a fantasy world to compensate. We do all sorts of funny things to avoid that hot place where we observed an unsolvable archetypal conflict. Often a person will deny his or her feelings, because one might wind up becoming like the parent with endlessly frustrated needs. Or one may deny the imagination, because when the parent expressed it, he or she couldn't make a decent living and was a failure; so why go anywhere near something which might be such a source of suffering?

Splits in a chart can yield a unique and rich and truly individual way of expressing in life, if there is some relationship between the opposite poles. But people so often crush their own potentials, and imprison important aspects of themselves because of the profound feeling that the problem is unsolvable. The greater the sense of collision between the parents, the greater the sense of hopelessness about one's own inner conflicts is likely to be. I should emphasise that the operative word is "sense," because it is a sense of hopelessness rather than an actuality. But telling oneself that is often not sufficient.

It would seem that the number of potential parental scenarios is limited, just as the number of planets is limited. This may be a rather crushing blow to anyone who feels that his or her parental pattern is utterly unique. Of course the circumstances are utterly unique, and so is the individual's potential to work with the situation. But the archetypal patterns tend to fall into distinct groups. In terms of what has "gone wrong," because something always does, one of the parents will usually be more powerful than the other in one sphere of life. If the mother is more powerful than the father, then images are constellated of the devouring, predatory woman and the impotent, castrated man. Usually the subjective feeling of the mother's greater power is reflected in the chart by an emphasised tenth house, with significators such as the Sun or

Pluto in the midheaven; or by many planets in Cancer, which is archetypally predisposed toward experiencing mother as Great Mother because it is matriarchal in consciousness. The mother might be experienced as stronger in an earthy way, materially more competent and better organised. Here the significators are often Saturn or Mars, or the Moon in an earthy sign strongly aspecting Saturn or Mars. Or she may have more power on an emotional level, either through sheer force of personality or through guilt-provoking manipulation. Martyrs are tremendously powerful people, and hold everyone around them in thrall, because one cannot bear to hurt someone who is already suffering so much. The significators here are frequently Neptune or Pluto in the 10th, or Jupiter displaying his Piscean dimension, or the Moon in a watery sign aspecting Neptune, Pluto or Jupiter strongly. The mother may be stronger intellectually, and this is not an uncommon situation. I have often heard people talk about mothers who were well-educated with a university degree while the father was a labourer with little education. You can guess which astrological factors tend to turn up here—Mercury or sometimes Uranus in the 10th house, or the Moon in one of the airy signs. The mother may be stronger socially, by being very extraverted with many friends and the power to draw people to her, while the father may be shy and retiring or socially awkward and clumsy. Here the significators for the mother may be Venus or the Moon in the 10th, or the Moon in Libra, or Aquarius, or Gemini, or Sagittarius. Or the mother may be spiritually more powerful, closer to God as it were. This is a typically Neptunian figure.

Audience: Can you explain what you mean by a significator? Do you always mean a planet in the 10th house?

Liz: Yes, that is part of it. I will try to go into this in much more detail later on. But planets in the 10th, and the sign on the midheaven, seem to describe many of the essential components in the image of the mother and therefore of the World Mother. Also, we have to consider the Moon by sign, house and aspect to other planets. All these factors need to be looked at. Synthesising them is sometimes complicated, because one often finds double messages. But I will try to illustrate this with example charts we will examine later.

I hope that you don't take these astrological significators too rigidly, by the way, because they are meant to be suggestions and not rules. A single indication in the chart does not automatically mean that a particular situation exists as a dominant in the psyche. A theme needs to be repeated more than once before we can look at it in that way. But hopefully this can give you some idea of the different kinds of power which the mother can wield in terms of the parental marriage. One needs to think of it in opposites, because that seems to be the way in which the human psyche perceives things. If the mother is emotionally powerful, then the father will usually be perceived as emotionally weak or detached, which is another way of describing someone who lives in his head and not in his heart. In the end, it is arguable whether the parents are really operating along a power-powerless axis, or whether it is the child who perceives this imbalance because of his or her own predisposition. I suspect that sometimes it is one and sometimes the other, and occasionally both together.

The presence of planets in the 10th or 4th house tells us something immediately about the subjective image of the parental marriage as well as about the individual parent, for they are a couple. Firstly, there is a kind of red light which says, "Look here. There is an archetypal figure masquerading as a parent." Secondly, there is the suggestion of a balance of power one way or the other, because if one of the parental houses is tenanted and the other not, then one parent is much more important to the individual than the other. I have sometimes met people in whom there is no real awareness of this "taking sides," and often the wrong parent is attributed with all the messes in one's life. It is a psychological truism that it is never the one you think it is that has had the deepest and most lasting influence, because the parent with whom one has the most overt and conscious conflict is usually the one with whom one feels safe enough to actually fight. It is really terribly paradoxical. But we can also look at it in another way. The presence of planets in the 10th or 4th house suggests that there is an archetypal issue which has been at work within the parent, and therefore within the parental marriage; and this issue has now passed to the child as a kind of psychological inheritance.

For example, Neptune in the 10th house suggests a suffering mother, a woman who has sacrificed her own self-expression in the name of love for husband, family, children or whatever, and who is one of life's victims. There are usually issues of guilt and emotional manipulation and overidealisation connected with the mother, and she wields great emotional power within the psyche of her child. But Neptune is an archetypal figure, an outer planet which carries a collective mystical vision, and it is not a real person. It might be more accurate to say that the archetypal image of the Suffering Woman, who has reached her apotheosis in myth as the Virgin Mary, is at work in the mother and probably in the whole maternal line, and the individual with Neptune in 10 must come to terms with this archetypal figure in a way more creative than either identifying with it, or rebelling violently against it and therefore against all emotional commitments. If the personal mother has not been able to work to integrate this "fate" creatively, but remains the victim of the father, then the child will inherit the dilemma and the challenge. And even if there are no planets in the 4th, one can make some educated guesses about who is causing all this suffering to the poor mother, because every victim needs a bully, and the woman who identifies so strongly with the theme of suffering and victimisation will either unconsciously choose a partner who helps her to suffer, or will work on the partner until he comes up with the goods despite himself. So there is an entire scenario about a parental marriage, just from the presence of Neptune in the 10th house.

If the mother is the figure of power, then the female side of life becomes terribly potent, and the male side is experienced as weak. This can provoke either contempt or overprotectiveness and overidentification. One can see that the effects of this spread beyond the sphere of relationships and can permeate one's creative expression, one's standing in the world, and one's connection with the body. If this kind of imbalance appears in a man's horoscope, then obviously women will seem terribly powerful to him, and so will the feminine side of himself. The emotions are too potent, the passions are too strong, the body is too dominant, the instincts are too overwhelming. The whole feminine realm looms as something potentially castrating, and the masculine world is felt to be weak and ineffectual. So this man will either struggle against the overpowering World Mother by beating down the feminine wherever he meets it, within and without, or he will simply fall passively into her embrace and sacrifice his manhood, as the priests of Kybele once did literally. Either way, it seems to reflect a very uncomfortable inner situation, because the harmony between the World Parents has been destroyed. One of them has swallowed up the other. I often feel, when I see a male client who has this kind of emphasis in the birth chart and who is interested in working psychotherapeutically on the dilemma, that it is a male therapist who might offer the most potential for healing. This is because in some way it might restore a better balance to that lop-sided World Parent, and provides an image of a stronger masculine figure than the father was. This is the ethic behind masculine "societies" like the Freemasons, which underline the power of the masculine spirit and invoke a feeling of potency in the face of the World Mother. You should all try to see a production of Mozart's *Magic Flute*, which is about precisely this issue. Although one cannot send in the birth chart and get a new one, I believe it is possible to bring the parents into a more balanced perspective and make a better relationship with the archetypal parents who stand behind them. Then the overemphasised feminine can provide a more creative outlet, such as work in a profession which is "feminine" in that it utilises the feelings and the imagination, while the individual man no longer feels castrated by the World Mother.

If the father appears as the more powerful parent in the birth chart, then there is likewise a situation of discomfort, because once again the World Parents are not in harmony. Here the male dominates the female, and the feminine realm is experienced as weak. The father may be more materially powerful, which may seem like a typical situation—except that, for a child, it is not necessarily the father's financial support that makes him materially powerful. It is his capacity to actualise things on the material plane that implies his power. This is experienced as a problem if the father's material dominance accompanies the mother's material helplessness or inability to cope. The mother may stay in a desperately unhappy marriage because she fears going out into life on her own, and uses money as an excuse; and money is therefore a symbol of control. Then the father holds the key to everyone's survival, and he becomes terrifying in his power. Or the father may possess the intellectual power, by being clever and articulate and reasonable. He may also be the emotionally powerful parent, or the sexually potent one, while the mother is experienced as cool and withdrawn and inhibited. The father's violent emotions may affect the entire atmosphere in the home, where his sexual aura fills the house, while the mother is hardly even in a body, but is disembodied and floating somewhere in the ethers, close to God. Then it is the feminine which is experienced as ineffectual and helpless, and the male becomes the oppressor. You can see what this says about our politics, can't you? The World Parents appear in society just as readily as they appear as inner splits within ourselves.

When the father becomes the Terrible Father, then the whole feminine side of life is suppressed or undervalued. Often this shows itself as a domineering animus in a woman, where there is always a nagging voice inside telling her that she must not be spontaneous, she must not show her messy feelings, her body is unacceptable, her needs are too demanding, her imagination is simply silly. That is the masculine beating up the feminine within a woman. This can happen within a man as well, and we can see what this may do to his feelings and his instincts. One will usually either fight desperately against the father's power, aligning himself with the victimised mother and himself becoming a victim of tyrannical authority in the world outside, or one will simply offer oneself up to the World Father and become a tyrant himself. But either way, the sense of internal imbalance and pain is there.

This internal discomfort arises instantly in any relationship which the individual enters later in life. One can be with a partner for five minutes and already someone is being oppressed. Whatever the partner does, there is a deep unconscious expectation that a power battle is bound to ensue, because the power battle of the parental marriage dominates the unconscious. So someone is going to have to win and someone is going to inevitably lose. Because these things are so deeply ingrained in us, we will shape our relationships accordingly. Usually we find partners whose parental backgrounds match our own in an eerie way, like twinsets with pearls. When one actually discovers the whole story about both parental marriages, one begins to see that the two mothers and the two fathers are virtually interchangeable in essence if not in behaviour. Often the same zodiacal signs appear. If the mother is the powerful parent in one's life, then very likely she was the powerful parent in one's partner's life as well. If the father is missing or weak or absent in one's childhood, then he will probably have played the same vanishing act in one's partner's childhood too. It is as though the archetypal dilemma with which one is challenged is the same dilemma that arises in the partner's life, and this complex draws two people into a relationship where the same issue is constellated and where a new chance to work with it creatively arises. I suspect this is why so many people have trouble with their in-laws. It is because they have met them already long before.

All you need to do is turn on the television, and the archetypal parental marriage scenarios appear there in all their glory. They are so classic and so universal that soap operas seem to go on and on eternally, with millions of viewers, year after year, repeating the same themes.

Audience: Like *Coronation Street*.

Liz: I must confess that I don't watch *Coronation Street*. I am sure I am missing a profound archetypal experience. But *Soap* might be another typical example. *Soap* contains a classic marriage scenario. Jessica is bright and frivolous and very intelligent and very flirtatious, and she runs circles around her rather thick husband. He is devoted and quite lumpish, and her infidelities only bind him more closely to her because he has no idea what to do without her, let alone with her. This is really a mythic marriage, and the Greeks, who always had a word for it, epitomised it in the story of Aphrodite and Hephaistos. Aphrodite, the goddess of love, is beautiful, vain, flirtatious and incurably promiscuous. Hephaistos, her husband, the smith-god, is ugly and lame, lumpish and clumsy, although he is a fine craftsman. But he is not very sophisticated company. He is completely enthralled by her beauty. She is forever cheating on him, and he is forever taking her back, after a few faint displays of outrage and protest. This is what I meant by a limited number of archetypal marriage scenarios. The marriage of Aphrodite and Hephaistos, which we can see modernised in *Soap*—although I have some question whether the scriptwriter really knows Greek mythology, or is just tapping the same eternal fountain—is alive and well and one of the typical enactments of the parental marriage.

One of the derivatives of the Aphrodite-Hephaistos pair is the large, overpowering wife and the small, thin, henpecked husband. This is very funny on television or in the theatre, but tragic when one's parents are enacting it, and even worse when one discovers one is enacting it oneself. American audiences seem to love this particular marriage situation comedy, with great overfed women inevitably a foot taller than their minute, rather diffident husbands and usually with loud, strident voices. The husband usually says, "Yes, dear," at frequent intervals throughout the programme. There is always canned audience laughter, but it is not funny to watch at home. And internally it represents a deep imbalance, because the Great Mother has castrated the poor impotent little son-lover. What can one hope for in personal relationships, if such an image dominates in the unconscious?

On a much less amusing note, another scenario which is often portrayed on the screen as well as at home is the physically violent father and the cowering, helpless mother. I have often wondered whether these scenarios are culture-linked, because the earlier one I mentioned, of the huge powerful woman and the diffident man who escapes into dreams or intellectual pursuits, is popular not only on American television but also in Italian films. Fellini, for example, has made a fine art of portraying such women. The violent father and the abused, suffering mother seem to appear with horrible regularity in the backgrounds of many Irish clients that I have seen.

Audience: Why do you think this is the case? Might it be a problem with alcohol?

Liz: I don't know. If it is a problem with alcohol, then both the relationship scenario and the alcohol problem spring from the same root, rather than one being the cause of the other. The archetypal relations between the World Parents permeate cultural values as well as the unconscious of the individual. Just as the image of god varies from one collective to another, so too does the nature of the bond between the World Mother and the World Father. My intuition may be attributing cultural differences which are not actually there, but my intuition also tells me that it is picking up something very interesting. But drunken fathers appear in every culture. So do violent fathers who don't need alcohol to set them off. The mother often has no refuge in life other than religion and sacrifice for her children. Mythically we can look at Ares, the war-god, who is described in Homer as a berserker. The violent, amoral father who explodes and starts smashing everyone and everything in sight is usually married to a Neptunian partner who just puts up with it. Curiously, she rarely leaves and goes off to make a new life. She just suffers, and tells the children, "Be quiet and don't upset him, he's drunk tonight." Someone for whom I recently did a chart described this kind of parental marriage to me. From around the age of ten or eleven she began to plead with her mother to leave her father because of his violence. But the mother kept replying, "I am staying for the sake of you children." But of course that is not why she stayed. If you think about it for a moment, you will see that this is arrant nonsense. The children would be considerably safer and happier in a household where someone isn't getting beaten up all the time. But the suffering woman needs a brutal male to help her suffer. Otherwise how could she fulfil the archetypal compulsion? In the chart of my client, Pluto appeared in the 10th house conjuncting Saturn and Mars, while the Moon conjuncted Neptune in Libra. Those of you who feel the 10th house represents the father might say that this grouping in Leo describes his violence very aptly. But I would also turn it around, and suggest that this rather aggressive collection in Leo describes the animus of the mother, who also drapes herself in the guise of the suffering Neptunian and acts out her own anger and destructiveness through a violent partner who can leave her feeling saintly and clean.

The unfaithful father and the resentful but loyal mother are another derivative of this dynamic. In myth, we can see the marriage of Zeus and Hera as an embodiment of this extremely common dilemma. In Teutonic myth, it is Wotan and Fricka who personify the wandering husband and the resentful wife who herself never leaves or has any affairs of her own. She just stays at home and smoulders. Zeus is of course Jupiter in Roman myth, and in astrology; and Jupiterian fathers often embody this wandering, promiscuous figure, although the wandering may be in fantasy rather than concrete reality. But a father whose erotic fantasy spreads itself over anything with breasts that moves can be more hurtful than one who acts it out, because one feels rejected all the time but cannot attribute the feelings to any concrete action. There is no feeling of security in the marriage but nothing to blame the anxiety on, and the daughter of such a father will often have a deep mistrust of men without any apparent cause.

Can you consider for a moment what this might mean as an internal dynamic? It is easy enough to see the Zeus-Hera scenario acted out in life. But the man who cheats and the woman who stays weeping at home also constitute a symbol, and represent something inwardly. Do you have any idea about this?

Audience: Sometimes the betrayed wife attacks the other woman.

Liz: Yes, but who is the other woman? Usually she seems to be opposite to the wife, or to whatever the wife represents. Perhaps the other woman is really the unconscious or unlived dimension of the wife, which is projected outside the marriage.

Audience: Then the other woman, or the other man for that matter, isn't really outside. She is inside.

Liz: The entire thing is inside. Try to think about what this kind of internalised parental marriage, which usually ends up in a triangle, might mean for the individual.

Audience: I think it has something to do with a lack of relationship between the spirit and the body.

Liz: Yes, I think so too. Zeus is a god of heaven, a spiritual figure. He is creative fire. He is not properly related to his earthy wife, who feels to him like a limitation rather than a creative partner who can offer a container for his creative inspiration. And Hera, the goddess of marriage and childbirth, is condemning of the freedom of the spirit. She wants her husband tied to her all the time. She cannot let him go away and come back. It is always via another woman that Zeus fathers the heroes or demigods like Theseus and Perseus and Herakles. Here is a split where there is no resolution, and the resolution is sought outside all the time, which only results in greater anger and frustration. The marriage of Zeus and Hera, which is often enacted in parental marriages, seems to represent a creative problem within the individual. Committing oneself to concretising creative potentials is tantamount to death of the spirit. It is earthly bondage, rather than accomplishment. One cannot be creatively free and also committed. And the earthy, instinctual side sees the flights of the spirit and the imagination as dangerous and threatening, and attempts to stifle them. What is needed is a middle ground, a new viewpoint between the two; but sadly, this middle ground always seems to appear as somebody else.

Different people will identify with one or the other of these two figures, and the "bad guy" becomes the unconscious potential which is crushed. If we identify with Father Zeus, then everything worldly and secure feels like a trap, and any kind of commitment might crush creativity. Then nothing is ever achieved, and we live in the world of the eternal youth, with endless potential and nothing ever actualised. If we identify with Mother Hera, then everything belonging to the imagination and the spirit of exploration is seen as foreign and unsafe. Only the home base and what is known and solid can be given value. Hera is an impossibly conventional goddess. Creative play becomes childish, irresponsible, or weird and abnormal. Women can identify with Father Zeus just as men can with Mother Hera. It isn't a sexist issue. But this archetypal parental marriage embodies a particular kind of conflict which confronts certain individuals.

What do you think might be a typical astrological configuration which suggests this pattern?

Audience: You already mentioned Jupiter. Can the mother be Jupiter?

Liz: Yes, of course. Jupiter can be in the 10th house, or in strong aspect to the Moon, or the Moon can be in Sagittarius. Certainly the mother can embody the spirit of Zeus, in which case she is the puella, the eternal girl for whom life must be one long and exciting adventure and for whom marriage, children and domestic responsibilities are really a kind of death. Sometimes one can see a kind of martyr-like figure when Jupiter is a mother-significator; but it is quite different from Neptune. Neptune is shrouded in a mystical aura, and the martyred woman of the Neptunian image is a sacrifice of the gods, an embodiment of human suffering. But Jupiter is an actor, and the martyred woman of the Jupiterian image plays it all to the hilt. Behind the apparent suffering, which is always portrayed with great style, one can see the inborn skill of the stage.

Audience: Then Hera might be suggested by Saturn.

Liz: Yes, Saturn can be related to her. The social codes and boundaries and respect for traditional values which are part of Hera's domain are Saturnian. The Moon also can embody Hera, particularly when the Moon is in the 10th house in an earthy sign. The Moon seems to symbolise the maternal face of the feminine, while Venus represents the erotic. Hera is too preoccupied with being the right kind of wife to be playful and coy like Aphrodite is. But if Hera were more whole, then Zeus would not be married to her, because together they create a unit. Sometimes Pluto can suggest a Hera-like figure, at least from the point of view of jealousy and possessiveness. But Pluto is much darker and deeper than Hera. If one finds a configuration such as Jupiter in the 4th house, or conjuncting the Sun, and in turn the Moon in Taurus or Capricorn squaring or opposing Pluto, then I think one can see the implication of a parental marriage which smacks of Zeus and Hera. With this dynamic at work on an internal level, there is often a problem around the issue of creative expression as well as relationship, because one side is always trying to fly and the other to build stable structures on the earth.

We all seem to have something of these typical scenarios within us, and they are not pathological; they are archetypal. But they are a challenge to us, because what the parents could not put together between them appears in the child. We are each the product of two parents, and both sets of genes are alive in us. So too are both parental psyches, and their dominant myths. I doubt that there is a way to get it right. But we might add something more creative to the archetypal pattern before it passes down to our own children. I think we call that evolution.

Audience: Do we then have an idea of the perfect couple, the perfect marriage, somewhere within us?

Liz: I believe we do. That is what the myths portray, when they present us with the image of the World Father and the World Mother together making the universe; and myths arise from human psyches. Life is of course not like that, and neither are horoscopes. But perhaps the hope that such a thing exists, somewhere, on some level, is behind what we call our spiritual striving over the ages. We not only try to embody the perfect World Parents in our love affairs and marriages. We also worship the divine couple as God. This is a religious as well as a relationship issue. Ultimately it is a wholeness of self that the perfect union embodies. The alchemical symbolism which Jung explored in such depth places the image of the coniunctio, the divine marriage, as the highest goal of the great work. The coniunctio puts together what we can never find in life. Just as we are collectively driven to reproduce ourselves, so we are also driven toward the image of that perfect union, which is both our source and our goal. The worse the parental marriage, the worse the internal split—and the more, in consequence, the individual is compelled to try to find a solution which is better than what the parents had because his or her own inner wholeness is at stake. One might say that, paradoxically, those bad parental marriages are really gifts in disguise, because they make so much trouble that we must grow large enough to encompass a better balance; so we have added some small individual contribution to the ancient unfoldment.

Someone asked me earlier, during the coffee break, about the image of King Arthur and the etiquette of courtly love. This is another great archetypal scenario, and it represents another kind of parental marriage. In some ways it is the answer of the collective under the Piscean Age to the models of union offered under the Arien and Taurean Ages. In the Arthurian legends, the figure of woman is split. There are horribly ugly women, or whorish ones, and there are beautiful, ethereal, unobtainable ones. The cult of Mary, which erupted with considerable power from the collective unconscious in the 12th century, is very bound up with the more prosaic and human symbols of courtly love. Here woman is represented as a kind of unattainable spiritual ideal, while the man must carry the burden of the wayward flesh that has to be mastered and transmuted in order to earn the woman's love. Although the woman may be desired sexually, the desire must not be consummated. That would destroy the whole point of the thing. The worship must be on a spiritual level, and it is a kind of alchemical work, where the gross fires of carnal passion are transformed through longing for what one can never have into poetry and gentle deeds. To attempt to pull the woman down to the man's carnal level would be an insult and a degradation to her. Here woman holds the spiritual power as an intermediary to God, just as Mary does in Catholic doctrine. She can offer grace and forgiveness. Man, being a lowly base creature of flesh, can be excused for satisfying his lusts with ordinary women whom he does not love, although he might marry them. One can see much of this in Dante's portrayal of Beatrice in the *Divine Comedy*. Beatrice is in heaven, while poor Dante must content himself with purgatory at best, unless she intercedes for him with the angels. In actual life, Dante never even spoke to Beatrice, but saw her once or twice across the Ponte Vecchio; and fortunately for the history of poetry, she died before he had a chance to take his projections back.

Another good example of this strange and curiously bittersweet scenario is Wagner's *Tannhäuser*. Elizabeth, the pure and saintly heroine of the opera, battles with the lecherous goddess Aphrodite for Tannhäuser's soul. She is willing to sacrifice her own life for him, as long as he can be freed from the filthy embrace of the goddess of carnal love.

This can also present itself as an archetypal parental marriage scenario, and as an inner dynamic. Very often, with this situation, the man finds that he cannot perform in bed with such a saintly woman. He feels ashamed and brutish, and idealises her too much to subject her to his disgusting lusts. He can perform with a prostitute, but not with his wife.

Audience: I don't know whether it was really like this, or whether it is just the way I perceived my parents, but what I experienced was two people who lived together in a completely closed little mundane circle. Unless I am totally deceived, neither of them had any affairs. They seemed to be happy together. But all they ever seemed to talk about or experience was the ordinary little things in life. Their lives were so banal. What does that do to a child?

Liz: Well, probably you could answer that better than I could. But I would expect that, if they were truly like this, they must have been making some strenuous efforts to keep out of their lives anything magical, unpredictable, extraordinary or threatening. No parent is just mundane and banal, any more than he or she is just a spiritual sacrifice, or just a promiscuous boy, or just an earth mother. Something must have been shoved quite violently into the unconscious, to keep things safe. It is that unlived life which I would imagine you have been infected by. One thing which might come from such an infection by the parental shadow is a horror of being ordinary, of being shut up in banality and mundane concerns yourself. It might then become very difficult to appreciate the positive side of earthy things. There must have been so much shut out of that parental marriage. Passions, great heights and depths, a quest for meaning, a need to strive. No life can exist within such a closed circle unless both people have unconsciously made a very stringent bargain to suppress anything that might rock the boat. In a sense, this means suppressing the archetypal realm with its compulsions and dramas and grandeur, which I have been describing this morning. If that is held back, then certainly peace of a kind is achieved, and security; but at the price of the soul. And the child will inherit the desperation of the trapped soul, and will perhaps be driven by it, to the exclusion of all else. It is the unlived life which you would inherit. What parental significators appear in your chart?

Audience: I have no planets in the 10th or 4th house. But the Moon in Taurus conjuncts the midheaven from the 9th house. I have several planets in fire signs, including Pluto conjuncting the ascendant in Leo. But I still do not understand whether my parents were really so closed, or is it my perception?

Liz: I don't know how much is them and how much is your perception. I would have to look more carefully at your chart to see just what your perception really is. But probably they behaved a lot like that on the surface. The people of your parent's generation lived through two world wars and saw everything they believed in torn down and transformed. Many of them retreated into the kind of marriage you have described. But what they were really like as individuals, inside and in the unconscious, is very likely quite different, and your conscious perception of them as you have described it might vary from what the chart portrays as your true and deep experience of them. In a way, what is just as relevant is the way your fiery nature makes you react to them. It often happens that two parents who are both fairly earthy will establish such a marriage, particularly if external events have driven them into their earth even further. And often fate confronts them with the unlived life in the form of a fiery child. What about your parents' charts?

Audience: I have no birth times for them, but you are right. They are both earthy. My mother was a Cancer with the Moon in Taurus, and three more planets in earthy signs. My father was a Capricorn.

Liz: It is also interesting that your Moon is in Taurus as well, but it seems that you disown it. Its conjunction with the midheaven, although it falls in the 9th house, suggests that your mother is identified with these Taurean qualities, and of course she is an excellent hook. You evidently project your own shadow on her, and she no doubt projects her unlived fire onto you. It is very mysterious how the child often incarnates everything which the parents cannot live. Your parents may have been quite happy in their little mundane world. But the archetypal parental marriage as it appears in your chart may portray the price they had to pay for that apparent happiness. What about your father?

Audience: The Sun in my chart is in Aries, conjuncting Mercury, Venus and Mars. They are all in trine to Pluto and in opposition to Neptune.

Liz: This is what I meant. It sounds as though the visionary and poetic quality of fire links you to your father, although since he was a Capricorn he was perhaps frightened of it in himself and stifled it. But it would be interesting to know his ascendant, and the rest of his chart. The aspects to the Sun, particularly the conjunctions to Venus and Mars and the opposition to Neptune, suggest a very different figure to the one you initially described. A Neptunian father is often a kind of absent figure, perhaps glamourously attractive or magical, sometimes idealised, but unavailable and beyond reach. I have a feeling that he was not mundane at all; or, at least, that his inner life was not. He only pretended to be, because he must have had a great sense of responsibility, and he allowed your mother to carry the weight of the material side of the marriage, the substance of it. That is the way that I would interpret the picture in the chart. You haven't said whether your Moon in Taurus is square to Pluto.

Audience: It is.

Liz: Well, the plot thickens. Perhaps we should take this material apart more carefully, and use your planetary placements as an illustration of all I have covered so far. The parental marriage as it is suggested in your horoscope would be reflected by the 4th and 10th houses, and by the aspects and signs of the Sun and Moon. That is as close to a general rule as we can come to. Let's see if we can put together a story out of these placements. Firstly, we need to look at the two parental houses, where there are no planets. Taurus is on the cusp of the 10th, with the Moon conjuncting the midheaven, and Scorpio is on the cusp of the 4th. In a very general way, that suggests that the mother is symbolised by earth—the one who was stable and emotionally much more present, and rooted in ordinary life. The conjunction of the Moon to the midheaven implies her emotional presence. In fact I suspect that she

was so present that you have a deep, although perhaps unconscious, identification with her and her situation in life as a woman.
Your own feelings and instinctual responses would probably be
very bound up with hers. But the preponderance of fire in your
chart implies that it might be quite a challenge to live out the
earthy qualities. So the mother becomes the "mundane" one, who
seems to live in a narrow, boring world. I would repeat what I said
earlier: that you might have a great fear of being ordinary and dull
and boring, and trapped, like your mother.

The aspects to the Moon seem to amplify this interpretation.
The Moon-Pluto square is an aspect which I associate very often
with depression and unhappiness and frustration in the mother.
The Moon as a symbol of mother is also a symbol of the life of the
body and the life of the world. This is the World Mother, the pole
of matter which balances the spiritual dimension of the World
Father. When Pluto is connected with the Moon, then the World
Mother carries a certain darkness and passion. This is the primitive underworld life of nature, which resists civilising and resents
rejection and separation of any kind. The myth which I mentioned
earlier, that of Zeus and Hera, is a reasonable illustration of this
kind of feminine figure. But she is deeper than Hera; and one
could also consider such mythic figures as the Gorgon, who
embodies outraged nature. The child absorbs all this, as it were,
with mother's milk. Being a woman in this image means frustration, resentment, and unfulfilled desires. But since she was a Cancer with a Taurus Moon, perhaps your mother felt that the home
and family were too important to risk a confrontation or a crisis of
any kind. I think she may have stifled all her emotional needs, and
hid in little banalities, and was probably quite depressed underneath it all.

The images around the father are quite different. They are
very erotic. First of all, Scorpio falls on the cusp of the 4th house,
which suggests that beneath the dour exterior you must have
experienced a powerful undertow in him. I suspect that your relationship with him, or your deeper feelings about him, might be
much more complex than you have intimated. The solar aspects,
particularly, as I said, the conjunctions with Venus and Mars, suggest an idealised and romanticised figure, a figure of erotic fantasy,
who remained forever inaccessible although adored. Sometimes
with this kind of situation, the man uses his mundane marriage

as a hiding-place, because he cannot cope with his passions and his wandering anima; but if there is a daughter, then usually she discovers those passions, because they trigger off her own developing sexuality and a great deal of fantasising ensues. Very often in this kind of triangle, the mother is cast as the perpetrator of the dull, mundane life which the parents live, and "if only" the father had had a more exciting woman—such as yourself—his real potential and creative imagination might have been able to live. Does this sound at all relevant?

Audience: Yes. Go on.

Liz: Are you sure?

Audience: Well, I did ask.

Liz: Yes. Well, I think this parental marriage resembles Zeus and Hera much more than it does two banal little people buried in material objects and daily tasks. I am increasingly getting the feeling, too, that you might perhaps have taken sides, and that it is the father who earned all your sympathy and idealisation, while your mother had to carry your own earthy shadow and became a rival—the one who, although dull and boring, still managed to get and keep your father. If we look at this as an archetypal parental marriage, then your own allegiances within it will say a great deal about your own internal dilemmas in life. You have both earth and fire, and somehow you need to find a way to give value to both in yourself. If you have become a father's daughter, then the fantasy-world of fire and spirit is the one in which you will feel most at home; but that will cost you your relationship with your body and with your feminine self, unless you can make peace with your Taurus Moon and its simple, basic needs. That I think is some of the challenge which your chart suggests, and which your parents in their marriage do not seem to have solved. They merely hid, which is not surprising considering the times they lived through and the social behaviour which was expected of them. I will ask you one very personal question which, obviously, you need not answer; but it might help you to see how this parental marriage continues to live in you. Do you have a propensity for triangles, for attachments to married men?

Audience: Oh, I see.

Liz: Good. Perhaps we can go on. I hope this was not too embarrassing.

I want to make sure that you are all following. Although I have said that these images in the horoscope are subjective pictures, nevertheless I interpreted the example which was kindly offered before as though it were all objective. I really don't know how objective a picture the parental marriage in the horoscope is. In my experience, it is indeed quite objective, although your guess is as good as mine as to how all that is arranged in the boardroom. But it is also subjective, and that is in many ways just as important if not more so. And selective perception comes into it. I interpreted the Moon-Pluto square earlier as something I associate with depression and repressed anger in the mother. Obviously a person is something more than just an embodiment of depression and frustration. She may have had many other qualities, some very creative and positive; and she also may have changed over the years. But if that square to Pluto is the only aspect that the Moon makes, then depression is the primary experience of the mother on the part of the child. Also, I interpreted the aspects of the Sun as describing an idealised and eroticised father-image. The father here obviously had other facets to his personality, notably the Sun in Capricorn, which is anything but a figure out of Arthurian romance. Probably his sense of self-discipline and moral law was very powerful and won in any contest with a more volatile and poetic nature. But the Capricorn qualities do not appear in the birth chart in relation to the father. That is selective perception. We might look at the Moon-Pluto not only as an image of an unhappy woman, but also as an image of great depth of feeling, and a tremendous force of instinctual life; and that is the positive side of the inheritance from the mother. We could also look at the solar aspects and see that the positive side of the father is his vision, his imagination, and his romantic nature, although none of this emerged in his overt behaviour. But as a parental scenario, we can also see that there are bound to be difficulties between the two.

A person begins life with a particular perception of how things are between the parents. That picture does not have to remain static. But as long as it is unconscious, it will not change, and then the individual becomes caught in a compulsive pattern which feels like a fate. Hence I made an educated guess about affairs with married men, and a flight from the ordinary world with its threat of becoming just another unhappy, frustrated woman caught in a marriage with a man who somehow slips through her fingers. The real parental marriage was obviously not "bad" in any conventional sense, and there were obviously many compensations; and it is pointless to suggest that these parents should have handled their lives any differently, since they made the best choice they could, and it worked for them. But the amputated life has come home to roost in the daughter, because such a solution is only partial, and there are more acts in the play. The World Parents are still in conflict, although the worldly ones have bought time. Mother Earth is stifling Father Fire, and is experienced as dull, crushing and life-destroying. Father Fire is beautiful, magical, and erotically fascinating, but he must always escape somewhere, or else he will be flattened by the weight of earthy life. The spirit and the body are perceived as incompatible; if one inhabits the body then the spirit is chained, but if one inhabits the spirit then the body is rejected and outcast, and the ordinary pleasures of earth life are spoiled.

Whatever the resolution might be to this dilemma, it will not come from doing what the parents did. Nor will it come from siding with one parent against the other, because these parents are archetypal and they are within. To cut off either one means amputating part of oneself. So some other path must be pursued, and that is always terribly difficult, because one must make it up as one goes along. The parents cannot be a model, nor can rebelling against the parents, which is really no different. Ultimately the dilemma which is reflected here is not only the dilemma of the parents' marriage, but the whole issue of being able to live creatively and with flair and imagination in a world which sets limits through incarnation in a physical body. That is the challenge of earth and fire, which are in our example carried respectively by mother and father.

EXAMPLE CHARTS

Now I would like you to look at the charts which I have put up on the board, so that we can examine more closely how one might interpret the parental marriage and its effects and meaning in the individual's adult life. We have the advantage with these charts of having a brother and sister, and their parents, although the mother's chart is lacking an ascendant. I also have the planetary placements for both sets of grandparents if we need to consider them later—and we might, because the mythic theme of the parental marriage is generally traceable through several generations in a family—although once again, as with the mother, there are no birth times given. But I think you will see how the stark outlines of the parents' essential character, even reflected only by planetary aspects and signs without the complete testimony of a properly calculated chart, is echoed throughout all the horoscopes which we consider. There is a lot of information to absorb with this group of charts, so I think we should proceed slowly, beginning with the son, whom I will call Bruce. Does anyone have any initial comments to make about Bruce's birth chart? (See Chart 2 on page 116.) Don't just consider the 10th and 4th houses. Try to get an overall feeling of the man first.

Audience: There isn't much earth in this chart—only Neptune in Virgo conjunct a Virgo ascendant. And the Neptune emphasis is very strong through the Sun in Pisces in opposition to it. I think he is a rather dreamy man, maybe quite dependent or vague. That is my initial impression.

Liz: In essence he is no doubt vague, dreamy and dependent. I think you are right. But in manner he is quite different. I will tell you something about him. He is a moderately successful executive in a large company, and is primarily occupied with the sales side of the business, so he travels a good deal. His personality on the surface is typically Virgoan in the less attractive textbook sense. He is persnickety and quite "straight," with a rather brittle persona. Behind this he has a bad drinking problem. His sister, from whom I have most of the information about the family, told me that when he was a child, he was extremely cruel and destructive, and not only teased her viciously, but was not above tormenting animals as well. This is a strange phenomenon which I have occasionally encountered with strongly Neptunian charts. Do any of you have any idea why this pattern of cruelty might occur with such a pronouncedly Piscean horoscope?

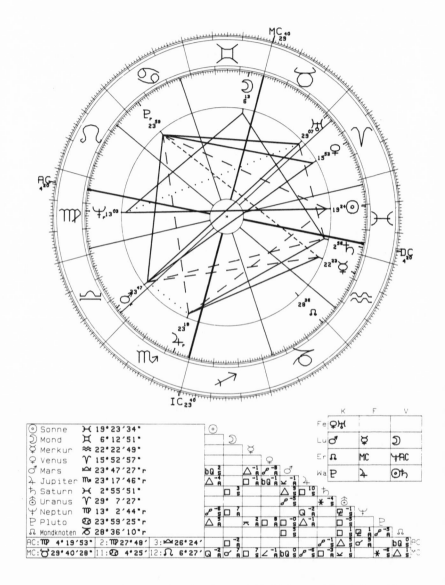

Chart 2. Bruce. The birth data has been withheld for confidentiality. Chart calculated by Astrodienst, using the Placidus house system.

Audience: I think it's the shadow-side of Pisces. Pisces is usually sensitive and compassionate.

Liz: We might look at it that way, and I think there is some truth in it. But I also think there are more subtle issues at work here, and we also need to be clear about just what "shadow" means. The comment about Bruce's dependency is perfectly true, and I believe in many ways this is a rather weak and unformed personality. But he is also someone who abhors being seen, or seeing himself, in that light. He projects his essential weakness and helplessness onto weaker objects, such as a younger sister or a pet, because he cannot bear these feelings in himself. Something falls into the shadow when it is not permitted expression in consciousness. It is Bruce's essential Piscean-ness, if I can be permitted to make up a word, which he will not permit into consciousness. He would much rather be an Aries or a Leo, and not a soft and sensitive and vulnerable Neptunian. Whenever he sees these qualities reflected back to him, it brings cruelty out of him, and he wants to hurt and destroy the thing which mirrors his own essence back to him. One sometimes finds this with Pisceans—I don't think it is that Pisces is secretly cruel, but rather that many Pisceans, women as well as men, cannot bear the experience of being what they are, because it means embracing some very vulnerable feelings. Pisces does not have strong boundaries against others, and this means always being receptive to the needs and sufferings of the collective. If this proves untenable, then the Piscean can easily start behaving like a fake Gemini or Capricorn, with apparently no sensitivity at all and a hyper-rational persona. And then I think the cruelty can sometimes come to the surface, if the person is reminded too forcibly of what is being repressed.

It is also interesting to note that Mars is retrograde in Libra, in a close square to Pluto and in opposition to Uranus. That, I think, also has quite a lot to do with the cruelty. There is a very powerful will in this man, and strong desires at work in him, particularly on a sexual level; please also note Venus in Aries in the 8th house, opposite Mars and also square Pluto. But he does not have the necessary strength and solidity to pursue those desires and really make something of himself. He is quick-witted and clever—Mercury is trine Mars—and he is probably good at handling people, because of the Moon at the midheaven and also the rising Neptune which gives him the ability to mirror back to others what he instinctively senses they want to hear from him. But somehow, with all the energy and power implied by those Mars aspects, he has never been more than mediocre in his life, and I think this is because of the essential blurredness of his personality. He is not really a crystallised person. I think his desires therefore burn away inside him, but he is not equipped to direct them toward a definite goal. There is enormous unconscious anger here, which I believe is also connected with his drinking problem. I think Bruce has a very violent streak in his nature. But the Sun in Pisces in opposition to Neptune cannot express such violence in any overt way—it must content itself with tormenting pets—because of the powerful need of others. Here the Sun is also in the 7th house, which emphasises his dependency on others to give him a sense of reality. And Saturn is in Pisces at the descendant, which I think also suggests that he relies on others to give him his support and security in life—although he would be the last person to admit it, and probably makes it very difficult for others to feel needed and valued by him.

So Bruce is really caught between two opposite needs which grind him in the middle. He cannot break out and ruthlessly pursue what he wants from life because he lacks the strength and self-reliance; but he also cannot simply give himself to others and live contentedly in devoted service to them, because he cannot bear to be thwarted or denied anything that he wants for himself. If Mars were stronger—say, in Scorpio or Capricorn—then I think he might have been better able to express the will and independence of the Mars-Pluto-Uranus configuration. But it is retrograde in the sign of its detriment. It is likely therefore to be overwhelmed by the aspects to it, and to be repressed and unconnected except on an intellectual level.

Audience: Is he married?

Liz: Yes, he is married, and has three sons. I don't have his wife's birth data, but I am told that she is a strong and earthy woman, who more or less runs the household and holds the marriage together. He has evidently found his 7th house Saturn in her. She tolerates his drinking and is effectively both father and mother to their children. But Bruce is always leaving the family to travel. No doubt he feels restricted by her.

Before I tell you about Bruce's parents, I would like you to try to piece together the signature of the parental marriage in his birth chart.

Audience: If I look for the father in the solar aspects as you suggested earlier, and then at the 4th house, there seems to be a contradictory picture. The Sun is in opposition to Neptune. That describes someone very mystical and maybe artistic, and otherworldly. Perhaps the father wasn't there very much. Maybe he was unformed and weak as you say Bruce is. But the Sun is also trine Jupiter, and from what you said before about Zeus, that describes a very different person. It's a much more adventurous spirit. And the Sun is also trine Pluto, which might mean great power or sexuality. I don't understand how to put these things together.

Liz: Neither did Bruce's father. That is exactly the point. And neither does Bruce. As you say, there is a contradiction here, or what I might call a split. The split lies in Bruce—we have been talking about it just now, in the opposing drives toward satisfaction of desire and self-abnegation for the sake of others—but it also probably lay in his father, who, I will tell you now, was also an alcoholic. You will usually find these contradictory pictures of the parent in the chart, and they are what comprises the inheritance from that parent on a psychological level. What the father has not succeeded in integrating within himself, Bruce will manifest as his own dilemma in life, and he is then challenged with coming up with a more creative way of handling the split than his father did. It is very rare that you find a perfectly consistent portrait of the parent in the horoscope, because most people are not consistent; and you can be pretty sure that with someone who has the kind of serious problems that Bruce does, the family background is going to be full of splits and dissociated psychic pieces lying about unnoticed under the carpet.

There is a dimension to Bruce's father, which also belongs to Bruce, that is indeed adventurous and Jupiterian. It expresses itself in Bruce through his need to travel, and it reflects a particular aspect of the father's life as well. The father left his rather claustrophobic Yorkshire background and travelled to London, where he eventually became, just like Bruce, a moderately successful business executive. Somewhere within himself he must have found a little Jupiter, to have made that transition from the North of

England to life in the big city. Evidentally he was also an actor *manqué*, and his great love was the theatre. That is also very Jupiterian. All his life he was involved in amateur theatrical groups. But he never managed to develop this passion into a vocation, and worked a fairly orthodox nine-to-five job. He was also, in his youth, an attractive and debonair figure, with a great deal of sexual charm. The Plutonian qualities are not so immediately recognisable, except perhaps in the lonely pursuing of his own destiny away from the family background; but as we go on, and examine the nature of this father's marriage, you will see that there was indeed a strongly Plutonian dimension to his personality.

I think you can begin to see how all three aspects to Bruce's Sun describe something about his father. But the father somehow could not put it all together. He seems always to have wished he could have been somebody else, and his daughter told me that he was very aloof and inaccessible in her childhood, vanishing behind a drink and a newspaper and the television. He lived somewhere in a dream-world where all his unfulfilled longings were satisfied, since his actual life seems to have been very dreary. That is the Neptunian significator, and it seems to be the facet of Bruce's father that is most painful and difficult for Bruce to understand and integrate.

This opposition, if we interpret it as Bruce's experience of and perception of his father, seems to suggest a "vanishing" father, a man with whom no real relationship was possible. He slid away from any direct effort at contact. I think that Bruce must have felt his psychic absence acutely, but just as he cannot face his own weakness with compassion, so too he cannot face his father's. I think that Bruce, on a conscious level, despises his father's ineffectuality, and this attitude in turn makes it even more difficult for him to confront a similar nature in himself. This is the weak and despicable father whose more heroic qualities, reflected by Bruce's solar trines to Jupiter and Pluto, must have been apparent but were never actualised to the son. At the same time, the Sun in opposition to Neptune suggests a great deal of unconscious idealisation of the father as well as disappointment, and perhaps Bruce secretly put him up on a pedestal and romanticised him, secretly blaming himself for his father's apparent disinterest and aloofness. The sister also told me that Bruce has a habit of appearing at her home wearing his father's clothes—his coat, hat, and so on. The father, by the way, is now dead. But somehow Bruce tries still to get close to this man whom he could never contact by wearing the discarded clothes. Of course he is unconscious of why he does this. But it is terribly sad, and you can see the secret idealisation and worship of the father who forever slipped out of his grasp.

Now I think we should consider the signature of the mother. Does anyone want to try to piece her together from Bruce's chart?

Audience: The Moon is in the 10th house in Gemini, square Saturn and also square Neptune. That seems to me to be another contradiction. On one side there is a restrictive, cold, conventional figure. On the other side there is the same helpless dreaminess and weakness as the father had.

Liz: Yes, you are right, this is another split. Try to think about it. Something about the mother is here very similar to the father; both are reflected by Neptune. But the mother's inner contradictions are different. This is not exciting Jupiter and powerful Pluto foundering in Neptunian fog. This is Saturn. What do you think?

Audience: I think this must be a conflict of romanticism and duty. I think she must have lived the Saturnian side. She had to put up with an alcoholic who could not relate to his family. She would have had to be the strong one, doing all the practical things. She probably had a strong sense of responsibility, so she couldn't just walk out. Her own weakness and dreaminess couldn't be expressed because there wouldn't have been room for both of them to behave like that. Probably both of them wanted life to be wonderful and beautiful and glamourous and full of magic. He drowned his disappointment in the bottle and acted out the Neptune, and she suppressed her disappointment and became dutiful. Have I got that right?

Liz: I think you have got much of it right. You have certainly got the hang of what I mean by piecing a story together. The mother is indeed a romantic, and was horribly trapped in a life which bore no resemblance to her dreams. The Saturnian significator, as you say, suggests that she tolerated it all out of a sense of duty, and no doubt made everyone around her pay for it. From the description I have been given, she was evidentally a rather intellectual type— appropriate for the figure portrayed by the Moon in Gemini in Bruce's chart—with varied cultural interests and pursuits, and was something of a socialite. But she was given to violent outbursts and black moods at home when none of her important social contacts was there to see it, and fought continually with the father and also, later on, with Bruce. She seems to have been disappointed that they were not wealthier and more socially "important," and the more the father drank, the more venomous were her attacks on him. She died of cancer when both children were still quite young.

Audience: I am unclear about that 10th house Moon. Does this mean that Bruce experiences her as very emotional and maternal? Or that he is very emotionally attached to her?

Liz: I think it means both. The mother is lunar to Bruce, and therefore changeable as the Moon, as they say. But she is Moon-in-Gemini lunar, which is much more the artistic, extroverted, butterfly-like face of the Moon. If the Moon had been in Taurus, or Cancer, then "maternal" might have been a more accurate description. But the flavour of the Moon in Gemini is one of charm, flirtatiousness, brightness and frivolity. It's like the heroine of *La Traviata*. That is the face which all her friends saw, and which Bruce saw as well, although he saw something else too.

But the presence of the Moon in the 10th also suggests that Bruce's own emotional nature is closely identified with his mother. It is interesting that he fought with her so strenuously, just as his father did. The 10th house Moon suggests to me that he was perhaps too close, and so the fighting was a kind of desperate struggle to pry himself loose from her, and to get closer to the father. Although the square to the Moon from Saturn suggests that he felt unwanted and rejected by her, the square from Neptune suggests that, as with his father, he romanticised and idealised her. All his feeling responses are unconsciously merged with hers, so his view of his father is going to be her view, and her bitterness and disillusionment with life are going to infect his own response to life. Bruce cannot easily separate from this mother, although she has been dead for a long time. As long as he is bound to her vision of life, then he cannot reconcile himself with his father, nor with the side of himself which is like his father. This is what I meant earlier by "taking sides." Consciously, Bruce has little good to say about his mother. But unconsciously, it is through her embittered eyes that he looks at life, his father, and himself. And he has created almost literally the same situation with his own life and his own marriage as did his father, although Bruce's wife is not explosive and moody. But she is a strong woman who props the household up, and so was the mother; and this is reflected by the Saturn as significator of both the mother and the marriage partner. Bruce is dependent upon his wife as he was upon his mother, and tries to run away through his travelling in much the same spirit that he fought with his mother earlier in life.

I think you can begin to get some of the feeling of what kind of marriage these parents had, and the planetary significators in Bruce's chart are confirmed by the facts of the situation as Bruce's sister has described them to me. Both the Sun and the Moon strongly aspecting Neptune suggest a theme pertaining to both parents: a general atmosphere of disappointed hopes, failed dreams, and general self-deception and evasion. There was a mother who had social ambitions and pretensions to cultural accomplishment, married to a man who disappointed her both emotionally and financially; and, I suspect and as you will see later when we compare the parents' charts, sexually as well. To her, he was a failure, and all the promise and excitement at the beginning of the marriage turned sour and bitter. She could not forgive him, so she attacked him constantly, and he retreated further and further into his Neptunian world. She was so preoccupied with her grievances that she had little to offer her children save Saturnian duty; and no doubt she did her best to turn her son against his father. She had to be the strong and practical parent when really she would have liked to play Scarlett O'Hara before a crowd of rich adoring suitors at her feet. She was so eaten up with resentment that she failed to discern how she sacrificed all her own creative potential—not because anyone asked this of her, and not because of any real love, but because she was essentially too weak and Neptunian herself to take charge of her own life and try to find fulfilment apart from her husband and family. The husband was supposed to give her everything, and when he did not, then she made him pay. And her resentment eventually literally ate her alive.

On the other hand, there was a father who started off life with a spirit of courage, adventure and romantic enthusiasm, leaving a narrow life behind him and trying to "make it" in the whirl of the big city. He had a lot of dreams of artistic achievement, but lacked the stamina and self-reliance necessary to try to put his talents to the test, settling instead for a humdrum job which bored him silly but which at least guaranteed him some financial stability. He married a woman who seemed to be passionate and exciting, and socially "higher" than him; but then he found that he had taken too much on board, because she demanded too much of him and he could not live up to her expectations, let alone live up to his own. He was not confident enough in his own masculinity to stand up to her, so he retreated into the world's oldest form of passive aggression. There is an enormous amount of aggression in alcoholism, although usually we think of the self-destructive side of the problem first. But there is also the desire to destroy others, and the suffering of the alcoholic's family is perhaps one of the unconscious objects of the exercise.

Audience: You could almost say that Bruce's alcoholism was inherited.

Liz: It certainly looks like that. It is not uncommon for the child of an alcoholic to become an alcoholic. But I don't think it is a physical inheritance. It is a repeating way of trying to deal with an essential split which the parent could not deal with. Bruce has a split between his Neptunian nature—something which he shares with his father in both its creative and destructive forms—and his Plutonian/Martial nature—something else which he also shares with his father. Neptune describes a quality of connectedness with the numinous world of the unconscious, and it offers on the positive side a glimpse of a larger, deeper and more meaningful cosmos which brings light and magic into the limitations of mundane reality. On the negative side, this same gift acts as a problem, because one's eyes are always cast on that magical world and one expects life always to live up to the perfect beauty and boundlessness that one has glimpsed within. Of course life cannot do this, and so the sense of disappointment, disillusionment and despair can become very great.

Had the father been better able to mobilise what in Bruce's chart is described as a Plutonian nature—a little "true grit" and survival instinct—then he might have been able to actualise some of that Neptunian vision. But he could not, for reasons which we will see when we look at his chart and *his* parental marriage. So the father acted out his own split by selecting a wife who could carry all his primitive and self-willed qualities for him, and in turn recoiled from these things and retreated into the other half of his nature. Bruce, when he was a child, displayed some of the less attractive Pluto–Mars qualities himself, but they were already twisted, rather than expressed as healthy aggression and power; and probably a small dose of his mother's passions went a long way, and he appears to have become more "civilised" with age. But he likewise has retreated into the same Neptunian stupour as did his father. I don't know where that more explosive side of his nature is displaying itself now. Certainly it is imploding through his drinking. I hope it is not directed against the three children. But I think it is mostly just deeply repressed, and the alcohol is both a covert manifestation of it and also a means to keep it locked in the basement.

Do you see the mythic overtones of this marriage? Obviously I could not have put together such a detailed scenario without the facts about the family background which I have given you. Bruce's chart does not say that he had an alcoholic father, although many people with Sun in opposition to Neptune do; and if the father is not alcoholic, then he has escaped in some other way, and the experience of pathos, sadness, disappointed love and sense of loss are the same. But the planetary significators—in the case of the father, Neptune, Jupiter and Pluto, and in the case of the mother, Neptune and Saturn—tell you something of the essential themes which belong to the parents and which therefore also belong to Bruce himself. Whatever the real characteristics of these parents, which we will explore in due course when we look at their charts, they appear here mythologised. The father is a romantic adventurer who has failed to cope with the demands of life—Jupiter-Pluto unable to make it and therefore succumbing to Neptune, drink, apathy and withdrawal. The mother is a glamourous extravert torn between the responsibilities of her mundane life and her dreams of romantic glory, vicitimised by a burdensome marriage and poisoned by resentment and disappointment—Moon in Gemini square Neptune and Saturn. These two are like something out of a Tennessee Williams play, although they are English. Neptune is common to both parents, and this is an outer planet, suggesting some ancient and collective aspiration which is being enacted in a highly personal way in the privacy of the parental bedroom. Both parents express this Neptune in different ways. The father reacts

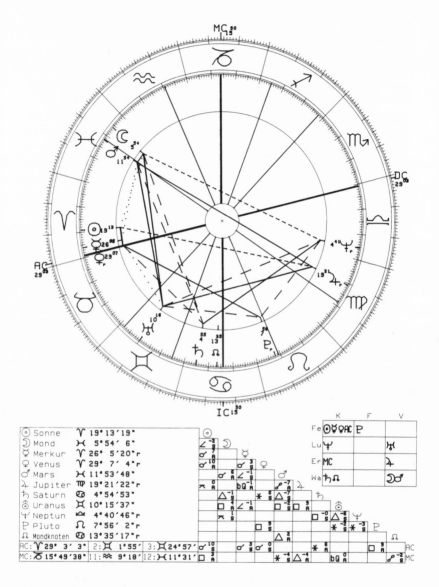

Chart 3. Susan. The birth data has been withheld for confidentiality. Chart calculated by Astrodienst, using the Placidus house system.

to his disappointment and disillusionment with passivity and disintegration, while the mother reacts to hers by becoming outraged and vindictive. And Bruce is bound also to Neptune through his Sun and Moon, so he is the inheritor of what might potentially be a great creative gift, but which has so far proven to be a canker in the family psyche. He must try to find a way to live with this quality of fantasy-making and contact with the numinous realm in a more creative form than did his parents. So far he has not succeeded. It would appear, from what his sister said, that so far he cannot even face the fact that there might be anything wrong. Like his father, he has succumbed to the blindness of Neptune without the creative dimension of it, and is suppressing all his more aggressive instincts. We do not know in what form these instincts will eventually surface, but they of course will do sooner or later as the psyche tries to redress the imbalance. We also do not know whether Bruce can meet this challenge.

Shall we look at Bruce's sister's chart before we examine the parental charts? I will call her Susan. What do you make of this chart? (See Chart 3.)

Audience: This chart feels a lot better to me than Bruce's does. There is a lot of fire in it—Sun, Mercury, Venus and the ascendant in Aries. But there is also almost no earth here, only Jupiter in Virgo. And the Neptune signature appears again in another form, with the Moon in Pisces. But I think she has coped better.

Liz: Yes, she has. She has her problems, but they are not so deeply destructive as Bruce's, perhaps because, as you say, she has plenty of fire and the typical Arien determination to make her life better. Bruce has only Venus and Uranus in Aries, and although fire can reflect many difficulties of its own, in the context of the kind of family background which we have been talking about, it is an invaluable help, because it reflects a capacity to sense possibilities in life which are greater and more positive than those of the background. Whatever its failings, fire tends to pick itself up and move on, unless the person is intensely introverted and lives the fiery intuition through an escape into the fantasy-world.

Susan originally had aspirations toward becoming a sculptress, although she has not succeeded in living out these early dreams. There seems to be a very sad proliferation of failed artists in this family. Perhaps that is the Neptunian significator running through like a red thread, and no one has yet been able to really embody and concretise that creative potential. Susan has lived with a successful painter for about fifteen years, although they have never married and have no children. That is also not surprising, in terms of what she saw enacted in the parental marriage. She is reasonably happy in this relationship, although still frustrated and unfulfilled in terms of her own creative potential. She was briefly married when she was much younger, but this marriage was a disappointment and she does not seem inclined to repeat the mistake through a formal contract to her painter. In this respect at least she has succeeded in accomplishing what her mother did not—leaving an unhappy relationship to seek something better for herself.

Now we need to see whether a similar parental marriage pattern appears in Susan's chart. Obviously we cannot expect to find precisely the same significators. But I think we can expect to find a similar story.

Audience: The Sun makes no major aspects, apart from its conjunction to Mercury. And it's in the 12th house. There is a quincunx to Jupiter and a semisquare to the Moon. I think this says something very similar to Bruce's chart. There is the Jupiter flavour, and the 12th house, which is like the Neptune-Pisces emphasis in Bruce's chart. It is as though the father disappeared into the fog of the 12th house.

Liz: Yes, it is a similar story, if you look at the Sun alone. Here indeed is the unknown and vanishing father, with sparkling promise but nothing to contact in the end after all. The lack of major aspects suggests to me a lack of outlets for expression of the self—which may be one of the reasons why Susan was not able to actualise her own artistic ambitions, as well as a reflection of the lack of contact with the father. And the Sun in the 12th house also suggests that Susan's own identity and self-expression are submerged in the family unconscious, as though she swims feebly against some powerful apathy which blunts the creative edge of the Aries. She has never really been able to break free from that sad family past, although she is much freer than Bruce, and seems to have a genuine relationship in her life rather than a carbon copy of her parents' marriage. But this lost father reflected by an unaspected 12th house Sun is only part of the testimony. Look at the 4th house.

Audience: Pluto is in the 4th. And it squares Venus. Does this mean that Susan is more affected by the darker Plutonian side of her father than Bruce is?

Liz: In one sense, yes, she is more "affected" by it, because it sits alone in the 4th house. Pluto appears as a father-significator in Bruce's chart as well, part of the grand trine of Sun-Jupiter-Pluto. Here it sticks out, as it were, as though it were a separate issue. I believe that on some level, probably an unconscious one, Susan knows that her parents' marriage was not as simple as a dragon-mother castrating a weak and impotent father. Bruce knows this too, but the issue which concerns him most is the Sun-Neptune figure, because firstly it is an opposition and therefore trouble-some, and secondly because he is himself a Piscean and it is the thing which is closest to his own identity. But with Susan, she knows that her father also carried something dark and destructive, which the mother carried and acted out. It is bound up with his sexuality and in turn with Susan's, because of the square to her Venus, which in turn rules her 7th house and therefore her atti-tudes and expectations toward the partner. I think this is the main reason why she has not married again, nor had children, although watching two parents slowly and quietly destroy each other is not conducive to a great deal of faith in the institution of marriage. But I would say from this 4th house Pluto square Venus that she is frightened of winding up at the mercy of a man's sexual manipula-tion, which I suspect is precisely what happened between the mother and father; although the mother has of course been cast as the villain of the piece because she was so spiteful and vituperative about her disappointment. But the sex-life of an alcoholic is not exactly dynamic, although the fantasies no doubt must have been; and chronic impotence, which is usually the long-term condition of the alcoholic, may be seen and is usually experienced by the partner as a tacit form of rejection and refusal.

Here is the split-off side of the father appearing as a powerful factor in the relationship with the daughter, who no doubt received some of her father's unconscious sexual fantasy-life and felt both excited and threatened by it. I would read this from the 4th house Pluto square Venus. A father will always relate differently to a daughter than to a son, for obvious reasons; and if there is a sexual problem between the parents, then the daughter will often be the recipient of the father's libido which flows away from the mother. Also, with Susan's Sun in Aries, which I associate on an archetypal level with the mythic phallic father-god, Susan is predisposed, because of her own inner psychic constitution, toward experiencing her father through an archetypal lens of great potency. Although she appears to have experienced no real relationship with him—suggested by the unaspected Sun in the 12th house—nevertheless there is a dark unconscious tie which is incestuous and manipulative in nature. So both significators, Neptune and Pluto, appear here in relation to the father as they do in Bruce's chart, although the emphasis is quite different. Even the third one, Jupiter, is also present. But it would seem that Bruce, with his Sun in Pisces and Neptune rising in opposition to it, is predisposed toward identifying the father with Neptune and will therefore experience him as weak and inaccessible, while unconsciously idealising him and searching for the heroic adventurer that he senses to be lingering somewhere in the mists. Susan, with her 4th house Pluto and Sun in Aries, is predisposed toward identifying her father with force and phallic power, and therefore fears his unexpressed sexual potency. What about the mother in Susan's chart?

Audience: The Moon conjuncts Mars. That is a very powerful and aggressive mother. That conjunction is square Uranus, which is maybe a reflection of the explosiveness and unpredictability of the mother's moods. But they are also both trine Saturn, so there is the dutiful and practical figure again.

Liz: Yes, once again we have a similar picture, although there are important differences. In Bruce's chart, the mother's explosiveness is not really reflected. Instead, there is a portrait of a collision between a romantic and idealistic nature and the hard limitations which life imposes on it. It is also a picture of a conflict between something fragile and other-worldly, and something tough and strong and self-reliant. The description in Susan's chart is more explicit and more turbulent. Perhaps we should remember that there were ten years between Bruce's birth and Susan's. I think the parental situation was much worse by the time Susan came along, and had flowered into the full-blown scenes from *Medea* which

Susan has described to me. The Moon-Mars conjunction in Pisces reflects, in part, the Moon-Neptune square in Bruce's chart, but in addition to the Neptunian vagueness and romanticism there is also a rather punchy Mars added as a significator. This is, as you say, a highly emotional and aggressive nature, full of passion, romanticism and a burning desire to be somebody in life. This of course also reflects something about Susan, and the presence of this conjunction in the 11th house suggests that she, like her mother, cares a lot about what other people think of her.

The square from the Moon to Uranus suggests a deep conflict about fulfilling the biological obligations of a mother. I suspect that by the time Susan was born, the mother did not really want another child; I think she probably just wanted to get out. But the Saturnian significator, which appears in both Bruce's and Susan's charts as a major factor in the mother's temperament and nature, would suggest a twofold obstruction to any escape from the burden of the marriage and of childbearing. Firstly, the mother probably had too great a sense of conventional responsibility. A "good" woman and wife stays in her marriage and bears her husband children, irregardless of her own secret feelings about the matter. Secondly, the mother seems to have had a problem with regard to aloneness and self-sufficiency, which are also Saturnian issues. This is the conflict between Saturn and Neptune, which may also be seen as a conflict between the necessity of being self-sufficient and the need to live through and for others. All the explosive anger which Susan described to me appears here portrayed very clearly, while in Bruce's chart the mother-image is not a figure of violent anger; she is someone sadly caught between romanticism and duty. The duty is still apparent in Susan's chart, but here it appears as a trine rather than a square between Saturn and the Moon. This perhaps implies that Susan appreciated this dimension of her mother as something positive, and she admired her mother's strength; while to Bruce it must have seemed cold and rejecting. There is another aspect here which none of you have mentioned, the quincunx between the Moon and Pluto, which points to something shared between the parents in Susan's experience of them—a dark sexual undercurrent which the mother acted out through castrating anger yet which the father possessed in equal measure, and which has powerfully, albeit unconsciously, affected Susan.

Audience: What do you mean by that? What do you think actually went on sexually between the parents?

Liz: I don't know. I can only speculate from the evidence of the charts. But I think that the father's anger toward the mother expressed itself as a kind of sexual manipulation—a teasing which always ended in disinterest. You will see later on that there must have been a powerful sexual attraction between these parents at the beginning of the marriage, because the mother's Venus conjuncts the father's Mars and the mother's Mars trines the father's Venus. I think she was very excited by him and very addicted to him sexually. I think he used this against her. We will go more into this side of the marriage later. Right now I want to finish with this material on Bruce's and Susans' charts. Are there any other issues about these parental configurations which anyone wants to ask about?

Audience: Are there any myths which might reflect this parental marriage? I have been trying to think of one, but I can't. It isn't really Zeus and Hera, because Zeus is strong and fights his wife. Or at least he has the strength to escape her and find other women. But Bruce's father couldn't escape, and neither can Bruce. He fought his mother on the surface, but I think she got him underneath.

Liz: Yes, I would agree: She got him underneath, on several levels. But this father is more Zeus-like than at first appears. His drinking is a form of escape, although unlike the escapes of Zeus it produces no creative offspring. But it is a pursuit, albeit blind and with no potential, of the anima; although the anima ends here in a *cul de sac*, and is revealed as a disguise for the depressive apathy of the Terrible Mother. But Bruce also runs away from his own marriage into his business trips.

Audience: Does he have affairs when he travels?

Liz: I have no idea. I doubt if Susan does either, since her brother is not the sort to discuss such personal issues with her. But I would guess that he does, judging by the 8th house Venus in Aries in opposition to Mars in Libra. I think that aspect has to come out somewhere, and Bruce is not yet sodden as his father was later in life. If I follow my intuition about Bruce, I have the idea that he goes for prostitutes while he is on the road, or very easy pick-ups, and he is possibly not very nice to them when he gets his hands on them; but no one ever hears about it. Maybe that is the reality and maybe it exists only in his fantasy life. But I suspect that he has a rather nasty edge to his erotic fantasy life. It is the aspects between Venus, Mars, Pluto and Uranus, involving the 8th house, that give me that feeling. There is a great deal of anger in him which springs from his sense of impotence and ineffectuality, and I think also that he must feel somewhat impotent with his very strong wife.

In response to your question, I am also trying to think of a mythic image for this parental marriage, but I cannot find one which is exactly right. Yet it is not an uncommon scenario. There is something Zeus-and-Hera-like about it, and the mother certainly has some of Hera's qualities; these are the Saturnian ones which kept her bound to the conventional roles of mother and wife. But the mother was more witchlike than Hera, and had a lot of Hekate in her, or the Gorgon, because of her poison. This is reflected by the significators for the mother in Susan's chart—Mars, Pluto and Uranus. The father, although he seems quite Jupiterian in some ways, is an introverted Zeus *manqué*. Once upon a time he wanted to be an actor, but nothing ever came of it. Instead of running away into the arms of other women, he has, as I said, run away into another form of anima, the bottle. He is a kind of inside-out Zeus who has lost his potency. In that sense we have traces of the Zeus-Hera marriage here.

But he also has a very vicious undercurrent, and I believe, as I have said, that he unconsciously thwarted his wife in deliberately cruel ways, so that her anger sprang not only from her own disappointed expectations, but also from some subtle humiliation which he inflicted on her. But this kind of thing never gets noticed, and no one can point a finger, so he comes out as the pathetic victim of a terrible woman's anger and scorn. He is indeed a victim, but of something within himself. There is really more a touch of the Kybele-and-Attis myth in this marital tale, with the frightening mother-goddess and the gentle and ineffectual son-lover who castrates himself. Or we might consider Atargatis and Ichthys, who are the Phoenician version of the same pair, because "Ichthys" means "fish." I think this is a close mythic picture of one of the threads at work in this parental marriage.

The other thread running through the story—that of the powerful and potent male manipulating and thwarting the female—is also echoed in myth. There are numerous tales about young girls threatened with the attack of hideous male monsters, like Psyche before she meets Eros, or Andromeda chained to her rock. There is something of this at work here too, because the father is also Pluto, and the mother the Neptunian victim. It depends upon which side of the prism you view it through; but it is the same myth, and it is about power. Both the male and female versions of the story pit Neptune against Pluto, and there is a power-battle in which someone plays the aggressor and someone the pathetic and helpless victim. I think this is one of the deep paradoxes of the parental marriage, and of the archetypal World Parents: Both are secretly reflections of each other, yet they divide the roles up between them so that conflict—and a potential new synthesis— can arise.

Perhaps it would be interesting now to look at the charts of Bruce's parents. (See Chart 4 on page 136 and Chart 5 on page 137.) These will naturally be no surprise to you, after all that we have discussed. Although it would be true to say that the images of the parents in Bruce's chart are his subjective portraits and therefore factors within his own psyche, the parents provide excellent hooks for his projection of these images.

Bruce's father has the Sun in the 12th house in Leo, trine to a 4th house Moon in Sagittarius. This Moon reflects the Jupiterian quality which both his children echo in their charts with their Sun-Jupiter contacts. The Sun in the 12th, which is repeated in Susan's placement of the Sun in the 12th, seems to reflect that vague and elusive Neptunian aura which the father carried for his children. It of course also makes a statement about *his* father in turn, but it describes him, like Susan, as someone whose own identity might have great difficulty in emerging from the sea of the family unconscious. This 12th house Sun in Bruce's father's chart points to one of the most interesting dimensions of the exercise of exploring the parental marriage in the horoscope, because this man himself seems to have experienced precisely the same kind of parental marriage—this would be the marriage between Bruce's paternal grandparents—as Bruce and Susan both portray in their own charts. Bruce's grandfather, with whom the father evidently identified closely, seems to have been a weak and changeable man, quite peaceable and pleasant but without much substance. This quality is suggested not only by Bruce's father's solar placement in the 12th, but also by the Moon's presence in the 4th, implying that the father is experienced as changeable and unreliable. Meanwhile, Bruce's paternal grandmother is represented in the father's chart as guess what—Pluto in the 10th house, in company with a Venus-Neptune conjunction in Cancer also in the 10th. This is underlined by the opposition between the Moon and Pluto. And there is one more planet represented as a significator for Bruce's father's mother—Jupiter, which conjuncts the midheaven in Gemini. Here are the same planetary significators for the parental marriage as we have found in Bruce's chart: Jupiter, Neptune and Pluto.

Audience: The father has the same ascendant as Bruce. Maybe this is one of the reasons why they have both reacted to their problems in a similar way. Virgo is not a very strong sign when it comes to emotional confrontations. Maybe this is also why the father never pursued the theatrical ambitions which seem to fit the Sun in Leo and the Moon in Sagittarius. The Virgo ascendant made him opt for a safe job instead.

Liz: I think you are right. Bruce, like his father, has also opted for a safe job. Not surprisingly, Bruce is also interested in amateur theatrical groups, although not to the extent that his father was, and I suspect more because it provides him with another one of those sad pseudo-links with his father than because he is really drawn to the theatrical world. But I think there are some extremely interesting things about this father's chart. Initially, when we look at it, it does not seem so inharmonious. There is of course no such thing as an "alcoholic" chart, any more than there is a "homosexual" chart or a "great composer" chart. But the Sun and Moon trine, according to orthodox interpretation, should give a fortunate life, and a good sense of self-esteem. It is an aspect with a lot of positive qualities, because the conscious goals and the instincts work in harmony, and it is not an aspect which one might expect to find in such a sad life. But I think that everything in astrology is double-edged, and the way in which an aspect works depends greatly upon the consciousness of the individual who has the aspect. In someone who is unable to live an individual identity, the Sun-Moon trine can work as a kind of insulation against life. Just as there are situations where squares and oppositions are very

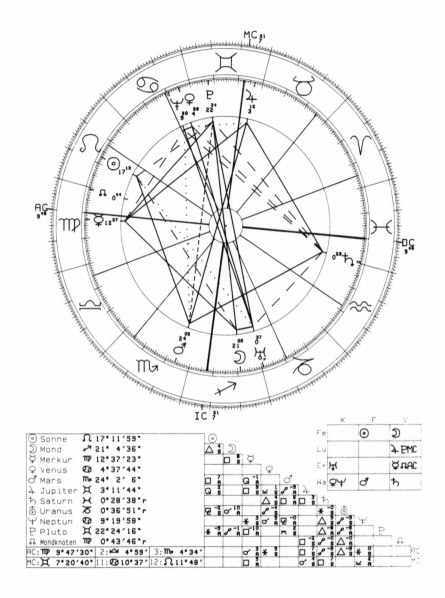

Chart 4. Bruce's father. Birth data has been withheld for confidentiality. Chart calculated by Astrodienst, using the Placidus house system.

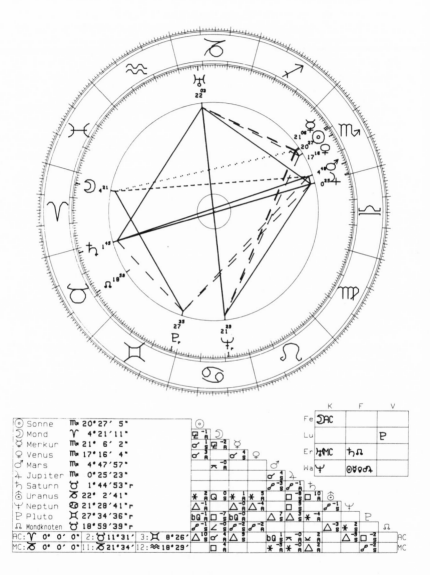

			K	F	V
⊙ Sonne	♏ 20°27′ 5″	Fe	☽AC		
☽ Mond	♈ 4°21′11″	Lu			P
☿ Merkur	♏ 21° 6′ 2″	Er	♄MC	♄♌	
♀ Venus	♏ 17°16′ 4″	Wa	♆	⊙♂♀♃	
♂ Mars	♏ 4°47′57″				
♃ Jupiter	♏ 0°25′23″				
♄ Saturn	♉ 1°44′53″r				
♅ Uranus	♉ 22° 2′41″				
♆ Neptun	♋ 21°28′41″r				
♇ Pluto	♊ 27°34′36″r				
☊ Mondknoten	♉ 18°59′39″r				

AC: ♈ 0° 0′ 0″	2: ♉ 11°31′	3: ♊ 8°26′	
MC: ♉ 0° 0′ 0″	11: ♉ 21°34′	12: ♒ 18°29′	

Chart 5. Bruce's mother. We don't know the birth time. Birth data has been withheld for confidentiality. A flat chart has been calculated by Astrodienst.

valuable because they give a good fighting spirit and a creative tension to the personality, so too trines can sometimes be quite lethal because one can escape into them. They are like safe little pockets where the struggles of the world cannot intrude, because there everything is harmonious and gentle and flows with ease. This Sun-Moon trine, which falls in watery houses and concerns the inner life, seems to provide a retreat from the outer world. The sense of self-satisfaction with a Sun-Moon trine can be very great, and while that can provide confidence in many people, it can also be smug and blind when one has bad problems. One can just pretend that everything is fine. Here is someone who I believe just vanished into his fantasies and shut the rest of the world out, while his body went to work and pretended to be a Virgo.

Audience: But why couldn't he live his individuality? He is a Leo, after all. Neither child seems to have that Leo quality reflected in connection with the father. And the Sun in Leo is sextile Pluto. Maybe that is the strong Plutonian quality which both Bruce and Susan have reflected in their charts to describe the father. That sextile should have given him some power. The Sun is also square Mars in Scorpio, which is a pretty strong Mars as well.

Liz: All that you say is true in potential. There are some excellent aspects in this chart. But I think there are a number of reasons why this man's potential was never actualised. At the risk of sounding redundant, one of the reasons is probably the nature of the father's own parental marriage. But I would like to look more closely at that a little later. I think the Sun-Mars square which you mention is actually one of the problems, rather than one of the strengths. Mars is a much more complex planet than one might imagine, particularly in a male chart where it is extremely important because it is connected with the sense of sexual identity. Mars is our capacity to know what we want and to go out into life after it. When Mars is square to the Sun in a man's chart, then these aggressive-competitive instincts may be experienced as inimical to the man's image of himself. It is a split between ego-consciousness and the crude male instincts, and that can result in a man's becoming dissociated from his essential masculinity. Both Mars and the Sun are male principles, but they are different facets of the masculine, just as Venus and the Moon are different facets of the feminine. The Sun, which the Greeks portrayed as the gentleman-god Apollo, is concerned with consciousness and creative spirit. Mars, who is a chthonic deity, is concerned with the power of the body. I believe that Bruce's father could not deal with his own aggression, and this problem is echoed in Bruce's own chart as well. And this is also suggested by the image of the parental marriage in the father's chart, where we can see once again the same theme of the weak or impotent man and the overpowering and controlling woman. Without a good connection with Mars, that lovely Leo-Sagittarius combination can express only on the plane of fantasy, because it does not possess good survival instincts and the necessary ruthlessness and competitiveness to put its grand dreams into practise. And fire alone, without something tougher to give it body, tends to hang around King Arthur's court a lot, and believes altogether too much in the good, the true and the beautiful. Life becomes something out of a fairy-tale, and all the nasties are banished to the outer darkness of the unconscious.

I think this is why Bruce's father never pursued his real love, the theatre, in any but a desultory way. It would have meant his battling for success. The theatre is a very aggressive business, with a great deal of jealousy, backbiting and fierce competition among some very driven and narcissistic people for every decent role available. Jupiter got him started, out of the northern background and into the city; but there was not enough Mars to see his dreams through into actuality, because Mars was pushed into the unconscious. So he could not achieve his ambitions, no matter how much talent he might have possessed—and I suspect that he possessed quite a bit. I think it is this, as much as the rather reticent Virgo ascendant, which helped to render him ineffectual. Virgo rising is, as you say, not a strong sign when it comes to emotional confrontation, and like Pisces it has a tendency to bend and slide away; and certainly the man displayed this kind of diffidence in the face of his wife's onslaughts. But in the work sphere Virgo is capable of a great deal of tenacity and self-discipline, and is not averse to diligent practise in order to get a technique right. I don't think the Virgo ascendant necessarily precludes success and the fulfilment of ambitions, although it no doubt made him rather passive in personal confrontations. But Mars square the Sun can sometimes suggest a person who wants all kinds of wonderful things from life—to be first, to be best, and so on—but who cannot bear experiencing himself as a brute, and runs in horror from behaving in what he deems to be a selfish and aggressive manner. So of course he can never get those wonderful things he wants. Also, he cannot stand up to an aggressive wife. This is a Mars problem, and as we have seen, Bruce also has a Mars problem in his birth chart—although there it is not Mars-Sun, but rather, Mars retrograde in Libra square Pluto and opposite Uranus and Venus.

The Scorpio Mars, which the father did not wish to own, got projected onto the mother, who cheerfully acted it out through her nasty cutting animus. She was an excellent hook because of her strongly Scorpionic nature. As you can see if you look at the two charts together, the father's Scorpio Mars conjuncts the mother's Sun-Mercury conjunction in Scorpio. It is this Mars in the father's chart, square to the Sun and also Saturn (albeit an out-of-sign square) and in quincunx to Pluto, which makes me suspect that there was enormous aggression behind this man's withdrawal. It is also why I feel he performed some subtle goading which pushed the mother into her fits of anger. Scorpio, as we all know, can be very vindictive if it turns poisonous, and here it is in the 3rd house, which reflects something about the way in which he must have expressed himself to her. Despite this Mars being strong in the sign of its dignity, I think that Bruce's father lived it primarily through the unconscious, because he could not cope with a hairy, sweaty Mars experience of himself. He must have seen himself as a bright knight in golden armour; most Leos do. I believe he feared his own violence. So he bottled it up and gave it to his wife, who in turn gave it back to him. For all these reasons, bound up with the Mars, he could not live out the creative potential which you quite rightly perceive in the Sun in Leo sextile Pluto.

Another reason lies, as I have said, in the nature of his own parental marriage. We saw already how this problem worked in Bruce, for without a positive father-figure on which to project one's early emerging masculine self, a man flounders without any clear sense of male identity. Bruce's grandmother is shown here as a Plutonian figure, both by the presence of Pluto in the 10th house and by its opposition to the Moon. The grandfather, in turn, is reflected by the Moon-Uranus conjunction in the 4th, and by the 12th house Sun in Leo. Just as Bruce is powerfully connected to the feeling-life of his mother, Bruce's father in turn is powerfully connected to the feeling-life of this grandfather, who I believe must have felt castrated and overwhelmed by his powerful partner. This grandfather, judging by the Moon-Uranus conjunction in the 4th, no doubt offered the same kind of response to his son as Bruce's father did to him: withdrawal which the son experienced as alienation and lack of interest. The grandmother, on the other hand, although obviously powerful and probably extremely manipulative, is also portrayed in this chart as Venus-Neptune in Cancer, which seems to imply that, on the conscious level, she must have appeared quite fragile and weak, and Bruce's father probably idealised her. She becomes the mythic damsel in distress which his intrinsically chivalrous nature always sought to rescue. He couldn't see that she really needed no rescuing. Like father, like son. So the grandmother's secret power was probably never obvious to Bruce's father, and he fell into the pattern of the man with the powerful mother-complex, one of the extreme forms of which is alcoholism—the negative Plutonian mother inside who defeats all his efforts at freeing himself and asserting himself as a man in his own right.

I would like to briefly mention one or two aspects which appear in the paternal grandparents' charts, so that you can see in what an eerily precise fashion these patterns have repeated themselves through the family. The grandmother, who appears as Pluto in Bruce's father's chart, had the Sun in Aquarius in an exact square to Pluto. That should come as no surprise to you. Sun square Pluto is a peculiar aspect in a woman's chart, because more often than not it is unconscious. The will to power, and the capacity to wield power through subtle emotional means, is not something which many women of that generation would admit; and even in younger generations it is not an easy aspect for a woman to live, because it is considered "unfeminine" by the collective. A good example of this is Margaret Thatcher, who has the Sun square Pluto. More often, the woman with Sun-Pluto will pretend that she is weak and helpless, and will apparently give the power away to another; but then she becomes a victim, and can manipulate through guilt. I have met many women with this square who try very hard to portray a fragile, fluttery persona, while underneath there is a stainless steel spine. They are about as fragile as the Rock of Gibraltar. We can see from the 10th house Pluto, and the Moon-Pluto opposition, in Bruce's father's chart, that on some level he was well aware of his mother's enormous strength and manipulativeness. But I think the Venus-Neptune contact made him romanticise her, which is why he could never get free.

The Moon in this grandmother's chart is in the last decanate of Leo—I am unsure of the degree because of the lack of a birth time—and it is also square Pluto. The issue of manipulation and sexual power-battles has been going on in Bruce's family for many generations. Interestingly, Neptune in the grandmother's chart is virtually without aspect, forming only a trine to Uranus in Virgo. So we might say that the Plutonian theme in the parental marriage comes down to Bruce and Susan through the father's side of the family, via the paternal grandmother.

The paternal grandfather, who in Bruce's father's chart is portrayed, as we have seen, by Moon conjunct Uranus in the 4th house, has, also not surprisingly, a Sun-Neptune conjunction in Taurus in his chart. This conjunction also pulls in Venus, which is placed at the end of Aries. Here is the gentle, peaceable, rather dreamy man who marries the powerful Plutonian wife, although the surface behaviour may have been more conventional according to the social demands of the time. And again not surprisingly, this paternal grandfather has a Sun-Mars square, just as Bruce's father does. So all that I have been saying about the problem of integrating the aggressive instincts applies here to the grandfather, and seems to have passed down to his son, Bruce's own father. We might therefore say that the Neptunian theme comes down through the father's side of the family, via the paternal grandfather; as does the problem of integrating the aggressive Martial impulses.

Now I would like you to look more carefully at the chart of Bruce's mother. I have said that this is a flat (untimed) chart, with no ascendant. But I think we can glean a great deal of insight from it anyway. There are no less than five planets in Scorpio in this chart, which I think would certainly earn her the appellation of a Plutonian woman. It is this group of planets which picks up the Mars in Scorpio of her husband, and which no doubt in the early days of the marriage picked it up in a much more exciting and erotic form. There seems to have been something about Bruce's father which was quite sexually hypnotic for the mother. Bruce, however, does not seem to have perceived this Plutonian quality in his mother. Pluto is not a mother-significator in his chart. What he has perceived is more Neptunian, because of his natal Moon-

Neptune square; and this Neptunian quality seems to be reflected in the mother's chart by the trines which her Mercury, Sun and Venus make to Neptune. For Bruce, the mother is vague and dreamy and romantic and elusive, and it seems that she was indeed so—at least in part—because of these natal aspects. The Sun conjuncting Venus in her chart also seems to reflect some of her cultural interests, and her need to be popular and liked by people.

But Bruce also sees her as Saturn. She is not Saturnian in the usual sense, as there is no strong emphasis in Capricorn (unless the ascendant is Capricorn) and there are no aspects between Saturn and the luminaries. We don't know if Saturn was placed on an angle in her birth chart. But there is a pair of oppositions here between Saturn and the Mars-Jupiter conjunction in Scorpio in the mother's chart, and I think this configuration reflects her intense anger and frustration. She must have felt a constant inner sense of impotence which perhaps contributed to her staying in a situation in which she was so miserable, despite the strength of the planets in Scorpio and powerful aspects such as the Mars-Jupiter conjunction trine Pluto.

The Moon in the mother's chart might be at the end of Pisces or the beginning of Aries. We have no way of knowing. I have a hunch, however, that the Moon is in Aries, because of the character whom Susan described—her general irritability and bad temper—and the resentment with which she sacrificed herself. The Moon in Aries is not cut of the cloth of martyrs, and no Moon in Aries will submit to such a role without at least some steam escaping. The Moon in Pisces, on the other hand, is generally much more willing to martyr itself, and does not complain so much, because there is more capacity for selfless devotion to another. Also, the impression of the mother in society seems to have been that of a lively, interesting and stimulating woman, and without including an Aries Moon we would have a chart so inundated with water that it is difficult to associate such a horoscope with such an animated personality. There is almost no air in this chart—only Pluto in Gemini—and with a Pisces Moon there would be no fire at all. That does not sound like the difficult and explosive woman who fought so violently with her husband and son.

Audience: What about the mother's parental marriage? I am beginning to feel as though we keep watching the same film over and over again. Her Sun conjuncting Venus in trine to Neptune seems to say that her father was another of those nice, gentle, artistic, passive souls. And if the Moon is really in Aries, then she would have a Moon-Pluto square. In fact they would be in square even if the Moon were at the end of Pisces. It's the same scenario again.

Liz: Of course it is. That is the punchline of all this wading which we have been doing through so many horoscopes. The mythic scenario of the parental marriage which we first began to explore in Bruce's chart, and then in Susan's, is not just an image which these two people carry. It is a family myth. There seem to have been several generations of Kybele-type women secretly devouring Attis-type men. Whatever the overt behaviour, this constellation appears to have been lurking underneath. And there seem likewise to have been several generations of these Attis-type men who fight back by the withholding of love, energy and erotic feeling, so that their women become the unhappy victims of sexual rejection and manipulation. In the end we are truly looking at an archetypal theme, and it runs like a red thread through this family. Bruce has recreated it in his marriage. Susan fears its recreation and has opted for a half-life in order to avoid it, which is not the worst of ways to break the chain, although it does cost a lot. And finally, this image of the powerful woman and the weak man is also the reflection of a dynamic at work within Bruce himself, where his unconscious—in the form of the dark mother-anima—overwhelms his masculine ego, which is too weak to stand and fight. Any individual is at the end of a long line of enactments of a relationship dynamic which is both a family inheritance and a mythic pattern of his or her own potential integration. Bruce is a sad example because he is not a very conscious person, and he is not trying to deal with the split in himself in any constructive way. Many people do try to work with these inherited things, and the parental marriage then becomes a kind of model of potential wholeness, if one can discover a creative way of bringing the two World Parents together.

Audience: Then what might the potential be of a better union between what you call the Kybele-type woman and the Attis-type man? What could Bruce become?

Liz: I think he could become a rare thing in a man, someone who combines sensitivity, compassion and imagination with great will and tenacity and the capacity to actualise his dreams. He has both components in him. He could be of great service to other people, something I suspect he would get considerable fulfilment from if only he could be all of himself—because there is a potential for considerable empathy and insight into others' difficulties, and a gift for articulating and explaining things in ways which others can understand. I think he should be working in a creative field—perhaps not the theatre, but maybe something in the writing, publishing or advertising spheres—where his ability to sense what others need, and what the market wants, might bring him some considerable success. But of course we don't know what will happen to Bruce. We would have to examine the transits and progressions to see where he is moving, and whether something might open him up. I have a bad feeling about it, not because of anything in the chart, but just because I have a feeling. But most of the world, faced with a dilemma like Bruce's, just muddles through and passes the problem to the children.

We could go on discussing these charts for another three days, and obviously there are many things which I have not touched upon. Also, my slant has been in a particular direction, because of the theme of the seminar. But I would like to move on now, as I think the point has been made.

Audience: My experience of these parental figures in relation to each other is that they appear in my dreams in the same way they appear in my chart. That is one of the things which made me begin to look again at my parents in ways which I had previously not thought of. Do you think the dream-figures of the parents are really the parents, or are they inner figures as well?

Liz: I think they are both. On one level, we can work with the figures of the parents in dreams in a reductive way, and a great deal of the feelings and experiences of childhood may come to the surface as the result of this kind of exploration. If you have always thought that your father was a sweet, lovable chap and he appears repeatedly in your dreams as an ugly rapist, then I think the unconscious is probably telling you something about other factors at work in your relationship with your father. On another level, the parents in one's dreams are also archetypal figures, and one can discern through the apparently mortal personalities the mythic figures I have been describing. For example, the father who appears flying a plane is a thinly disguised Zeus or Uranus, the puer aeternus up in the air. That is another fruitful line of exploration, because then one can get closer to the mythic background behind the parents, and see more clearly what drove them. But in the end these archetypal figures, as well as the more personal dimensions of them, are inside us. The ugly rapist-father may describe one's own unconscious aggressive feelings, and the puer-father playing at being a pilot may be one's own inner adolescent needing to distance himself from life by remaining up in the air. On both a personal and an archetypal level these figures are alive and well in the unconscious, and they personify masculine and feminine components in ourselves. One very fruitful way of working with the dream-parents along these lines is to try to see where such a figure is expressing in one's own life in an unconscious way.

For example, if your recollection of your mother is of a quiet, serene, uncomplaining, devoted woman, yet you keep dreaming of her as someone angry and aggressive who constantly attacks you verbally or physically, then this might be seen as a revelation of the unconscious side of the personal mother. It may contradict your conscious impression of her as a loving and sacrificing parent, and may point to her unconscious anger and frustration and desire to destroy her child. You cannot take one or the other; you must try to put them together, and see the whole person that conscious and unconscious jointly describe. So that may be very valuable in helping you to understand why, for example, you are so frightened of criticism and attack from other women, without any apparent cause.

But this figure might also be seen in a more archetypal garb. The angry Hera, jealous of the daughter-rival who might take away her wandering husband, or the vindictive Gorgon who vents her own frustration and unhappiness on her child because she cannot bear to see someone else better off than her, are mythic figures, and might shed some light on something for which the mother cannot be blamed, but which has caught her from the collective unconscious. One might find something in one's own birth chart such as Mars conjunct Pluto in the 10th, or Moon square Mars. But in the end, this angry woman is also a figure in the unconscious of the dreamer, and it may point to a shadow-side of your own personality of which you are not yet conscious. And unless you can become conscious of such a figure in yourself, she will express herself in covert ways, and undermine your confidence and your relationships with others. And the aggressiveness in such a figure also may not be wholly bad, but might be a needed cutting edge which is missing from the conscious personality and which is trying to get itself integrated. As such, this angry archetypal mother is not wholly pathological; she is archetypal. Her qualities may need to be included in life, for without her you cannot defend yourself, or be true to your own feelings, or instinctively sense when another woman herself wishes you ill.

You should probably read Erich Neumann's book, *The Great Mother*,[1] which is a marvellous and complex analysis of the many faces of the mother-archetype. It is a great pity that he never wrote a companion volume on the Great Father, although some of the material about the World Parents which I have touched on comes from another of his books, *The Origins and History of Consciousness*.[2] One of the themes which Neumann pursues is the multitude of faces which the mother-archetype can wear. I can give you a very rough summary of it, because it is relevant to our theme of the parental marriage and the mythic figures which comprise the World Parents in the individual horoscope. Neumann gives a diagram of a cross with two axes, each of which has a positive and a negative pole. One of these axes represents the maternal dimension of the mother-archetype, and at the negative end of it is the Terrible Mother in all her guises—gorgon, harpy, witch, snake, dragon, sickness, depression, poison and so on. At the positive end of this axis is the Good Mother, imaged by those aspects of life which nourish and sustain—milk, harvest, bread, breast, nature, trees, cornucopia and so on.

This maternal axis of the archetype incorporates many of the facets which we have touched upon in our examination of the charts of Bruce's family. There is a dominance of the negative end of the axis in that family, suggested by the strongly Plutonian feminine image that comes across in several of the charts. This arche-

---

[1] Erich Neumann, *The Great Mother* (Princeton, NJ: Bollingen Foundation, Princeton University Press, 1955; and London: Routledge & Kegan Paul, 1955).

[2] Erich Neumann, *The Origins and History of Consciousness* (Princeton, NJ: Bollingen Foundation, Princeton University Press, 1954; and London: Routledge & Kegan Paul, 1954).

typal figure is not only expressed through images such as Kali or the Gorgon; she can also be experienced through psychic conditions and states such as depression, apathy, impotence, paralysis and addiction to drugs or alcohol. When a figure like this appears in a person's dream, then it pertains on one level to the destructive and devouring side of the personal mother. This will usually be echoed in the birth chart by Pluto connected with the Moon or the 10th house. Behind this personal mother stands the archetypal negative mother, and it might be a truer way of looking at things to suggest that the personal mother was caught in the grip of this archetype, rather than that she *was* this archetype. No parent is an archetype. This kind of mother-experience is not uncommon, and that is the reason why so many people experience similar feelings about their personal mothers. All these Plutonian mothers are not the same as individuals, and there is no factory in Yorkshire that produces them, although one sometimes gets the feeling that there is, because of the similarity of the subjective experience for so many people. There are not many planets, after all, and astrological language reduces the multiplicity of individual experience to certain essential archetypal themes. "Hell hath no fury like a woman scorned," says the poet, and the outrage and resentment and spite of a rejected woman who has been hurt and humiliated through devaluing of her instincts is an archetypal experience which astrology describes as a Plutonian mother. The rejection and humiliation may not only be at the hands of the partner; they are, more importantly, at the hands of the mother's animus. But such a figure when she appears in a dream is not only mother, and also Mother, but something within the dreamer which is both mother and Mother. And I think that ultimately it does no good to learn all these mythic and astrological bits of insight, fascinating though they are, without eventually trying to apply the knowledge to where this figure might be at work within oneself.

Audience: I have Pluto in the 10th house in my birth chart. I want to understand what this means. I can see that my mother fits this in a number of ways. She was very depressed, and I was always aware of her misery and pain. But you said that it would be truer to say that the mother was herself in the grip of the Plutonian archetype.

Liz: What I mean by that is that your mother as a person is not Kali, or the Gorgon, and not someone whom you should hate or ultimately blame. But probably she was identified with the archetypal figure of the Suffering Woman, and therefore she could do nothing to help her life situation. If you can understand this, then you will not feel guilty if you are happier than she was. If you cannot understand it, then the unconscious inheritance of this identification will lie somewhere in your own psyche, and you will unwittingly put yourself in a life situation where you too are made miserable and depressed just like your mother, and will not be able to help yourself.

Audience: But you seem to be saying that this is the only side of the maternal axis which I have experienced, and so therefore I can only express this negative side of the Great Mother. I don't think I have been a terrible mother to my children. If anything, I have tried hard to do the opposite of my own mother.

Liz: I don't think I said that. You said it. Because you have Pluto in the 10th house, it does not mean that this is the only aspect of the maternal principle which is available to you. But I suspect that your defensiveness about it springs from the fact that this complex is still very much alive and at work in you. When I say that your mother was infected by, or identified with, this negative aspect of life, that means that she was identified with the position of suffering and resentment, and that she could not see past this to any more creative or positive vision of life. An archetype among other things is a particular perspective toward life. If a woman views life through the lens of the Terrible Mother, then she will see woman, and her own femininity, as the victim of oppression and denigration, and she will react accordingly, both to her relationship to her man and to her role as mother. Then it seems that her freedom has been taken away, that she is undervalued and unappreciated, and that she has had to sacrifice her own identity and her own desires to raise children who will ultimately leave her anyway, and leave her with nothing.

Audience: Yes, that is certainly my mother.

Liz: If you have this archetypal experience reflected as the World Mother, half of the parental pair, then this is the main theme which your mother has passed on to you about what it means to be a woman. This does not mean that it is *your* only theme. It might not be your theme at all. But it does mean that sooner or later your personal journey will bring you into contact with that particular facet of life, and you have met it in childhood via the catalyst of the personal mother. It is therefore somewhere within you, and if you are unconscious of it, and simply try to model yourself on what you believe to be the opposite of your mother, you have not found a solution to the problem. If you try to deal with this inheritance in such a way, it will still lie in the unconscious, and you will be unconsciously setting yourself up to act it out. I have no idea what kind of mother you are. I am sure you are not "terrible." But then, probably your own mother wasn't either. She was no doubt a complex woman, and you are particularly tuned in to one facet. This facet is a certain perspective on life, and I would go so far as to say that you probably have this perspective within you on an unconscious level. That is why you strive so hard to be a "good" mother, rather than just being yourself. It does not mean you will be terrible to your children. It means that somewhere within you you probably carry much of your mother's depression and sense of hopelessness, over which you plaster a strenuously cheerful face. I think you must try to remember that as a woman the entire spectrum of the feminine is your inheritance and your nature. But different women seem to be called upon by their destiny, or by the Self, or by whatever name you want to give it, to deal with a particular aspect of that vast archetype which we call the feminine. No woman is all things. Do please try not to take what I say according to your own fears.

No mother deliberately sets out to be Pluto, except in Greek tragedy and the occasional Mozart opera. I am sure that your mother also tried very hard to be a good mother. That is exactly the problem. If you try very hard to be something according to a fixed picture in your mind, or your animus, then this means suppressing what you actually are; and that is the source of the depression and the resentment. It is when a woman desperately tries to model herself after some collective and sterile image of a totally good and perfect mother, without acknowledging that there are two poles to the axis and that they are forever conjoined, then all negative feelings such as anger, aggression and the need to put oneself first are repressed and forced into the unconscious. What starts out as healthy negative feelings becomes infected on that unconscious level with the archetypal experience of anger and aggression, and then in walks the Terrible Mother with her outrage and grievances. Then no matter how nicely and self-sacrificingly you behave, fate has a nasty way of putting Pluto in the 10th house of your children's charts, or slipping it into conjunction with their Moons. What you have hidden from yourself cannot be hidden from them, any more than what your mother hid from herself was hidden from you. And also, it means that the other person in the equation—the father—must carry the other half of the archetypal pair, and the natural pairing to the Terrible Mother with her seething resentment and hurt feelings is a cold bastard, the Terrible Father who lacks all feeling and crushes all feminine value. So the father, too, gets dragged into the archetypal polarity, because he had something for it to be hooked into, and then you have a certain type of parental marriage in your horoscope.

Very often an individual will polarise with the parental significator of the same sex in the chart, trying to model himself or herself on the opposite of all those qualities. This is the attempt to be "anything but" mother or father. In doing this, the parental figure naturally falls into the unconscious, but it of course has not been erased from the birth chart or the psyche by such sleight-of-hand on the part of the ego. Pluto, Neptune and Uranus are very conducive to this type of polarisation when they appear in the 10th or 4th houses, and so is Saturn. That is because these are all uncomfortable planets for the ego to express and experience. But in the end the person inadvertently falls into the opposite, because whichever end of the axis one leans on, the other end will lie in the unconscious and will sooner or later manifest itself either in covert behaviour or through the partner's behaviour. It is better to face the thing within oneself than to try to construct an artificial opposite. And lest we forget, there are no malefic planets. Even Pluto, which can so easily lend itself to the imagery of the Terrible Mother, might mean something else if one did not place an animus value judgement on it. This is the power of the raw instincts and the animal passions, and it is the cold and critical animus that decides that such feelings and needs are disgusting and unwelcome. And the Terrible Mother too has a place in life, because the transpersonal face of this figure is Fate, and an embrace of it means coming to terms with the laws of one's own physical and instinctual nature. That is a positive thing, rather than a negative one. The Hindus know about this when they worship Kali, whom they call the "destructive power of God in the form of the Dark Mother."

When a particular facet of the maternal archetype is emphasised in an individual horoscope as a mother-significator, then the natural consort to this figure is also constellated, and this forms the mythic backdrop of the parental marriage. The Terrible Mother is always found hand-in-hand with a weak redeemer-son-lover, who in turn may appear as "good" because he promises the rewards of the intellect and the spirit. We place our own value judgements on these figures. Or the Terrible Mother appears as the Suffering Mother, who has been hurt and repudiated by an unreliable, cold, unfeeling or promiscuous son-lover. Then she becomes "good," although angry and spiteful, and he becomes "bad" because it is all his fault that she suffers so much. These two figures always pair off, which is why suffering women always seem to marry men who make them suffer. Secretly they are bound together, and the anima or animus of the one is embodied in the other. It seems to me that one of the main benefits of exploring this peculiar terrain in the horoscope is that we might achieve a broader and less judgemental perspective, and a more balanced perception, of the two halves of the parental pair. Neither can remain "good" or "bad" for the sake of our psychic health. Both are inside us.

One of the hopeful products of such a shift in perception, when it is deep enough and not merely an intellectual exercise, is that one is not so fated in one's relationships. But perhaps we can never wholly integrate these figures, because they are archetypal after all, and can never become the personal property of one's ego. They are our guiding myths. But one can become richer as a person through some contact with the inner figures and a better relationship with them, not only because one is more real, but also because it allows more room for the opposite end of the axis to express also. When a person is locked into violent polarisation, there is no freedom for anything to express naturally. If you are trying vehemently not to be Plutonian, then any truly individual qualities of loving that you might possess as a mother are going to be stifled and blocked from expression under the weight of "oughts" and "shoulds" which accompany your animus opinion of what constitutes a "good" mother—which is anything but your own mother.

Audience: You said there were two axes. What is the other one?

Liz: The other is what one might call the soul axis. This is not the maternal feminine, which contains and holds, but the soul or anima dimension of the feminine, which guides and inspires. This axis, according to Neumann's diagram, also has two poles, a positive and a negative one. The "good" end of the anima is the spiritual dimension of woman, which is not incompatible with erotic feeling but which lifts consciousness out of its mundane rut and into a deepening and widening. The most transpersonal figure in our era for this pole of the axis is the figure of Mary. Wisdom and compassion belong to this pole of the axis. Another, older image for this inspiring face of the feminine is the postive face of Aphrodite, who brings sexual joy and opens the heart to beauty and grace. This is woman as companion, playmate, inner guide and muse. Through her life becomes magical, meaningful, joyful and full of purpose. The dark or negative pole of the anima axis is the siren, who lures the ego down into chaos and madness and disintegration. Here the inspiration is worked through enchantment and seduction rather than through love and joy, and the result is the destruction of life rather than the expansion of it. This is the role of those nasty *femmes fatales* in old Marlene Dietrich films. The personal mother can appear in the chart of a man or woman as this kind of figure, positive or negative, just as easily as she can appear as one of the facets of the maternal feminine. Planets such as Venus or Jupiter in the 10th or in strong aspect to the Moon can suggest her in both her dark and light guises; sometimes so can Neptune and Uranus, and Mercury, and the Sun. The unlived life of the personal mother is not always Plutonian and full of spite and resentment. It can be furiously erotic and full of unfulfilled sexual magic and creative inspiration. Just as the maternal axis of the feminine, dark or light, sits in natural partnership with a son-lover, the soul axis sits in natural partnership with a patriarchal or paternal axis in the masculine. Figures in myth, such as Aphrodite the courtesan, are inevitably married to heavy father-types like Hephaistos, and Mary is of course the bride of God the Father.

I must ask you all once again, as I always do, not to take these mythic images too literally. They have a way of behaving in a very protean fashion and slipping through one's fingers if one tries to force too structured linkups with astrological placements. No horoscope shows only one characteristic to the mother. There are always several, as we have seen, and often they contradict. Also, each planet has several faces. Neptune square to the Moon will suggest the sacrificial and suffering face of the victim-mother, while a Venus-Neptune conjunction in the 10th might suggest an exalted quasi-erotic, quasi-spiritual figure. You need to try to use some imagination and some knowledge of human behaviour to put together the different threads. And also you need to try to learn to think in opposites. If you have a feeling of the imagery around one of the parents, consider the natural companion to that figure, because the World Parents always travel in pairs. The seductive, girlish siren-mother—the puella who is still flirting with her Daddy—is usually paired with a heavy-handed and patriarchal father-type, and if you happen to be the son of such a pair then you are very likely to fall into the role of Hamlet and try to rescue the mother-beloved from the old tyrant's grip. If you are the daughter of such a pair, then you are likely to fall into the role of Psyche and feel that a more sexually powerful and beautiful woman keeps your chosen father-lover from you. The dark, smouldering, possessive maternal mother is usually paired with a charming but unreliable and sometimes unfeeling youth. The conventional, earthbound, security-conscious Hera-mother is usually paired with a randy, unfaithful, fascinating adolescent. No parents are like this. These are caricatures of human behaviour, and individual parents are complex creatures with individual natures. But mythic figures behave like this, and so do our complexes. We cannot separate the World Parents, and if one of them is strongly delineated, then the natural partner will be there by implication. I think we saw this illustrated in the family charts we looked at earlier.

Audience: When you were talking about the positive end of the soul axis, you mentioned Mary. Is that the only collective symbol we have for this dimension of the feminine in our culture? We don't worship Aphrodite any more. It seems rather lopsided to me.

Liz: Mary is the only recognizable religious symbol we have. But we create our own feminine symbols who are far more rounded than Mary and worship them in the cinema, in novels and poetry, in music, and in our everyday lives. You are right—Mary is lopsided, in the sense that she has no erotic dimension. I am sure this has been a collective problem, ever since we got rid of foamborn Aphrodite. Mary embodies many positive functions of the anima, as spiritual guide and intercessor, and as the compassionate intermediary between humanity and the remoteness of God. The only trouble with Mary is that she has no body. Then all the sexuality drops down to the negative pole of the axis, to the siren who lures men to destruction. That was certainly the medieval view of woman, whose body was the tool of the devil and who inspired men to sin. But Aphrodite appears to be alive and well in the unconscious of the individual woman, and lately we do not pay so much attention to collective religious symbols any more. This Aphrodite often appears as the shadow-side of a repressed and sexually inhibited mother, who may appear as Venus in the 10th house, or Venus conjunct or opposite the Moon in her child's chart.

Audience: But if Mary is our emblem for the highest form of the feminine, then it is very difficult for a woman to value the positive side of her sexuality. It always gets linked with the siren.

Liz: It does if a woman is identified with collective values. I have found that women who get most upset about this collective lopsidedness are often the ones who are unconsciously the most collective. It is where we are least individual that we are most prone to such splits. I would say that we do not pay much attention to Mary any more. But a generation or two ago, this figure was more powerful on a collective level, and it still is for the devout Catholic. It is an issue if you have an animus with a very collective voice, which can then be projected outside as the voice of society. Neumann's axes are drawn for the purpose of elaborating what happens when the conscious ego tries to approach the archetypal realm. It has a terrible time seeing double. To be spiritual and sexual at the same time is a big mouthful for the ego to swallow, and yet on the archetypal level there is no conflict. And it is completely indigestible if the ego is entrenched in a set of collective values which declare that the twain shall never meet. But if one can become a little more aware of both sides in oneself, with some genuinely individual feelings about what is right and comfortable for oneself, then I think there is much less guilt and repression, and less identification with these collective problems. One can actually enjoy one's contradictions. Then of course one has also broken the spell of the parental marriage, where one lopsided end of that axis must always be paired with a particular kind of spouse. Mary always manages to get herself paired with a father-god who demands perfection yet who behaves in a thoroughly unreasonable and destructive fashion. Often he is thoroughly carnal as well, and forces her to submit to the excesses of his "lower nature." The siren always manages to get herself paired with one of those higher-minded paternal types who is so preoccupied with the welfare of humanity that he has no time for her charms. I am drawing rather sardonic portraits, but I think they are true as far as they go.

Ambivalence is a characteristic of all archetypal figures, and it is this ambivalence which consciousness finds so difficult to contain. That is why Neumann winds up drawing such neat axes. It is also perhaps why the parental marriage, and the marriage of the World Parents, inevitably appears to us as a collision of opposites where two people have polarised over an issue which secretly belongs to both of them. The maternal axis which I mentioned before is a good example. The archetypal mother contains both a creative and a destructive dimension. Mothering includes both. But it is very difficult for a woman to experience herself as both. Usually there is a horrible feeling of guilt when one bumps into the destructive side of the mother in oneself. The feelings which a woman has toward a young child are often a very complicated mixture of love and hate, need and power. We take the love for granted as the main and necessary component of maternity. But there is inevitably going to be hate, because the birth of a child marks the death of the puella in a woman. Along with the mundane issues of responsibility on a practical level and the next fifteen years signed and sealed with a "never again" feeling about the loss of personal freedom, there are also deeper symbolic issues which are concerned with fate, time, age, and the leaving behind of eternal girlhood; and also with separation from one's own mother, and from identification with the eternal daughter who can always go back home again. That is the death-marriage which is embodied in the Hades-Persephone myth. There is often a great deal of negative feeling in a woman toward her baby, and although this is natural and inevitable, it is disturbing if one is identified with the collective opinion that one must be completely and sacrificially loving all the time or one is a Terrible Mother. The desire to destroy is often part of the experience of giving birth, and there is an aspect of this which is archetypal. Many animals act this out, as though one gives birth in order to provide food for oneself to feed on. Fish, for example, do this immediately; they swallow their offspring and it is the best meal in weeks. But to acknowledge such feelings raises a deep moral problem, because there is a difference between experiencing something and acting it out. Often refusing to experience it forces one to act it out unconsciously. If this challenge is not met, and the negative feelings are totally suppressed, then the unconscious of the child will pick them up. The Terrible Mother always lives side by side with the Good Mother. It is no different with creative work, which also constellates the archetype of the mother. There is not only the urge to bring something forth; there is also often the urge to destroy it, and many artists are quite accustomed to ambivalence and confusion about their efforts. But the collective does not blame the artist, whereas it does blame the mother.

I think you can see that the degree to which the actual parents can allow ambivalence and flexibility of feeling into their marriage and their consciousness has an enormous influence on the degree to which the child become adult can allow such ambivalence within himself or herself. The greater the repression in the actual parental marriage, the more these things will fester in the unconscious and the more power they assume over the individual's life later. In that respect, the parents as people wield enormous power and shoulder enormous responsibility, although this is an uncomfortable thought and would no doubt frighten many couples into never having children as a result.

Audience: Can I ask something about the siren? You seem to have described her primarily as a sexual figure. But I was thinking of women like Cleopatra, who seduce with power as much as with sexuality. Is this also part of the anima axis?

Liz: Yes, I believe it is. It is a quality of both ends of the axis. The creative or positive side of the anima can inspire one toward aiming for higher goals, and fulfilling potentials that have previously been undeveloped. The negative side seduces with promises of power that are inflationary, and drive the individual beyond his or her capabilities and limits. Then the road to self-destruction opens up. The operative word with the siren is "seduce." You are quite right, seduction can be through many things besides sexuality. The siren will often whisper things like: I am the only one who understands your talent. You are a misunderstood genius. Only I am on your side. Stick with me and I'll make you into something. The role of the anima is, on one level, to constellate the inner unconscious potentials in a man, and bring them forth into outer life. The anima is the medium who intuits what a man might become and what his destiny is really about. There are many women who align themselves with this pole of the feminine, and are often the muses who inspire a previously uninteresting or unfulfilled man into creative activity. The negative anima, the siren, will use this vision of a unique destiny for her own purposes, and will often bring about an inflation in a man who then tries to extend himself beyond his real capabilities. As you say, Cleopatra played this role with Marc Antony. The siren is the inner companion of the "misunderstood genius" who cannot accommodate his talents to the world's requirements, or whose talents are not up to the world's requirements but who cannot face such an unpalatable truth as that he might be ordinary. The siren is a dimension of a man's anima, and also a dimension of the psyche of women. And she can also be a mother-significator. The sexuality of the siren is not just the promise of a really good screw. It always implies or infers something else, and is often withheld and kept as a promise or a "reward." It is a kind of teleological sexuality, as though the sex were really the opening lines for a much lengthier play which ultimately concerns the future destiny of the man.

Literature is full of examples of this kind of feminine figure. And she sits side by side with, and is often undistinguishable from, the muse who inspires. On the archetypal level they are the same. Fairy tales also have many of these strange and rather ambiguous siren-types who promise something wonderful but are really quite wicked. I suppose it is an illustration of my point that when we meet such figures in fairy tales, they are usually "good" or "bad." It is rare to find a genuinely ambivalent and whole character. Good literature produces much more complex figures, because the archetypal polarity has been processed through the insightful consciousness of the artist. Fairy tales, on the other hand, are usually highly polarised, because the archetype is naively divided into several figures who are really facets of the same figure. There is often a wicked stepmother and a good fairy, and so on.

Audience: The good mother is frequently dead in fairy tales, and no one is around except the wicked stepmother. I was thinking of Cinderella.

Liz: Yes, the good mother is "dead," which I suppose means "unconscious," which is the critical situation at the beginning of the story. Fairy tales always begin with a critical situation; the miller loses his money, or the queen cannot bear a child, or something has gone wrong with the kingdom. Fairy tales are expressions from the unconscious of a mode of unravelling and healing a situation of split or polarisation. So the dead "good" mother is the loss of a certain value, and the negative mother has taken over consciousness; and the heroine is depressed and devalued because of it. That is another way of saying what I was talking about before in relation to the 10th house Pluto and the mother who identifies with the Terrible Mother. The "good" mother has died, and the woman, like Cinderella, lives in metaphorical rags and has to clean the fireplace because the "bad" mother tells her how worthless she is. But the good mother always appears transfigured and restored in the form of a good fairy who takes the side of the hero or heroine and fights the wicked stepmother. I think we could take these motifs in connection with the question which one of you asked earlier, about whether a person is connected with only one dimension of the archetypal mother because a particular planet is placed in the 10th house. The fairy tale presents us with a situation where the positive image has fallen into the unconscious—usually because of some crisis which has occurred earlier in the story or the family history—and where the ego is at the mercy of something very self-destructive and depressive. But the positive image always reappears in another form, generally in a more transpersonal one, and although there are very specific rituals or tests which must be passed through, this implies that the positive image exists somewhere within although the individual may begin life caught in the spell of a destructive complex.

The material which fairy tales offer us about the parental marriage is in some ways similar to the material from mythic images, because they are really the same figures. Kali returns as Mother Holle, and Eros and Psyche reappear as Beauty and the Beast. But there is something different which fairy tales seem to provide, and that is a "method" or "formula" for working with the problem which is described at the beginning of the story. Also, fairy tales frequently describe this magical reappearance of something which was thought dead. Without this sense that a disconnection from a more whole experience can be reconnected again, studying the issues of the parental marriage would be horribly depressing. After all, each preceding generation slips further and further back into the maw of the collective, and the opportunities for individual expression available to our parents and our parents' parents decrease in proportion to time past. We are all faced with a positively terrifying parental backlog of repressed muck for which we are ultimately responsible as individuals, in terms of how we deal with this heritage. No one escapes. The horoscope will emphasise a particular kind of parental marriage and a particular kind of imbalance. It will not necessarily tell us how to heal that split, nor even that it is possible to heal it. Many people never heal it, and their children must then deal with the problem. But there is the strange testimony of fairy tales to comfort us—that the dead "good" mother or father reappears as if by magic at the critical moment, to throw his or her weight on the side of the breaking of the evil spell. The secret unity of the "good" and "bad" figures in fairy tales can be glimpsed just as it can in myths, although myths are more overt in combining the opposites within one figure. But we depend ultimately on that magic which cannot be forced by the ego, or by an act of will. The good fairy does not always appear to every deserving or righteous person. I think there is a very mysterious process by which we begin to bring some light into the dark corners of the parental marriage.

I am certain that we do not accomplish this by trying to be the opposite of our parents, through an act of conscious decision. In the end I believe we cannot do this because the parents are within us, and we cannot become somebody else. I have found that an effort to face and experience in oneself the figure which has been projected upon the parent can open many doors. But one must bring one's own feeling values to it, and respond according to one's own individual understanding rather than according to collective rules—or the rules of the parents. I suppose I am trying to say that the parental marriage is a kind of fate, and running away from it on the external level will only constellate it on the internal one. And often people do not know that they are running away, because they do not know what their inner perception is of that parental coupling. It is through a reinterpretation of it, rather than an avoiding or transcending of it, that I think we live our own charts in a creative way.

PART THREE

SUBPERSONALITIES AND PSYCHOLOGICAL CONFLICTS

A personality is a full congress of orators and pressure groups, of children, demagogues, Macchiavellis . . . Caesars and Christs . . . .

—Henry A. Murray

The Inner Congress

In his book *What We May Be*, Piero Ferrucci writes that "each of us is a crowd." The English humanistic psychologist, John Rowan, once spoke of an internal society composed of the different people inside us. The Portuguese poet Fernando Pessoa writes, "In every corner of my soul, there is an altar to a different god."[1] These quotations express the same idea—that a person consists of a multiplicity of selves. We exhibit one kind of behavior at work, another at home, another in social gatherings and yet another alone on a country walk. Very often we slip in and out of our different identities without much awareness that we are doing so.

To put it simply, we all have different parts or different bits. One part of us may want one thing; another part of us wants something else. Each of our different parts—what we call subpersonalities or subselves—may have its own way of walking, its own way of talking, its own type of body posture, its own drive, will and particular wants. Subpersonalities are "psychological satellites" which co-exist within the personality.

Obviously this concept relates very well to the birthchart because the various planets and signs also represent different bits or parts of us. You can look at a chart and ask yourself what does this placement in the chart look like, what does it want and how does it present itself? For instance, consider Chart 6 on page 166. We'll call her Kathy. What might Kathy's Venus rising in Virgo look like? How might it approach people? What does it need or like?

Audience: It likes looking neat, tidy and efficient. It's probably cautious and reserved.

Howard: Yes, that is one bit of her, and that part may work well with other parts or it may not. Venus in Virgo is one of the instruments in her orchestra. But what about her Uranus in the 10th?

---

[1]Piero Ferrucci, *What We May Be* (Los Angeles: Jeremy Tarcher, 1982; and Wellingborough, England: Turnstone Press, 1982), 48; John Rowan, reading from "The Internal Society," a paper presented at the British Psychological Society Annual Conference in 1974; Pessoa, cited in Ferrucci, *What We May Be*, 47.

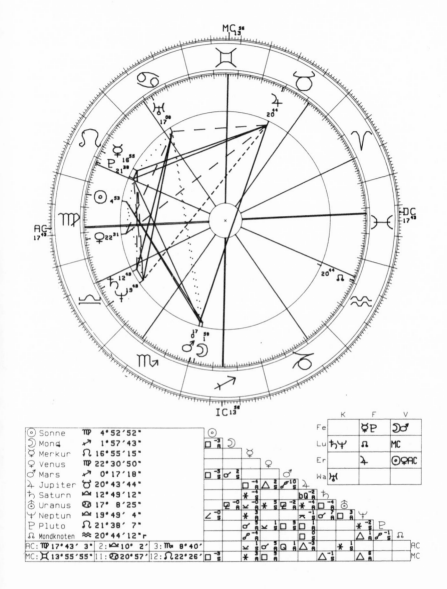

⊙ Sonne	♏	4°52'52"	
☽ Mond	♐	1°57'43"	
☿ Merkur	♌	16°55'15"	
♀ Venus	♍	22°30'50"	
♂ Mars	♐	0°17'18"	
♃ Jupiter	♉	20°43'44"	
♄ Saturn	♎	12°49'12"	
♅ Uranus	♋	17° 8'25"	
♆ Neptun	♎	19°49' 4"	
♇ Pluto	♌	21°38' 7"	
☊ Mondknoten	♒	20°44'12"r	

| AC: | ♍ 17°43' 3° | 2: ♎ 10° 2' | 3: ♏ 8°40' |
| MC: | ♓ 13°55'55° | 11: ♋ 20°57' | 12: ♌ 22°26' |

Chart 6. Kathy. Birth data has been withheld for confidentiality. Chart calculated by Astrodienst, using the Placidus house system.

What might that want or be like? Does it want the same thing that Venus rising wants?

Audience: Venus wants to be liked; it wants to please and harmonise. Uranus in the 10th doesn't care much about that.

Howard: Indeed! So, already we are getting a sense of her different parts—her subselves. The concept of subpersonalities fits easily into chart analysis and you'll see later that subpersonality configurations build up around various planetary placements or sign placements of the Sun, Moon and ascendant, etc. But hold on, we will come to all this.

RELATED CONCEPTS

Allow me to be intellectual for a minute and give my "Little Professor" subpersonality a chance. Here is a straight, formal definition of subpersonalities. Subpersonalities are "patterns of feelings, thoughts, behaviours, perceptions, postures and ways of moving which tend to coalesce in response to various recurring situations in life."[2]

This concept—that we are a multiplicity of selves—is not new. Transactional Analysis defines a parent, adult, and child state in all of us. Sometimes we "come from" our parent, sometimes our child. Gestalt Therapy refers to the "Top Dog" and the "Underdog." The Top Dog says, "you should go on a diet," while the Underdog replies, "But I can't stop eating chocolate cake." The philosopher Gurdjieff made a remark about how one part of you may decide to get up early the next day, but another part of you does nothing about it.[3] Jung indirectly spoke of subpersonalities

---

[2]Taken from Molly Young Brown's thesis, *The Art of Guiding: The Psychosynthesis Approach to Individual Counseling and Psychology* (Johnston College, University of Redlands, California, 1979), p. 14. This thesis is in the Psychosynthesis and Education Trust Library, 188 Old Street, London, EC1.

[3]For further information on Transactional Analysis and the child, adult, and parent state, the reader is referred to Eric Berne, *Games People Play* (New York: Grove Press, 1967). For further information on Gestalt and the top dog/underdog split, the reader is referred to Erving and Miriam Polster, *Gestalt Therapy Integrated* (New York: Vintage Books, 1973). For further information on Gurdjieff's concept of a multiplicity of selves, see Ouspensky, *In Search of the Miraculous* (San Diego, CA: Harcourt Brace Jovanovich, 1969).

when he talked about complexes. A man may be taken over by his mother complex. He can be in a present situation with a woman and then start viewing her from his mother complex. He doesn't see the situation clearly and objectively, but through the distorting lens of a complex. Or you might be taken over by your inferiority complex and interpret life from that point of view. Or a woman might be taken over by her animus; we say she is animus-driven. Or a man may be taken over by his anima, or "feminine" self; or your shadow may be triggered. These are all semi-autonomous bits of the psyche which take over and act independently of the objective reality of a situation.[4]

Clinical psychologists and psychotherapists are familiar with the idea of subpersonalities. Academic psychology isn't. John Rowan reported that he spent a whole day trying to find a reference to subpersonalities in the indexes of various academic psychology books. None were there. Of course, you do have mention of some extreme cases of personality dissociations, such as *Sibyl* or *The Three Faces of Eve*, but these are extreme. Subpersonalities are not necessarily such powerful dissociations. "Normal" people have different subpersonalities which they exhibit and identify with.

NAMING SUBPERSONALITIES

It's often useful to give subpersonalities names: you can have the bitch, the hag, the idealist, the hurt child, the critic, etc. Giving a subpersonality a name is a way of identifying it and working with it. Each subpersonality will have its own story, its own mythology and its own history. Some are more easily recognisable than others. They may come and go; new ones appear and then change again. Also, remember one general point—a role we play in life may contain more than one subpersonality. I don't want you to confuse the concept of subpersonalities with roles. Roles are broader. A businessman may draw on a few subpersonalities in his role as a businessman. He may come from his "striver" subpersonality, or his "pragmatist" subself. That same businessman may

---

[4]For further reading about Jung's concept of complexes, see C. G. Jung, *Psychological Types* (San Francisco: C. G. Jung Foundation, 1971; and London: Routledge & Kegan Paul, 1971).

have a very strong "mystic" subpersonality, but he may not choose to bring this out in business. Can you imagine just as he is about to negotiate a contract for a big deal, he says, "Well, it doesn't make any difference anyway—we are all one, man." Or he is about to land the big contract and his mystic subpersonality comes in and says, "You should be sacrificing and letting go of things." Of course, you could get an efficient mystic, or a mystical businessman.

THE ARCHETYPAL CORE

Every subpersonality has an archetype at its core. This is very important to remember. (Similarly, Jung wrote that every complex has an archetype at its core, i.e., the core of the mother complex is the mother archetype.) Deep within a subpersonality—what gives rise to and builds up a subpersonality—is an archetypal drive, urge, or principle. A particular principle will draw to it different personality elements or different ways of being in order to fulfill itself. It is the archetypal centre of a subpersonality which holds together various personality elements so that the subpersonality can express itself. Let me give you an example to make this clearer. I did some ongoing work with a woman who had Mars conjunct Uranus in Cancer on the ascendant, sextile Saturn in Virgo. She had a subpersonality which built up around this placement which she called "Ros." She was a social worker, and Ros came out when she did community work and she had to meet and negotiate with high-powered lawyers at the legal aid centre or wherever. She said, "and then I would become Ros." She described Ros to me. Ros would drive up in her Morris Minor and confidently open up the door, get out and walk in a determined manner to the meeting. She wore a scarf, had a white jacket on, neatly pressed slacks and carried a briefcase. She was ready to get things done (Mars conjunct Uranus sextile Saturn). What was the core of Ros: what organised her to wear that scarf, and those slacks, to walk like that and behave like that? The core was the archetype or principle of efficiency and effectiveness. That archetypal or core principle drew together—collected around itself—various elements of her mind, body and feelings to support efficiency and effectiveness coming out.

In other words, a subpersonality is a synthesis of various traits and other psychological elements. A subpersonality has drives, feelings, emotions and its own way of standing and walking. But in order to have such a synthesis of different personality parts, there must be a centre around which this synthesis occurs. In a subpersonality, this centre is an inner drive or urge which is striving to be expressed. This central inner drive has the power to attract and hold together what it needs to create the living entity of the subpersonality.

The same woman with the Ros subpersonality also had a subpersonality she called "the blob." (She had her Mars square Neptune.) After a few years of being Ros, she flipped over into the blob. She described the blob to me: her shirt hung out, she got overweight, she went all loose and undefined. She "blobbed out"—one face of Neptune. But what is the core of the blob? What is its essence? Even though the blob looked and felt unpleasant, at its core was the need to relax, to dissolve, to let go, to flow— "to be" as opposed to "to do." The blob was about not being so straight and determined, but definitely related more to anima needs. So even though the blob came out a bit distorted and extreme, there is something at its core which this woman needed to fulfill herself and to balance her more animus side. I had her imagine that she was holding Ros in one hand and the blob in the other to see if she could feel the difference between the two. Subpersonalities have a different weight, a different kind of palpability which you can actually feel if you imagine them in your different hands. The Neurolinguistic Programming people take this a step further. They do something called "the visual squash technique." In short, you imagine one subpersonality in one hand and then a conflicting one in another. Then you slowly bring your two hands together and gently squash one into the other. The idea is that by doing this you get a sense of the synthesis or blending of the two. It gives you an experience of how they might unite or combine and blend together. That is, of course, providing you don't splat them both in the process.

PLANETS, SIGNS AND SUBPERSONALITIES

Planets and signs represent archetypal drives and principles. Subpersonalities build up around archetypal drives and principles.

Therefore, subpersonalities can be seen to build up and form around the various signs and planetary placements in the chart. Ian Gordon-Brown, one of the co-founders of the Centre for Transpersonal Psychology, was very struck by this. He wrote:

> ...My colleague Barbara Somers and I ran a workshop in Transpersonal Psychology for a group of astrologers. We did our usual exercises to help the group identify their subpersonalities, based on images. We were fascinated to find that in a significant number of cases the subpersonality structures that emerged seemed to represent or symbolise some of the key configurations in the birth chart.... There is room for important and fruitful research here which would benefit both astrology and psychology. I emphasize that the exercises that raised the subpersonality material were nothing to do with astrology.[5]

They did exercises to locate subpersonalities and the astrologers soon realised the connection. "Hey, that's Uranus on my ascendant," or, "That's my Moon square Saturn."

Let's play around with this. What kind of subpersonalities could form around something like Mars conjunct Jupiter in Aries on the ascendant or midheaven? If Mars conjunct Jupiter in Aries were the archetypal core of a particular subpersonality, what personality elements would it draw to itself: how would it walk, talk, feel and go after things? What comes to mind?

Audience: Something like a warrior god.

Howard: Yes, I thought of a warrior as well. Someone who needed something to battle for.

Audience: The knight. Someone who fights for a cause.

Howard: How would this subpersonality hold itself?

Audience: Proud—upright, but leaning forward slightly as if it were ready to attack. The energy would flow up and out.

Howard: Excellent, you're really getting what I mean. What sort of subpersonality might form around the Sun in Capricorn trine Saturn in Virgo? What images do you get?

---

[5]Ian Gordon-Brown, "Transpersonal Psychology," the fourth section of "Psychology Today," Faculty of Astrological Studies, Diploma Course, 14.

Audience: Someone with a lot of stability.

Audience: Someone with a lot of stiffness.

Howard: This is very interesting. We have two comments here—a subpersonality which reflects stability as its core, but another which looks stiff and rigid. An archetype can express on many different levels. The archetypal principle of earth or Saturn can manifest as stability *or* stiffness or a combination of the two. So the Sun in Capricorn trine Saturn in Virgo could give rise to a subpersonality that is orderly and efficient, economical and not wasteful in movement. But, on the other hand, it could be a subpersonality which is tight, rigid and very anal, like the stereotype of the headmaster of a strict school. Now compare this in your mind to a subpersonality building up around the Sun conjunct Uranus in Gemini on the ascendant. What would that be or look like?

Audience: It could be a rebel subpersonality, someone with a quick and inventive, or erratic side.

Howard: Yes. Compare how this subpersonality might stand or hold themselves in contrast to the previous one we mentioned (Sun in Capricorn trine Saturn in Virgo). Take a few seconds to feel the difference in your bodies as you imagine this

Really, you are not doing anything different here today. You are just interpreting placements in the chart. But I want to enhance your interpretation of various placements by encouraging you to see how a planetary configuration gives rise to a certain kind of person inside you. All the different configurations in your chart give rise to a whole group inside you. As with any group, some of the various components of the group may not get along. You need to make friends with the different members of the group and help them relate better together. If one member of your group is particularly difficult, then you may need to spend more time with it in order that this part can be better integrated into the overall medium of your personality.

How To Recognize Subpersonalities

Some of today is experiential, and I want to lead you in an exercise to deepen your understanding of subpersonalities. The more you can ground this concept by looking at your own subpersonalities, the better able you'll be to utilise this theoretical framework in chart readings or in your own chart.

Before we begin, I'd like to say a little about the exercises we'll be doing today. Most of you in the group are familiar with the use of guided imagery techniques as a way of exploring the psyche. Some guided fantasies can be very powerful and stir up pretty deep feelings. But the ones I've chosen to use today are very gentle. This is a learning group, not a therapy group, and the exercises are to help you learn more about the concept of subpersonalities in relation to the chart. If, while doing these exercises, anything too unpleasant begins to surface, I suggest you just come out of it by opening your eyes and maybe writing a little bit about what you were experiencing. Also, please feel free to discuss your experiences with me, either within the group or, if you prefer, at one of the breaks. Many of you are in some form of personal therapy, so if something significant should happen in one of the exercises today, I trust that you will take whatever material comes up and bring it to your own therapy sessions. As you know, one of the requirements for our three-year training is that you are in therapy for at least a year. We make this a rule because we believe that if you intend to work as a psychological astrologer and probe other people's psyches, you had better have a good idea of what is going on in your own.

In previous seminars, some of you have asked me if you can or should do these kinds of exercises with your astrology clients. Let's clarify subpersonality exercises right now. If you are working as an astrologer and you are only intending to do a single session on the chart with your clients, then I strongly recommend that you do *not* use guided imaging with them. Should something difficult come up your client might be left stranded with it. So in a once-off session, I would steer clear of using guided imaging techniques. However, even in a once-off session, I see no reason why you can't introduce your clients to the *concept* of subpersonalities—that is, explain the theory and discuss the kinds of subpersonalities the chart suggests without necessarily taking them into an exercise or guided fantasy technique. As I said earlier, people usually catch on pretty quickly to this concept, and it is an effective way of highlighting the kinds of inner paradoxes and dilemmas we all experience between various conflicting urges and drives which battle for priority inside us.

If you are working in an ongoing way with your clients—that is, seeing them on a weekly or regular basis, then it is assumed you have the adequate psychological training or supervision to constructively incorporate guided imaging techniques into your work and to deal with whatever issues these kinds of exercises might bring up. You really shouldn't work in an ongoing way with clients unless you have completed a psychological or astrological training which equips you to do this competently, or until your supervisors or trainers have given you the go-ahead. I hope I make my point clear: in no way can the irresponsible use of these techniques be condoned. Now, let's begin the exercise.

1) Close your eyes and take a minute to relax—let out any excess tension in your body with your breathing.

2) Now, pick out one planetary placement in your chart. Your Venus in Virgo, or Mars in Sagittarius, or Leo ascendant, or whatever. Just choose one placement.

3) Now, become aware of the part of you this placement reflects. Allow an image to emerge which represents this placement. The image might be a woman, a man, an animal, an object or anything. Just let it emerge as if you were watching a screen and didn't know what was coming next.

4) Once you have the image, give it a chance to reveal itself more. Don't judge it or interfere with it. Let it do anything it wants to do.

5) Get in touch with the general feeling that emanates from it. If the image wants to talk, then let it talk. Give it space. Find out what it needs. Have a discussion with it. This is one of your subpersonalities. It has life, drive, wants and needs. I'll give you a few minutes to be with it.

6) Okay, now take half a minute to slowly open your eyes and return back to the room. Make some notes on what happened. If possible, give this subpersonality a name. Write a little about its habits, traits and idiosyncracies.

Now divide up into groups of two and discuss with your partner what happened during this exercise. It's good to talk about it to bring it clearer into focus. For my own curiosity, I'd like to know how that exercise went for people. Anyone wish to expose themselves?

Audience: I worked on my Moon in Cancer which is also square Neptune in Libra. The image I got, not surprisingly, was a large crab. This crab comes from deep down where there is a lot of water. The pincers are dangerous and it wants to hold on and not give up. It has a a lot of primitive, creative energy which it enjoys but it wants to stay uncivilised and unformed.

Howard: If the image you get is from the early animal kingdom, then it might mean a part of you which is still shadowy. Perhaps it's a part that hasn't been worked on enough, or paid enough conscious attention. Now that you have this crab, take time to talk to it, find out more about what it is up to. Observe the situations in which it comes out.

Audience: I worked on my Sun in Virgo and I got something I named "the Fix-it-Ferret."

Howard: There are a lot of animals in this room.

Audience: The Fix-it Ferret has to find out everything and make sense of everything. And when it has found out everything, then he can fix it. It wants to know everything so that it can organize and control. I also have Gemini rising. Maybe this subpersonality is born from the combination of Virgo Sun and Gemini rising— both Mercurial signs.

Howard: Yes, Gemini is more knowledge for knowledge's sake. It likes to know a little bit about a whole lot of different things. Virgo gains knowledge so that it can be put to practical use. Virgo will go deeper into fewer things. Abraham Maslow once wrote that knowledge helps to give us security. If we know about something, if we can understand how it works, if we can label it and classify it, then it is less frightening to us. People used to worship what they found scary, now they do scientific investigations into it. And after studying it, they try to dominate it. The archetypal core of your little ferret is wisdom and intelligence.

● ● ●

Did anyone have trouble with imaging? If you couldn't get an image for the placement you were working on, don't worry. Just think about the placement and try to figure out what subpersonality in you might be connected with it. You don't have to work with images in this case—let your mind do the exploring. We are going to do some more experiential work later in the day.

Over the years I have come to believe in the chart completely. Sometimes a person is sitting in front of me appearing a certain way and something in the chart doesn't fit with that. In those cases, I believe the chart, not the person. There are too many instances where what is in the chart has proven more true than what the person was trying to show me. The chart is a diagnostic tool useful in assessing subpersonalities which might even be hidden from the person. Charts also help us to get to the archetypal core of subpersonalities, because you can see the planets and signs involved, But there are other ways of ferreting out subpersonalities. You can do something called "The Evening Review." (It sounds like a periodical, doesn't it?) Every night before you go to bed (after you've brushed your teeth and provided you are not busy with other things) you run the events of your day backwards in your mind. It's like rewinding a video. You are then meant to just witness or observe these events as they pass through your mind. Do this in an objective, detached and non-judgemental way. Try this every night for a few weeks and you'll begin to notice that there are certain distinct ways you deal with different situations or that various situations provoke certain kinds of responses from you. Then you can begin to form a good idea of your subpersonalities.

Or you can start by asking yourself what different faces you show to the world in various circumstances. You'll find clues if you consider the different roles you play in life. How are you with different types of people—with authority figures, younger people, your wife, the people under you at the office? What comes out of you at home, on holiday, at work?

Once you have a subpersonality you can name it and then give it a general character sketch. Find out its needs and desires and maybe even do a drawing of it. Note the circumstances which evoke that subpersonality. Pay attention to its strengths and weaknesses and how it interacts with other subpersonalities within you.

Audience: How many subpersonalities does a person have?

Howard: John Rowan did some work with subpersonalities back in 1974[6] and he said that some people had as many as eighteen subpersonalities. He feels, however, that four to eight is the normal range. Otherwise you get into duplicating them. Or a few are really a facet of one. I don't think you can work with more than four or five at the most.

So, to sum things up. The first step is to recognise your subpersonalities. After recognition comes the acceptance stage. You cannot accept something until you have recognised it. (On the other hand, you can recognise something and not want to accept it.) After acceptance comes co-ordination: this means getting the subpersonalities to converse and relate to one another and finding out which ones like each other and which ones don't. Then comes integration—trying to get these subpersonalities to work better together so that they function more harmoniously and constructively and work towards realising your overall goals and purposes. The different parts of you need to know they are part of a larger whole. Otherwise, they may not necessarily be acting for the good of the whole.

FINDING SUBPERSONALITIES IN THE CHART

We are covering very basic material now. I want to discuss key configurations which might give rise to subpersonality placements in the chart. First, let's look at subpersonalities in a general sense.

1) *The Sign Placement of the Sun, Moon and Ascendant*: You may find three different subpersonalities in this way: one based on the sign of the Sun, the other on the sign of the Moon and the third built up around the ascendant sign. For instance, I worked with

---

[6]John Rowan, "The Internal Society," a paper presented at the British Psychological Society Annual Conference in 1974. The reader is also referred to Rowan's article "You're Never Alone with Yourself," which was published in the British edition of *Psychology Today*, January, 1976.

someone with the Sun in Taurus who had a subpersonality he called "Falstaff." Taurus is a sign which has to do with being in the body and enjoying the material and physical world. We already had an example of the Sun in Virgo with the "fix-it ferret" subpersonality. Moon placements also give rise to subpersonalities. If the Sun and Moon are in conflicting signs or elements, then you might find a conflict between two different subpersonalities which have grown up around each placement. For example, take someone with the Sun in Aries and the Moon in Cancer. What kind of subpersonality could form around the Sun in Aries?

Audience: The Sun in Aries could give the hero, someone who has to conquer things and be powerful.

Howard: What about the Moon in Cancer then?

Audience: The Moon in Cancer could give a subpersonality that is more sensitive—taking in rather than giving out. The Aries subpersonality may want to act and do something and conquer some new fields while the Cancer Moon subpersonality prefers to sleep or potter about around the home, or feels insecure or vacillates about whether it should do what the Sun in Aries wants.

Howard: Yes, I like that. You have sensitive, "chewing-things-over" Cancer with aggressive and forward-moving Aries—regressive urges versus progressive urges. The Sun may want to move forward, take classes, give lectures, pursue degrees, or open businesses. The Moon might prefer to stay in bed or not do anything because it feels frightened or fearful of leaving what's known. In general, if you have the Sun square Moon, one part of you needs to do something for your growth and unfoldment (the Sun) and another part may not particularly feel like it at the same time (the Moon). You may have to give a lecture, but really feel like being home in bed. Similar dilemmas could arise between subpersonalities which grow up around conflicting Sun and ascendant placements, or Moon and ascendant placements. In fact, if someone didn't have a subpersonality which grew up around the Sun or ascendant, then I would feel quite concerned. Where is that part of him? If someone had Capricorn rising and there was no part of him with a sense of order or even rigidity, then I would be very worried. I would wonder if I had the birth time right. I would worry that this person was not in touch with himself enough. The

Sun and ascendant are likely to produce subselves which are central to our most basic identity and purpose, to what we need to develop in order to grow into what we are meant to become.

2) *Planets on an Angle*: A planet placed on one of the angles may form the basis or core of a subpersonality. I'm not just talking about planets on the ascendant or midheaven, but the descendant and IC as well. A planet on the IC suggests something deep within us which may not be obvious to others unless they know us very well.

3) *Stelliums*: Three or more planets in the same sign will give rise to a subpersonality forming around the sign in question.

4) *Element Predominance*: Look at the elements in relation to subpersonalities. If you have six planets in water, then you may have a subpersonality which has something to do with the principle of water at its core. If you have six planets in fire, then you get a subself with a fiery core, one that needs to create from inside the self, to flare up and be creative. A predominance of earth can give rise to a pragmatist subpersonality.

Audience: Could the most inferior element give rise to a subpersonality?

Howard: Yes, this is a good point. So, if you have a lack of fire (undifferentiated or inferior fire), then there is probably a subpersonality lurking in the shadow that desperately wants to be all the things that fire can be, or which reflects the more negative, primitive, or unsophisticated qualities of fire. Good. Thanks for that. If you read Liz's book *Relating*,[7] she deals with the kinds of personalities associated with the elements very well. I would also recommend a book called *Jung's Typology*, which contains essays by James Hillman and Marie-Louise von Franz.[8]

5) *Unaspected Planets*: Unaspected planets may give rise to a subpersonality. If a planet is unaspected, it doesn't mean that it is not important. Unaspected planets have a way of acting indepen-

[7]Liz Greene, *Relating: An Astrological Guide to Living with Others* (York Beach, ME: Samuel Weiser, 1978; and Wellingborough, England: The Aquarian Press, 1985), 52-60.
[8]Marie-Louise von Franz and James Hillman, *Jung's Typology* (Dallas: Spring Publications, 1971).

dently of the rest of the planets in the chart. If you have an unaspected Moon, for instance, it doesn't mean that you don't have feelings. It does mean, however, that your feelings are not tempered or modified by other planets in the chart. There may be times you act totally without feeling—because the Moon is not connected to anything. Conversely, there may be times when you *only* act from the Moon, in other words, just from your feelings and nothing else, because the Moon doesn't pull anything else along with it. It has also been said that unaspected planets can act autonomously. Subpersonalities often act autonomously as well; they split off and act independently of the rest of the personality.

6) *Anima and Animus Planets*: I naturally associate some planets with masculine or animus type drives and others with anima or feminine urges. The Sun, Mars, Jupiter and Uranus are animus energies; there is the need to assert, strive, push forward and affirm the identity. The Moon, Venus and Neptune are feminine or anima energies; they blend, merge, fuse, receive, adjust, compromise, etc. Are you with me?

Let's say that you have two animus planets brought together by aspect—the Sun conjunct Mars, or Sun square Uranus, or Sun inconjunct Mars, etc. With two masculine planets brought together, you get a double dose of the masculine principle. There is a great deal of energy, will, drive, striving, competitiveness and maybe even belligerent tyranny. So quite a pushy or belligerent subpersonality could grow up around two masculine planets in aspect. However, if you have two feminine or anima planets in aspect—Moon conjunct Venus, Venus inconjunct Neptune, Moon trine Neptune—this configuration would give a subpersonality which has anima qualities at its core: love, flowingness, service, sacrifice, even to the point of sickly sweetness. Two anima planets in aspect may give a subpersonality which overdoes the feminine, adjusts too much, goes too far with it. Two masculine planets in aspect may give a subpersonality which is excessive in the expression of its animus traits.

Audience: Can subpersonalities themselves have shadows?

Howard: Yes, I believe so. Someone with a strong love subpersonality might be harbouring resentment and anger: "When is it *my* turn for someone to give to me and look after me for a change?"

A strong masculine or animus subpersonality may have a fear of not being loved or appreciated hidden within it.

Now, if you have an anima planet in aspect to an animus planet, then you could have two different subpersonalities in conflict with one another. Say you have Mars square Venus. The Mars subpersonality wants to assert its individuality but the Venus subpersonality wants to blend and be loving and form unions. You get the bully, the me-first subpersonality in conflict with the balancer, the diplomat, the fair one.

All these things I've mentioned are general guidelines for recognising subpersonalities in the chart. Please remember that any placement might form the basis for a subpersonality. But these are the obvious ones to look for.

THE DEGRADATION OF ARCHETYPES

Again, I must give credit to Piero Ferrucci and his work with subpersonalities for he discusses the degradation or distortion of archetypal energies.[9] Similarly, any one subpersonality may be the distorted expression of an archetypal principle or planetary principle. For example, a madly fanatic subpersonality may be a distortion of the archetype of enthusiasm or the planet Jupiter.

Heinrich Heine wrote a book called *Exiled Gods*[10] in which he explores through a study of myth and legend what happened to the Roman and Greek gods when Christianity took over. What did Mars, the god of war, become? What did Jupiter, the king of the gods and the protector of the people, turn into? What happened to Venus/Aphrodite? According to Heine, the Greek and Roman gods declined after Christianity took over and ended up shadowy type figures, hanging out with the owls and toads at night. They were dethroned. Mars became a mercenary soldier; Mercury a shopkeeper; Venus earned her living as a prostitute; and Jupiter hunted and sold rabbit skins. They maintained something of their original flavour or archetypal essence but they were expressing it on lower levels. The pure expression of the archetype was stepped down.

[9]Ferrucci, *What We May Be*, Chapter 4, 54-58.
[10]A brief synopsis of Heine's book is given in Ferrucci, *What We May Be*, 52.

An archetype is like an elevator in a department store. The same elevator can let you off on the first floor at woman's shoes, on the second floor for men's clothes, or you can go straight to the restaurant at the top. Similarly, any archetype can express on many different levels. There are different notes in a chord. The feminine archetype can express on so many different levels: it can be mother, nanny, girlfriend, feelings, vases, coffins or even night-blooming flowers! What I am saying is that any content of the psyche can be degraded. Joy can become mania; enthusiasm can become fanaticism; compassion can become pity; peace can become inertia and intelligence can turn into cunning.

So let's say you have a subpersonality which is inert, a blob. It is possible that inertia is a distortion of a deeper archetypal quality at the root of the subpersonality—the quality of peace. If you deny or want to throw out your inert subpersonality, then there is the danger that you will throw away your connection to the quality of peace. If an archetype has been degraded, it can be elevated again. The idea is to first recognise and accept the inert subpersonality and then do some work to find the archetypal core it represents which has been distorted. Then the subpersonality may be able to find ways to give expression to its core principle other than just on the level of inertness.

Stay with me and this will become clearer. Back to basics again. This is all a bit Margaret Hone-ish, you know, *The Modern Textbook of Astrology* written in 1951.[11] Now, I don't want to make fun of her—this book is very useful and it helped me a lot in the beginning of my study of astrology. Anyway, take the principle of the Sun and think about what is the positive expression of the Sun principle. What are the negative expressions? Think of the Sun principle in terms of the degradation or the elevation of an archetype.

Audience: Some positive Sun qualities are nobility, dignity, being an individual in one's own right, self-expression.

Howard: Margaret Hone would be proud of you. What about the distortions?

Audience: Sun distortions might be arrogance, haughtiness, expecting others to bow to you.

---

[11]Margaret Hone, *The Modern Textbook of Astrology* (London: Fowler and Co., 1951).

Howard: Right. So you can have a haughty subpersonality which is a distorted expression of the purer archetypal quality of nobility, dignity and self-assurance. That subpersonality is a degraded specimen of a principle which is a valuable and potent part of life. Before you can reconnect to the more positive Sun qualities, you may *first* have to connect to your haughty subpersonality. The haughty subpersonality is the way in. Archetypes can be distorted by such things as fear, doubt and rigidity, thereby coming out in an impure form, or short of their luminous essence. Let's continue with this. What about the Moon—what is the spectrum here?

Audience: A subpersonality based on the Moon could be receptive, responsive and sensitive to others. But the distortion of the Moon principle could indicate a person who is living off another person's identity and just reflecting others and not being who he is in his own right.

Howard: In extreme cases they are a kind of "psychic vampire," sucking up your energy to feed themselves. While some Moon-type subpersonalities might be overly dependent and draining, others express the Moon's more positive nurturing and mothering qualities. What about Mercury?

Audience: The upgrade expression is brightness, awareness, alertness, adaptability and versatility. But negatively it can be persnickety, dilettantish, finicky and very quicksilver—here today, gone tomorrow. A kind of trickster.

Howard: And Venus?

Audience: A subpersonality with Venus at its core could have a strong perception of beauty, taste, love and a desire for union. A distorted Venus subpersonality might be envious of others getting more attention, or may try to enhance itself at the expense of the partner, or so attached to beauty that everything has to be perfect.

Howard: Good. And Mars can be courage or recklessness. Jupiter is expansiveness versus inflatedness. Saturn is order versus rigidity. Things like that. I'm sure you get the picture. Generosity can turn into wastefulness. A need for order can turn into compulsive obsessions. It helps to get your brain moving to think of the different levels of any archetypal quality.

IDENTIFYING SUBPERSONALITIES

I have to thank Lady Diana Whitmore, the founder of the Psychosynthesis and Education Trust, for this next section. She taught me that once you find a subpersonality, it is helpful to ask it three questions: *What do you want? What do you need?* and *What do you have to offer me?* You can work with these questions in this way. Take a placement in the chart and see if you can come up with an image for that placement. Then you can dialogue with that image and ask it these questions. In this way you are exploring the subpersonality further; you are doing some therapy with it.[12]

Let's say you have a subpersonality who wants a flashy car. You have Jupiter conjunct Mars in Sagittarius in the 5th house. You image that placement and your picture is one of a racing driver—a Peter Fonda type. So you ask this subpersonality, "What do you want?" and it replies, "I want a flashy car." The want is very gross, very specific and very exact. When I had my Jupiter return in Sagittarius, I fulfilled an adolescent fantasy and went out and bought a used English sports car. I couldn't wait to put the top down. Of course, it was December. It's funny, I was looking forward to the Jupiter return because I thought it would make me more spiritual. Okay, enough of that.

After you ask, "What do you want?", then ask "What do you need?" to the subpersonality. All right, you want a flashy car, but what do you need? It may answer, "I need recognition." The need for recognition is more subtle than the gross want of a flashy car. The need for recognition could be fulfilled in other ways than just buying a flashy car. If you have another subpersonality which is frightened of driving fast or which is stingy with money (for instance, Saturn in Virgo square the Mars-Jupiter conjunction) then you will have to find some other way to fulfill the need for recognition than just buying such a car. Once you get at the need, however, it opens up the possible ways the want can be fulfilled.

---

[12]Subpersonality Seminar (1979) led by Diana Whitmore under the auspices of what is now known as the Psychosynthesis and Education Trust, London.

Finally, you have the third question to ask the subpersonality: "What do you have to offer me?" When you ask that question, you are probing for the archetypal core quality of the subpersonality. In this case it could be, "I have energy, drive and will-power to offer you."

Or take another example. Let's say that you have a subpersonality that wants chocolate. All it wants to do is to eat chocolate cake, biscuits, mousse, etc. A glutton subpersonality. Now ask it, "What do you want?" It will say, "I want chocolate," obviously. Now ask it, "What do you need?" What might it say?

Audience: Chocolate.

Howard: Very funny. A lot of chocolate eaters here today. What do you need? It might answer, "nourishment."

Audience: It might answer sugar!

Howard: How many times do you crave chocolate when what you are really needing is nourishment or comfort? Once you establish that the deeper need is nourishment, then you can find other ways to satisfy that need rather than just by chocolate. I know this is just a general example, but do you see what I mean? Then you have the third question to ask to the chocolate-eating subpersonality: "What do you have to offer me?" Okay, what does it have to offer?

Audience: Chocolate.

Audience: A coronary.

Howard: What a bunch of comedians here today! Come on, how might it answer, "What do you have to offer me?"

Audience: Love, nurturing, the opposite of deprivation, the urge for fulfillment.

Howard: Yes, somehow, under all that craving for chocolate is an archetypal quality which has to do with nurturing, love and fulfillment. The compulsive chocolate-eater may have a problem with those things.

● ● ●

The chart blanks I use have a dot in the middle. When I do a reading for someone, I try to get them to stand on that dot in the middle of the chart and from there peruse the different placements in the chart. The dot in the middle represents your "I-ness," or your "Is-ness." That I-ness or Is-ness has different planetary energies and signs through which to express itself. The dot in the middle also represents the conductor of the orchestra. The different planets and signs represent the different instruments in the orchestra. The good conductor needs to get to know all the different instruments and help them play harmoniously together.

The value of subpersonality work is not just in identifying your subpersonalities and working with them. It helps in another way. Identifying subpersonalities helps you become aware that there is a part of you which *has* these subpersonalities: that you are an "I" with a hurt child, a bully, a mystic, a pragmatist subself, etc. There is that part of you which can say, "Sometimes I'm the bully and sometimes I'm the mystic and sometimes I come from my hurt child." Who *you* are is not just any one of these things, but *you* are the one who shifts from one to another. In this way, you are strengthening your sense of having a higher organising centre or higher unifying centre which can identify, work with, contain, and make room for your various subpersonalities. This is a two-fold process. The first phase involves *identifying* subpersonalities and "owning" them. The next phase is to *dis-identify* from them and realise that you are not just them: you are an "I" who can move into that one or into another one. This is what I mean about the dot in the middle, or the higher organizing centre. From this central point, you have a greater degree of awareness and choice than if you are identified with just one or another subpersonality.

A CASE HISTORY

This case history will help you appreciate how the subpersonality theory can be put into practice, both astrologically and therapeutically. (See Chart 6 on page 166.) Kathy came to see me when she was twenty-nine. Yes, I see all your ears perking up and knowing nods. What is special about the ages twenty-eight to thirty? Yes, the famous Saturn return. Everybody knows about the Saturn return now. People ring me for a reading and they don't know very much about astrology but they tell me they are going through their Saturn return and must see me. Someone should market Saturn return cards, "So sorry to hear about your Saturn return," or "Wishing you all the best for your Saturn return." Everyone is so relieved when it's over—I hate to tell them about the first square Saturn makes to its own place after the return. I found that just as challenging.

Back to Kathy. She was twenty-nine when she first came to see me and she wanted to do some ongoing therapy work. Her presenting problem was that she was running into difficulties setting herself up as a freelance designer. She worked part-time as a Girl Friday for a well-known artist. This was sufficiently well paid to support her daily existence and, in theory, should have left her time to develop her own work into something commercially viable. Instead, she frittered away her free time or she ended up using it to run errands and do things for her boyfriend.

Very generally, this is the way we worked over twelve sessions. During our first session, I introduced Kathy to her chart and pointed out to her some of the personal conflicts represented by her astrological placements. She has the Sun in Virgo in the 12th house, often indicative of one who puts her own needs aside for others, or one who has difficulties in establishing boundaries between herself and others. Venus is within a few degrees of her ascendant in Virgo, accentuating the love qualities of balancing, blending, serving and harmonising with others. All these placements suggested that Kathy identified herself through serving others and adjusted considerably to maintain peace and balance.

However, Kathy's need for freedom, personal expression, and space to do her own thing is accentuated by the placement and configuration of Mars and Uranus. These are self-assertive planets and conflict with her more servile, self-abnegating side. Mars conjuncts the Moon and squares the Sun, accentuating self-expressive drives. Just think about it a moment—what would it be like to have Mars aspecting both the Sun and Moon? She doesn't want to sit back and go unnoticed. There is also a wide sesquiquadrate (135 degrees) between the Mars-Moon conjunction and Uranus, which suggests the need to give expression to her creative originality. Moreover, the Sun is the midpoint of Uranus-Neptune. In other words, the Sun is caught between the wilful and independent Uranus and the sacrificing and self-dissolving planet Neptune. If you picture the Sun as the hero going down the road of growth and individuation, Kathy has Neptune pulling on one arm and Uranus pulling on the other. This mid-point structure nicely sums up her dilemma between serving others or doing things for herself.

I went over the symbolism of Sun in Virgo in the 12th, Venus on the ascendant, and the Sun semi-square Neptune with Kathy. She immediately recognised this aspect of her personality which she herself described as "the Super-Server." Now we had a definite subpersonality to look at which had formed around those astrological placements. Kathy explained that super-server is terribly efficient getting things done, but normally these are things done for other people. Super-server also secretly enjoyed the recognition and approval she won for her efforts.

We did some spot imaging and inner reflection on super-server. Kathy was sitting there talking from her super-server subpersonality when I noticed her posture and face changing. I asked her what was happening and she said that suddenly she felt very young. Then she said, "I know who this is—it's Good Kathleen!" In this way, Kathy discovered "Good Kathleen," a kind of prototype for super-server, who lurked just beneath its surface.

Good Kathleen was about four years old and wore her hair in plaits. She was *the* good little girl; she was never disruptive. Good Kathleen lived with her mother and father in a tiny top floor flat in New York City. Her parents were not getting along well and it didn't feel safe for her to add to the discord by causing any trouble. Kathy spoke as good Kathleen: "I have to be good. If I set a foot wrong, something terrible might happen." Those were her words. In such an environment where things are explosive and crowded, she didn't feel safe enough to be spontaneous or express herself freely. She felt as if the home environment couldn't take any more pressure. (Note that the ruler of her 4th house, Jupiter, is square Mercury, the ruler of the 10th and also square Pluto.) As a child, Kathy learned to derive her identity by being what the environment needed her to be. For her it seemed the safest way to ensure her survival. Remember, all through her childhood, transiting Pluto is slowly creeping up to her Sun. Somewhere deep inside she sensed Pluto not far away, creeping up on her. Transiting Pluto moved into her 12th in her first year of life—there were threatening undercurrents around. It actually didn't conjunct her Sun until she was eight or nine and that was when her parents' marriage finally fell apart. Now, if you sense Pluto coming at such a young age, what do you do? You hide under the table—you try to be good as a way of preventing it.

When Kathy spoke from good Kathleen, she sat very erect and straight on her chair. However, as she continued speaking she became aware of another presence. She exclaimed to me: "Wait, there is somebody else around. I know this person and it's someone who is looking very disparagingly at good Kathleen. It's the Imp!"

At that point, my ears perked up. Who is this imp? I got excited. I suggested we find out more about the imp, suspecting it might be her Mars-Uranus side coming out. (Elementary, my dear Watson.) We brought forth a chair for the imp and I asked her to sit there and become it and show me how the imp sat. Kathy crossed her legs and put her hand on her chin, resting her elbow on one arm of the chair. It looked to me as if the imp was sulking. Suppressed Mars-Uranus energies often appear first as angry or whining, or more indirectly, as sulking.

I asked her if the imp had anything to say to good Kathleen. The imp spoke, eyes downcast, in a monotone voice, into the hand resting on her chin: "I don't like you Kathleen. You are so priggish and self-conscious. At least I've got a sense of fun. You let yourself be sat on. You are so boring. You feel so responsible for everyone else. . . . " I sensed that the imp, once freed and transformed, would provide Kathy with the necessary qualities to achieve in her own right, to express her own creative energies. At that time the imp was in a sulky and angry place. You would be too if you had been sat on for so many years. The imp was closely aligned with the natural, spontaneous child which Kathy never really had a chance to experience. All that natural creative energy was boxed in and had turned angry and depressed. Getting in touch with the anger would be the first step in freeing that energy so that it could be directed in more creative ways.

Kathy's pattern had been to hold back the imp. If the imp could be let in more, then the pattern could be broken. Now, at this time when we were meeting, transiting Uranus was beginning to move closer to her Mars-Moon conjunction and square the Sun. It seemed appropriate that the imp should be released, that Uranus should free up some of her Mars energy and that she should be breaking her pattern of holding back her Mars-Uranus side. You can't make something come out if it is not the right time—you have to honour what another person is ready to experience. It's wrong to shoot at somebody's unconscious. But the transits to Kathy's chart suggested and confirmed it was the right time to bring out Mars.

Over the next few sessions we made a deal to explore the imp further. We allowed space within each session for her "whining and sulking child" to express itself. I asked her what percentage of the time was she good Kathleen and what percentage of the time was she the imp? She said that in her life right now she was good Kathleen/super-server about seventy-five percent of the time and the imp about twenty-five per cent. In other words, I was asking what percentage of time did she give to Neptune and what percentage was devoted to Mars and Uranus. When she had given me the percentages, I then asked if she was happy with them. (If you are happy, why bother?) She admitted she wasn't. Then I asked her how she would like it to be? She wanted a balance. "So what is stopping you from having it that way?" She was afraid to assert herself and take time for her own design work because she was frightened she would upset other people if she wasn't doing what they needed her to do. She was still the good little girl trying to please mommy and daddy and not cause any trouble. To the little girl still alive in her psyche, asserting herself meant risking being abandoned and perhaps dying. As a child she tried to be what the environment needed her to be in order to win love and keep the family together. Later on in her life she was still doing this, even though now she certainly didn't need her parents to survive. She clung to an obsolete defence mechanism.

As the weeks went by, the initially monotoned and withdrawn imp began to express its feelings more and more demonstrably— both in and out of the sessions. Kathy became more lively and energetic, and her childhood fears that she would lose love if she expressed the imp began to diminish. We didn't change the name of the imp, but maybe we should have. In naming subpersonalities, there is a danger that you might get stuck in the name. Remember, if the subpersonality starts to change, it might be appropriate to alter its name as well. The imp could have been changed to "Spontaneous Kathleen."

What eventually happened was one of those synchronous experiences. The more Kathy felt it was all right for her to express

Mars-Uranus, the more the environment seemed to give her opportunities to do her free-lance designing. Opportunities arose for her to further her career as a designer, culminating around the time of our twelfth session in an important commission for her work from a chain of stores. Kathy also felt less frustrated when her free-lance work met with obstacles; she felt safer in asserting herself, in defining her boundaries and stating her needs. She spent more time pursuing the goals she had set for herself.

Previously, so strongly identified with super-server, Kathy felt *compelled* to serve and adjust to the needs of others, while the frustrated and undeveloped imp harboured unconscious resentment towards those she served. Now that Kathy recognised herself as someone who could safely assert her needs, she could more freely *choose* to be adaptive or of loving service to others.

Audience: Did Kathy know much about astrology before she came to you?

Howard: Just a little. She had her chart done once before. But I find that people catch on quickly to the concept of subpersonalities and that it sometimes can be used in the first session. I will start the session by telling the client to imagine he or she is standing in the middle of the chart—remember, the dot in the middle. Then I say that we will be looking at the different personality parts and that the planets symbolise those different parts. One part of the client may want one thing—one planet or configuration may want one thing—but another part or another planet may want something else. People relate to this easily. I can see if the client is understanding what I mean when halfway through the reading he or she points at one planet or placement I have mentioned and says, "But this part doesn't get along with this other part," and points to another position in the chart. Not only have the two subpersonalities been recognised but the clients have begun to sense the "I" that has them and which can work with them. As I said earlier, the whole point of subpersonality work is not just to identify subpersonalities, but also to dis-identify from them and reconnect to the "I" that *has* the subpersonalities—the "I" that shifts from one to another. Diana Whitmore uses this analogy to explain the difference between *being* a subpersonality and *having* a subpersonality. She says that if you *are* a dog that bites, then you bite. But if you *have* a dog that bites, then you can choose to let it bite, or choose to put a muzzle on the dog or teach it not to bite. If you are totally identified with a subpersonality, then you just act it out. But if you realise a subpersonality is something you have operating in you, then you can do something to change, alter, or transform it.

When you become more conscious of some dynamic operating inside you, then you are less likely to be unconsciously dominated by it. When Kathy was unconscious of the imp, she was dominated by it: the imp kept sabotaging and disrupting what she wanted to do. After spending more time working with the imp, she could channel its energy constructively.

SUBPERSONALITIES WITH LOVE AT THEIR CORE

Normally we have a few or more subpersonalities with the principle of love as their underlying archetypal drive or motivation. These subpersonalities display persistent urges towards belongingness, relatedness and inclusiveness. Subpersonalities with love at the core are usually highly sensitive and receptive to the environment. The signs which most strongly exhibit these qualities are Cancer, Libra and Pisces. If the Sun, Moon or ascendant fall in any of these signs, or if a predominance of planets occupy these signs, strong subpersonalities based on love will most likely be found within the individual. The needs and drives associated with the Moon, Venus and Neptune are also those of receptivity, belongingness, relatedness and inclusiveness. If these planets are found to be on or near any of the angles of the chart, or if they are found to be in close aspect or angular relation to one another, subpersonalities based on the love principle can safely be assumed. The placement of the Sun or Moon or a conglomerate of planets in the 4th, 7th or 12th houses might be another indication of love-type subpersonalities. Finally, a heavy emphasis of planets in the element of water, which is associated with Jung's concept of the feeling function, gives strong love-needs and the possibility of subpersonalities forming around them.

Love subpersonalities in their most positive expression are nurturing, caring, protecting and harmonising. However, the archetypal quality of love coming through the personality and interacting with the environment can easily be distorted by things like fear, doubt, insecurity, fixed attitudes or negative conditioning. For instance, the principle of love can be distorted on the personality level by insecurity, thus giving rise to strong dependency needs—the need to be constantly reassured you are loved, or the fear of doing something wrong and losing the loved one. In other words, distorted love-needs may take the form of over-dependency, ultimately finding its expression in a subpersonality which might be named "the sissy." Other distortions of the love principle are found in subpersonalities which exhibit too great a reliance on the environment—"the environment tells me what I need or who I am," or "the environment has to love me." Such subpersonalities operate from an excessive tendency to conform in order to win love. They can easily be too concerned with what others think about them. They may try to figure out what other people need or expect and then mould their personality or behaviour accordingly. Rather than being true to something inside which might go against what they believe someone else wants from them, they sell out and side with what keeps the peace or what will not ruffle others. Subpersonalities based on love may also suffer from a lack of discrimination, a difficulty in establishing clear boundaries and problems eliminating negative circumstances from their lives. They don't know when to say no. If someone in the environment has a problem, then the love-type subpersonality will somehow feel responsible for it.

Love subpersonalities structure their being as a defence against their greatest fears—those of rejection, loneliness or isolation. A person with a strong love subpersonality may hold back expressing or doing what he really feels for fear of hurting or alienating others and for fear of losing love as a result.

As we saw in the case history of Kathy, a child with the Sun, Moon, ascendant or a conglomerate of planets in Cancer, Libra, or Pisces or with a prominently placed Moon, Venus, or Neptune, or a strong 4th, 7th, or 12th house emphasis will exemplify these characteristics. For all children—but especially for the love-type—winning love is a way of securing survival. If the child is loved, then he (or she) feels he will succeed in extracting from the environment the kind of care and support necessary to keep him safe, comfortable and alive. Distortions of present love-type subpersonalities can be tracked back to childhood when we felt we needed to conform to win love or survive.

Stifling those parts unacceptable to the environment as a child may have been appropriate and necessary at one time. The problem is that we often hang onto childish defence mechanisms far too long. Far into adulthood we foster subpersonalities which cling to the notion that survival is dependent on adapting to the needs or expectations of others when, in fact, the adult is quite able to look after his or her own survival needs. It is the child-in-the-adult who fears drastic consequences should it step out of line or express its true individuality.

Subpersonalities with love at the core may have a pattern or statement about life which goes something like, "If I am not good, if I do not do what others want, if I am not what others expect, then there will be a disaster." This is the hidden agenda or context from which a love subpersonality might structure his or her choices in life.

Invariably, anyone who continually suppresses his or her own individuality, who is primarily centered around being what others want, need or expect, will probably be feeling a good deal of anger and resentment. This is the shadow side of the love-type subpersonality. The person may not express this directly, but it can be heard more indirectly through such remarks as, "All I have done for you and look what thanks I get," or, "If it hadn't been for you, I could have. . . . " The other person is blamed or put at fault for not being appreciative enough, or for being too oppressive, when in reality these are the exact things the love-type has done to his or her own self.

I have been dwelling on the distortions of the love principle and how these might express through certain subpersonalities. But I don't want to desacralise love any further. Love is a most beautiful and important force. Love is a way of reconnecting to wholeness. Love allows us to transcend isolated, individual identity. Underlying the love subpersonality is a very legitimate and beautiful urge to be connected to others and to transcend the separate-self sense.

Audience: In the exercise we did, I had a clear love subpersonality. I imaged on my Moon in Pisces and saw a woman in a long dress, totally flowing and all encompassing.

Howard: Yes, she represents a certain part of you then. The under-lying principle of love is very beautiful, but watch out for the dis-tortions I have mentioned.

WILL TYPE SUBPERSONALITIES

There is a whole group of other subpersonalities which may orga-nise themselves around the archetypal principle of the *will*. These express a drive for power and a need for self-expression in contrast to the inclusiveness and harmonising needs of love subpersonali-ties. Love is *yin* and will is *yang*. The signs which most strongly exhibit qualities of will are Aries, Leo, Scorpio, Aquarius and Capricorn—also Sagittarius and even certain qualities of Taurus (the will to maintain) to some degree. I keep changing my mind as to which signs should go with will.

Subpersonalities formed around the will principle may be found if the Sun, Moon, ascendant, or a predominance of planets occupy these signs. Will-drives are also associated with the Sun, Mars, Uranus and certain qualities of Jupiter, Saturn and Pluto. If these planets are found on or near any of the angles of the chart, or if they are placed in close aspect to one another, subpersonali-ties motivated by the will-principle are likely, whether or not these are conscious to the individual.

In addition, important placements in the 1st, 5th or 10th house could be a further indication of will-type subpersonalities. Fire is the element most associated with the drive for self-expression and recognition, so if the chart shows many planets in this element, the need for assertive self-expression will be strong.

Will subpersonalities, in their most positive expression, strive for excellence, strength, directness, and clarity. They have the potentiality to use their drive or power to serve a larger purpose or promote a greater cause. However, the archetypal quality of the will expressing itself in the personality can be distorted by, say, rigidity, into the power-tripper or the bully, who always has to have his will, or who is determined to turn his will into law. The will principle could also distort into behavior that is overly selfish, competitive, controlling, or ambitious. Will subpersonalities struc-ture their lives very often as a defence against their greatest fears—fear of losing control, fear of losing power, or fear of impotency.

If you remember from the *Stages of Childhood* seminar, we said that love is the central archetype of the first few years of life. Will, as an archetypal principle, emerges more clearly around the age of two. The development of the will is closely linked with separating from an over-dependency and over-identification with the mother and establishing one's own separate identity and individuality. Of course, the mother (or other people) doesn't always like the way we choose to do this. The development of the will gives rise to many conflicts and battles with parents, friends and authority figures. And yet, the will provides us with the energy and power to master the environment and gives us joy, greater self-esteem and a sense of achievement. Did anyone here today have a will-type subpersonality show itself?

Audience: I was imaging around my Pluto conjunct the ascendant in Leo. There was a very strong person trying to come out from behind something, but he wouldn't quite come out. He wanted to control the whole chart and the other planets. He wanted to come out and use the other principles for his ends.

Howard: How did that feel for you? Did he feel legitimate or okay?

Audience: Yes, he felt reliable. He said he would come out when he was ready to come out.

Howard: So, he was asking for time. Have you ever noticed him before?

Audience: No, today was the first time he came up.

Howard: He sounds as if he is worth working with. You can take some time at home to dialogue some more with him, talk to him, draw a picture of him. The more attention you pay it, the more you will help to activate that principle.

THE LOVE-WILL DILEMMA

The will-type subpersonality needs the freedom to be and do what it has to do. Subpersonalities with will at their core ask that others adjust to them. How very different from love-type subpersonalities who are busy adjusting to others.

You can have a chart with a love-will dilemma. This happens when there is a strong placement of planets, signs, or houses which indicate love-subpersonalities as well as other placements which suggest prominent will-subpersonalities. If this is the case, the person will experience some conflict or lack of integration between his or her love and will needs. You see a person who is deadlocked between, "When do I blend, adjust, and balance," and "when do I say no, you adjust to me." Hopefully, charts that show such a love-will dilemma will be able to find some way of bringing these two principles together constructively. Or at least they can learn to make room in their lives for both ways of being.

Two love planets in difficult angle to one another produce too much of the love principle. Two will planets in difficult angle to one another yield too much wilfulness. But a love planet in difficult angle to a will planet produces a dilemma between love and will. I mentioned the case of Mars square Venus earlier—Mars wants to assert its individuality and Venus wants to blend. The Sun square Neptune or Mars opposing Neptune can be another version of the love-will dilemma. One may be suppressed in favour of the other, but sooner or later the denied side will cause some trouble. If the needs of one subpersonality or planet are overlooked in favour of the needs of another, the neglected subself (or planet) builds up a kind of pressure in the unconscious. It may burst out irrationally from time to time. It may have to find a devious route to fulfil itself. Frustrated will subpersonalities become angry, whiny, sulky, sick or depressed. Frustrated love subpersonalities may be hiding hurts or a sense of not being loved and included.

The love part says, "If I am too willful, then I might lose love and people won't like me anymore." This is often a hangover from childhood when we were afraid that people wouldn't love us if we were too demanding or not what they wanted us to be. But will has its fears as well. The will part says, "If I am too loving, then I will be taken advantage of." Somewhere in the past you may have been very loving and open, and then let down and hurt. The will part says, "Be careful, if you give them an inch, they'll take a mile. If you adapt too much to them, you'll lose touch with who you are—you'll be swamped." Will is afraid to be loving—afraid to lose space and freedom. Love is afraid to lose contact.

A classic example of someone over-identified with a will-type subpersonality may be the businessman with a big striver subpersonality, something like Mars conjunct Jupiter in Capricorn in the 10th opposing Neptune in Cancer in the 4th. He is compelled to compete, to struggle, to get to the top. Later in life he may regret the lack of attention paid to his love-needs when he realises he is alienated from his wife or children. He may have achieved, but at a cost to his under-developed personal and emotional life. Or, he may find himself the victim of a stroke at age fifty-five, which leaves him partially paralyzed and in a position of having to be almost totally dependent on others. The denied love side has swung back and hit with full force. The businessman suffering the after-effects of the stroke is left virtually weak and helpless—the two things he probably never acknowledged were in him to any great degree. Or, he was always trying to prove his strength to compensate for a fear of weakness. Spending more time with his Neptune in Cancer in the 4th sooner, rather than later, might have made things work out differently.

If the astrologer can formulate the right questions, the chart is an invaluable diagnostic tool in assessing where a person stands in terms of love and will. Does the chart indicate an innate over-balance of will and the need to bring out more of the love signs and planets? Does the chart indicate an imbalance in favour of love, and perhaps the need to more fully develop will-subpersonalities? Or is there such an equal balance between the two that there is a perpetual indecision? An equal balance between love and will could also give rise to an ideal synthesis of these qualities—a natural ability to be loving when it is appropriate and to be more wilful when that is necessary. You could then be loving without losing your individuality and wilful without being over-bearing.

However, in many cases where the chart indicates a potential balance between love and will, this doesn't exist. The reason for this lies in the fact that the ego hates ambivalence and if it is confronted with conflicting choices, it will choose to identify with one principle and suppress the other. As already explained, the suppressed principle invariably surfaces later in one way or another, and often not in the most pleasant manner.

When we discussed Kathy I used percentages as a way of approaching her love-will dilemma. What percentage of the time are you coming from your will side and what percentage of the time are you coming from your love side? Are you happy with that percentage? If not, how would you like it to be? What is blocking you having it that way? These kinds of questions can get some good work going.

You might try the concept of *time-sharing* with subpersonalities. I know a lot of you don't think this works, but I still feel it's worth a try. Time-sharing involves getting an overview of the personality and its components and then consciously alloting certain times for the expression of one subpersonality and certain times for the expression of another. In this way, no one component of the self feels unrecognised, so there is less danger of it explosively accumulating or acting out in such a way that might sabotage the drives or needs of other parts of the personality. Speaking very simplistically, this may mean working out some schedule of time-sharing like this: Monday, Wednesday and Friday I give time to the love-subpersonalities, but on Tuesday, Thursday and Saturday I give time to my will-subpersonalities. Obviously in real life it is very much more complicated than this. But remember, if you choose to be loving as opposed to being self-assertive and individualistic, then tell your will-side, "Don't worry, I haven't forgotten about you. I'm coming from love now, but you'll get your turn to be wilful when it's the right time." It is important to acknowledge the side you are inhibiting and to let it know that it will get its needs taken care of as well. This way it doesn't feel neglected and need not go to obnoxious extremes to be heard. It's like when the conductor tells the strings to come in and the brass to shut up.

Audience: I just thought of another problem with the love-will dilemma. What about the person who is too easy going and adjusting at work where he should really be more wilful and tough; and that same person is too tough and pushy at home, where he really needs to be more loving and understanding of others?

Howard: Yes, that is a good one. There is a kind of displacement going on.

Audience: I was interested in the example you used about the businessman who might get a stroke in his fifties. I did a reading the other day for a woman whose husband just had a stroke. He had always been very efficient, organised and effective in the world.

Now she has to comb his hair and dress him and he just cries a lot. She had never seen him cry and she is amazed at what is there. I didn't see his chart, but she had transiting Neptune conjuncting the 7th house cusp.

Howard: Yes, that is just what I mean. Sometimes when people with obvious love-will conflicts in the charts come to see me, I work with them in this way. I try to explain to them the value in both ways of being. Being loving, adjusting, and reflective is right and good sometimes. Being tough, wilful and assertive is also right at the appropriate times. In other words, one principle isn't better than the other—both are okay. So it's okay to be your Mars-Jupiter conjunction in Leo and it's also okay to be your Moon conjunct Neptune in Libra. But the real crunch is knowing *when* to be each one, when to bring Mars-Jupiter in, and when to bring Moon-Neptune in. So I ask people to stand in the middle of their charts and take a barometer reading in different life situations. How is it going at work—do you need more love *or* will there? If you need more will, then bring in your Mars-Jupiter side some more. How is it going at home—do you need more love *or* will there? Is it appropriate given the situation to bring in your Mars or your Neptune now? Or I may suggest that someone bring in Neptune now, but in three months, if he still feels rotten, he should bring in Mars and get tough about what is going on. Transits and progressions may help here. If someone is having an important Neptune transit, then it probably is a time to bring in Neptunian qualities. However, if Uranus is touching everything off, I'm not sure I would advise someone to sit still and be patient and adjusting.

CHANGE VERSUS MAINTENANCE

Let's move on to some other subpersonality configurations and the possible dilemmas between different ones. Let's consider a dilemma called change versus maintenance. In its purest expression, the maintenance drive offers us anchoring and deepening, patience, and a sense of rhythm and timing. Maintenance offers us consolidation, a sense of waiting for something to be right. It's like waiting for something to cook or watching something grow. Maintenance means being with something and staying with something. It offers us structures which serve life and forms through which our being can manifest. Maintenance gives us time to ground ourselves in something and accepts the need to live within boundaries and recognises the limits of our human-ness. Subpersonalities with maintenance urges at their core reflect all these qualities.

The signs I most associate with this principle are Taurus and Capricorn and to some degree Virgo and Cancer. A predominance of earth signs may give rise to a maintenance subpersonality. A strong Saturn does so as well. I would also look at important placements in the 2nd, 6th or 10th houses.

However, the drive or urge for maintenance can be distorted into stubbornness, hanging on, inertia or keeping the status quo because of fear of the unknown. Maintenance can turn into crystallisation and rigidity. Too much staying with something when it has outlived its time is a problem with these subpersonalities. Things turn *tamasic*; they grow stale, outworn, rotten and sterile. Maintenance can dig its heels in and say, "So what? Why do you want more? Be happy with what you already have—stop dreaming; come down to earth."

Now compare this with subpersonalities which have the principle of change at their core. In its purest form our need or drive for change is very important: change allows for progression, for harmonious step-by-step development, for growth, transformation and blossoming. The bud has to burst to become a rose. You have to break an egg to make an omelette. Change subpersonalities are not so attached to form as maintenance types are. Change subpersonalities wake up one day and have a different view or vision of things and will disrupt what is already there in the name of what is new, untried or unknown. Maintenance subpersonalities sign a contract and ten years later they will uphold that contract, even if they feel very different about things now. Change subpersonalities will act on the idea of something new, while maintenance types are attached to existing forms.

The signs I first associate with change are Aries, Sagittarius, Gemini and Aquarius. If someone has a Gemini Sun, Sagittarius rising and an Aries Moon, you don't necessarily have a sense of them sticking to one thing for very long. The planets I associate with change are Mars, Jupiter, Uranus and, of course, Mercury.

The elements of fire and air are more prone to subpersonalities based on change.

Audience: What about Venus and Libra?

Howard: To the extent that Libra is an idealistic sign, I would associate it with change. Libra is looking for the more ideal relationship, the more ideal political system, or whatever. However, the balancing urges of Libra makes it a little less changeable than Gemini or Aries.

Audience: What about Pluto and Scorpio? They like to tear down to make room for something new.

Howard: Yes, I would also put them here but in brackets—Scorpio is a bit too fixed in many ways. But it is true; eventually Pluto or Scorpio, for the sake of change and evolution, will clear something away which is outworn or not working. It just takes a long time to build it. Compare it to Sagittarius, who sometimes changes just as soon as the going gets tough.

What are the distortions of change? The distortions can be very destructive—changing for the sake of change. Change subpersonalities may have the attitude that all boundaries and barriers are bad and are not to be recognised. They can be attached to change because of a fear of rooting or settling. They hate to lose any alternatives, therefore they don't stick with any one thing. They may even be insensitive to the needs of their own bodies, seeing the body as another limit that they don't want to respect. They may not give enough credence to the limits of one's humanity and commit a kind of *hubris* by aiming too high or being too idealistic. Like Prometheus, they may try to steal fire from the Gods and be punished. You don't get a Virgo thinking that everything is possible. Earth says, "Wait a minute, you are going overboard." Aries, Sagittarius or Aquarius will say, "No—if you believe it, you can make it happen." Change subpersonalities have something of the eternal youth (the puer) in them. Maintenance subpersonalities have more of senex.

The greatest fear of change subpersonalities is being imprisoned in form. Just as Zeus hated to be trapped by Hera, spirit hates to be imprisoned in form.

Audience: So, if somebody had Saturn square Uranus in the chart, could that give rise to a subpersonality based on Saturn in conflict with a subpersonality based on Uranus? The Saturn one would be cautious and conservative and the Uranian one would be more restless, unconventional and changeable.

Howard: Yes, I would see it that way too. What are some other combinations of change and maintenance dilemmas?

Audience: Someone with a few planets in Capricorn but also some in Aquarius as well. Or someone with a strong Taurean side but also a strong Sagittarian side. Or someone with Aries strong but who has Saturn conjunct the Sun or Capricorn rising.

Howard: Yes, you are getting the picture. There are a variety of combinations. Just refer to our list of change planets and signs and maintenance planets and signs and look for different combinations of them.

Audience: Isn't there a middle ground?

Howard: Yes, I am always looking for a synthesis of different sub-personalities if possible. So there may be a way to keep the best of the old but make room for the new. But in general watch for subpersonalities which say, "I must change, I must grow, I must transform, keep moving, evolve," in conflict with other ones which are more inert or which need stability and security.

It may be possible to first get a home base and some security and then travel or move around. Or some people may do it the other way. Take an airy or fiery chart with Capricorn rising. In the first part of life, they live from their change and adventure side and then around thirty or thirty-five they begin to come into the Capricorn. A new subpersonality emerges which says "Gee, wouldn't it be nice to settle down, buy some property and be more down to earth and ordinary." Some people hate the idea of being ordinary and just human. Other people are terrified to explore their farther horizons and risk being different from the norm.

THE MYSTIC-PRAGMATIST SPLIT

What we have just been discussing leads nicely on to another dilemma between conflicting subpersonalities—what is commonly known as the mystic-pragmatist split.

In the Stages of Childhood seminar we said that in the womb (or somewhere in the past) we have had an experience of being immersed in an oceanic totality. It is a state which is pre-subject/object, a feeling of non-differentiation, with no sense of a separate self yet formed. From the ascendant to the 6th house we develop a sense of a discrete•self, separate and distinct from other selves. We move from an ego-less state to having a sense of "I." From the 7th to 12th houses we relinquish this separate-self sense in order to merge with others or the greater whole again. What I am talking about is a basic existential human dilemma. One part of us wants to develop a separate self-sense, define ourselves more clearly and form boundaries. And yet there is another part which has a persistent urge to dissolve back into that uroboric wholeness again. We intuit that our innermost being is universal and unbounded, yet we inhabit a body which distinguishes us from others.

Now some people are more inclined towards distinguishing and differentiating themselves from others and with making boundaries. Other people, however, are more concerned with dissolving boundaries and merging with others or with God. The pragmatist is the one trying to make distinctions and boundaries; the mystic is seeking transcendence of the separate-self sense.

Subpersonalities can form around mystic urges or pragmatist urges. Let's look at the planets, signs and houses involved on either side to make this clearer. Pragmatist subpersonalities often form around the earth signs, Virgo in particular. Gemini is also into making distinctions and looking for differences. Mercury and Saturn are the planets to look to in this case and the 2nd, 3rd, 6th and 10th houses may play a part in giving rise to these kinds of subpersonalities.

Pragmatist subpersonalities have the ability to deal practically and efficiently with the environment. In fact, a measure of health in contemporary society is the degree to which an individual is adjusted to the environment. People are judged from a pragmatic stance, by how well they relate to the environment or cope with the everyday world of form and matter. In extreme cases, this can be judged in a most rigid, materialistic manner. Someone with two cars in the family garage must be better than someone with only one car. A person is judged by his position and place in the world, by whether he has a good job or family. These are all tangible things and that is what matters most to the pragmatic mentality.

Those with strong pragmatist subpersonalities are more concerned with *what is* as opposed to *why is*. Earth, Virgo, Gemini,
Saturn, Mercury, the 3rd and 6th houses also correspond to left-
brain activity as opposed to the mystical right-brain. The left brain
compartmentalizes, pigeonholes, analyses and labels. The left
brain gathers facts.

Pragmatists make good bureaucrats, researchers and civil ser-
vants. They like to see concrete and tangible results for their
efforts. The pragmatist subpersonality will have a "me-in-here"
versus "you-out-there" reality. They like to figure things out,
divide things into parts and see how it all works. If you know how
something works, then you can use it to your advantage, or you
can improve it and make it better if necessary. Positively, a pragmatist subpersonality can deal well with the everyday world and
encourages achievements and accomplishments. The pragmatist
can take ideas and put them into action and materialize things.
One of the main pragmatist distortions, however, is "If I can't see
it, then it doesn't exist." At some point in the life, a person who
has come from the pragmatist side may suffer what is called an
existential crisis. They are successful in a practical and material
sense; they have the job and house and family, but they don't
know what it all means. During an existential crisis, they may
wonder, "What is it all for?" or, "What am I here for?"

Do you get the picture of that side? Now let's compare the
pragmatist approach with that of the mystic. First of all, what
signs, planets or houses would you put on the mystic side?

Audience: Neptune, Pisces and the 12th house. These all have to
do with dissolving boundaries and transcending the ego.

Howard: Yes, that's right. Any other mystic significators?

Audience: What about Jupiter, Sagittarius and the 9th house?

Howard: Yes, Jupiter, Sagittarius and the 9th house have a lot to
do with searching for meaning in life and journeying beyond the
boundaries of the everyday and mundane. The 9th house entails
a quest for answers to the whys and wherefores of existence. Let
me elaborate on the mystic type subpersonality a bit more.

I associate the right brain with the 9th and 12th houses and
Jupiter and Neptune. The right brain sees wholes. You can show
the right brain a bunch of dots and it can visually connect them

into a picture. Marilyn Ferguson, who wrote *The Aquarian Conspiracy*,[13] summed up the distinction between the left and right brains very succinctly: "The left brain takes snapshots, the right brain makes movies."

Mystical types (9th, 12th, Jupiter, Sagittarius, Neptune, Pisces) often live in the realm of possibilities. Someone with these placements prominent may have a Walter Mitty or Billy Liar type subpersonality: they dream their life away in fantasies of glory and heroism. Mystics reach for the ineffable. Someone strongly identified with the mystic is just looking for one peak experience after the next. They don't like the mundane realities of everyday life. They want the heights, the glamour, the other-worldly—not cleaning the sink and paying the gas bill. They are looking for the ultimate knowledge which will release them from bondage. They are looking to be swept up into something. They need a great deal of space or freedom to broaden their awareness and explore farther-out realms. Their anathema is restriction, being bounded or tied down. One of the main mystic distortions is, "In order to be spiritual, you have to drop out—you have to live on a mountain—you can't have a nine-to-five job." A related distortion is, "In order to be spiritual, you have to destroy the ego—you shouldn't have any ego or individuality."

While the pragmatist may suffer an existential crisis, the mystic may suffer what is called a crisis of duality. This is when they have all these spiritual ambitions and high ideals of love and unity and self-images of being all-loving and enlightened, *but* they still feel like killing anyone who rings up or disturbs them in the middle of a meditation. They suffer because of the discrepancy between where they believe they should be and where they are. Or there is a huge gap between their ideals and what is going on in their gut.

The pragmatist is threatened by a mystic takeover and fears losing his or her boundaries—fears formlessness. The mystic however fears being trapped in a prison of material concern or petty, everyday trivialities. But in actual fact, the mystic and the pragmatist need each other. The everyday personality is the vehicle through which higher awareness is expressed. The mystic has the

---

[13]Marilyn Ferguson, *The Aquarian Conspiracy* (Los Angeles: Jeremy Tarcher, 1981; and London: Granada, 1981), 82.

vision and bigger picture, while the pragmatist has the ability to bring the vision down to earth and make it practical. The mystic may have healing powers, but the pragmatist knows the techniques which enable that healing to be channelled. Do you see what I mean? If people come to you with this dilemma, the way to work with them is to make them aware that the two parts need each other. The mystic can make life more meaningful for the pragmatist; and the pragmatist can help the mystic to accomplish things. Not to accept the pragmatist is akin to not wanting to be a separate individual—not wanting to grow up—or saying no to life.

If you have a client who has the mystic-pragmatist split, or if you feel it yourself, you can try this technique. Have three chairs in the room. Have one chair be the pragmatist, another chair be the mystic and the third chair be the observer chair. Sit in the pragmatist chair and talk from there—just spout all that it believes in and values. Then sit in the mystic chair and talk from there. You can move back and forth from the pragmatist chair and the mystic chair and the two of them can have a dialogue or argument or whatever. Then sitting in the observer chair, comment on how the two might get along better or reach some sort of synthesis. You may think this sounds silly, but I've tried it often and it does help to sort out these different sides. So if someone has the Sun in Virgo, Moon in Capricorn and Pisces rising with Jupiter on the ascendant, she might try this. Or if someone has the Sun in Taurus in the 2nd house but six planets in the 9th and 12th houses, then he could see how this works.

Audience: I think pragmatists worry more about little details.

Howard: Yes. Let's say you have to give a lecture. The pragmatist (a strong Gemini, Virgo, 3rd or 6th house for instance) will struggle trying to get every word in the lecture sorted out before having to speak. But the mystic (more 9th and 12th, Jupiter and Neptune) may think, "I'll just leave it to the night I give it and the cosmos will make sure the right words come out." The mystic can be so "up there" that he trips over the furniture. The pragmatist may be so narrow-visioned that he can't see the bigger picture.

I attract a lot of clients with the mystic-pragmatist dilemma. In some cases, one year they come and see me and all they talk about is how they want to be enlightened and just go away and meditate all the time. The next year they come back again and tell

Table 1. Subpersonality Structures

Type	Basic Drives	Signs	Planets	Houses	Elements	Distortions
Love Type	Strong need to belong, relate and be included. Sensitive and receptive to the environment.	Builds up around placements in ♋, ♎, ♓	Builds up around a prominent ☽, ♀ or ♆	Strong 4th, 7th or 12th	Emphasis in water signs	Too concerned with what others think. Lack of discrimination. Difficulty establishing boundaries.
Will Type	Expresses a drive for power and self-expression; "you adjust to me."	Builds up around placements in ♈, ♌, ♏, ♑, ♒, (also ♉ and ♐)	Builds up around a prominent ☉, ♂, ♅ (also ♃, ♄, ♇)	Strong 1st, 5th or 10th	Emphasis in fire signs.	Power-tripping; selfishness; over-competitive; over-controlling; boundaries too tight.
Change Type	Driven by a need for progress, transformation, and change	Builds up around placements in ♈, ♐, ♊, ♒	Builds up around a prominent ☿, ♃, ♅, or ♂	Strong 3rd, 9th or 11th	Emphasis mainly in fire and air	Changing for the sake of change; an inordinate fear of boundaries and limits.

Table 1. Subpersonality Structures (continued)

Type	Basic Drives	Signs	Planets	Houses	Elements	Distortions
Maintenance Type	Strong need to consolidate and contain; desire to ground, anchor, preserve and maintain.	Builds up around placements in ♑ and ♉ (also ♋ and ♍)	Builds up around a strong ♄	Strong 2nd, 4th, 6th or 10th	Emphasis in earth signs	Stubbornness and inertia; too much conventionality; maintaining the *status quo* because of fear of the unknown
Mystic Type	Seeks escape from the mundane, transcendence and spiritual expansion; right-brain types.	Builds up around placements in ♐ and ♓ (also ♒)	Builds up around a strong ♃ or ♆ (also ♅)	Strong 9th, 11th or 12th	Emphasis mainly in fire and water	You have to "drop out" or "destroy the ego" to be spiritual; too much dreaming and living in realm of possibilities and not enough grounding
Pragmatist Type	Exhibits an urge to make boundaries and draw distinctions; ability to deal practically with the environment; left-brain types.	Builds up around placements in ♉, ♍ and ♑ (sometimes ♊)	Builds up around a prominent ♄; or a strong ☿ in earth	Strong 2nd, 3rd, 6th or 10th	Emphasis mainly in earth signs	Too down to earth; not enough vision; lack an over-view of life. "If I can't see it, then it doesn't exist."

me that they just want to earn a lot of money and get some security. Table 1 on pages 208 and 209 summarises some of the subpersonality structures and their possible astrological significators we have discussed so far.

HEAD, HEART, AND BELLY

I've been working with the idea over the last year that life can be lived on three different levels—the head, the heart, and the belly. Helen Davis, a psychotherapist in London, stimulated my thinking in this area. Subpersonalities can form from head, heart, or belly energy. Let me explain this more clearly.

Anything that is going on inside or outside us can be experienced on these different levels. For example, let's say that somebody is meant to meet you and they have kept you waiting for an hour and a half and they still haven't shown up. You can deal with this situation via the head. The head may try to understand what is happening: you check your diary to see if you have the right time or place. The head may look for some sort of conceptual framework to understand what is going on. The head may even think that the reason the person didn't show up is because you are meant to do something else that day. Aquarius, Gemini, Libra and Sagittarius are head signs who try to figure things out or see their meaning. Cerebral type subpersonalities can build up around these signs. Also, Virgo and Capricorn are heady in part, because they try to make sense of things as a way of keeping their feelings under control.

Or you can relate to being stood up from the heart. You feel sad that the person didn't come and worry about them being all right: "I hope she didn't get in an accident coming to see me—wouldn't that be terrible—it would be my fault." Or the heart goes home and writes a poem about how sad life is—"two ships passing in the night" sort of thing. The heart universalizes its emotion, feeling the sadness and poignancy of it all, making a meal of feelings, and perhaps even enjoying a wallow. Cancer, Pisces, and Leo are obvious heart signs, and subpersonalities with a lot of heart may build up around these signs.

But what is going on in your belly? What is going on in your gut if you have been kept waiting over an hour and a half for someone you really wanted to see? And it's raining out as well. The belly is churned up and agitated. You can't help the belly getting agitated—it is the body's innate, gut response to being let down. The instinctive side may be thinking, "I hate him, I'll kill him, how could he do this to me? . . . wait till I see him again, I'll get him back." The belly may even be churning up other times in your life that you have been let down—like when you were four months old, flat on your back in your cot screaming for mother to come and she doesn't come. The present situation will trigger any time in your life you have been betrayed, expectant and left hanging. I associate Scorpio, Aries, and Taurus with pure belly energy. Cancer is a mixture of heart and belly. Capricorn is an odd mixture of belly—strong gut feelings— and head, trying to rationalise and figure out and hold down. Subpersonalities with strong gut reactions may build up around these signs, or if, for instance, Pluto is on an angle or conjunct the Moon.

A woman came to see me for a session—a Gemini with Virgo rising. There you have a strong head, a person trying to be understanding, rational, and cerebral. But she also has a t-square involving the Moon in late Cancer square an opposition of Mars in early Scorpio and Jupiter in early Taurus. The Moon square both Mars in Scorpio and Jupiter in Taurus suggests a strong, gutsy, reactive side. She followed a spiritual teacher and lived in a commune. For years she suppressed some of her deeper belly-feelings because she thought she *should* be more understanding and compassionate. So she had one subpersonality built around the understanding Gemini and Virgo, and another more repressed, angry and reactive subpersonality which formed around the t-square. She suppressed the more instinctive subpersonality and now is being treated for fibroids: all those years something was growing and festering inside her, even though she was trying to be reasonable.

This does not mean we have to act out and unleash belly subpersonalities on everyone, but we do need to accept them and find ways of working with them. There was a good play on television some months back, *Duet for One*, with Frances de la Tour, which amplifies what I mean. She played a violinist who was stricken with multiple sclerosis. Her husband suggested she go into therapy, and the play is about her sessions with the analyst. In the first session, she enters in a wheel chair, yet holding herself very erect. She is coming from a very adult subpersonality; she is very much in her head and has everything all figured out. She says that she knows it is a drag that she has the illness and can't play the violin anymore but she has sorted it out, she will make the most of things by taking on music students and helping her husband with his work, and this will make life meaningful for her.

For a second you think how noble and mature she is—how together she is handling things. But the analyst doesn't buy it. Over the next four or five sessions he proceeds to break her down until by the fifth session she is collapsed on the floor screaming and raging about her condition. A very angry and hurt subpersonality has emerged. She is also yelling about when she was nine years old and her father wouldn't let her play the violin because she had to go out and work at a chocolate factory or something like that. Anger and rage are coming out about all the times she has been blocked or held back in her life.

What the analyst does now is interesting. It is at this point when she is the most broken down, collapsed, and unleashed, when she is most overtaken by her angry and raging belly subpersonality, that he intervenes and says, "Okay, now we are going to talk about you taking on students and helping your husband." He brings her right back to what she had cerebrally decided in the beginning of therapy; but it is only now that she has contacted the angry and pained subpersonality deep inside her that she has freed the energy which will be needed to get her proposed projects going. Before that she was using her head subpersonality as a way of avoiding facing her deeper feelings. All her energy was used in holding feelings back and there was no energy available with which to move forward. It was only when she had contacted and owned her deeper belly feelings that she had something to shift— that she had energy to move into other things.

Contacting your raging and angry subpersonalities does not necessarily mean acting them out on others. It means bringing them to light, looking at them, being with them within yourself, accepting them and containing them until they are ready to shift. You can't transform anything you are condemning or denying, so it has first to be accepted. If you just act your negative feelings out all the time however, you may get stuck in them. The alternative between living them out or suppressing them is accepting them and bringing them into light. They may not feel very nice, but once accepted, there is the chance that you can take the energy contained in these subpersonalities and re-direct it into some other form. Remember, it is only when Hercules lifts the Hydra monster out of the swamp and into the light of day that it loses its power and is transformed into a jewel. I'm not sure we can eliminate or get rid of *everything* that is dark or negative, but once it is accepted or recognised, then it can possibly be transformed. Or at least you can think of forming a better relationship with it. We all have to accept death as part of life. We can't change the fact we are going to die one day, but we can work on our attitude toward death.

WORK VERSUS PLAY

You may have certain subpersonalities which are compulsive workers—workaholics. I've seen these build up around placements in the 6th or 10th house, or where there is a strong emphasis on Saturn, Virgo, or Capricorn. These can be in conflict with subpersonalities which want to play. Play subpersonalities could form around Jupiter in a fire or air sign, or around a strong Sagittarius placement. I have this dilemma. It's between a compulsive worker and a "goof-off"—do you have that word here?—"goofing off"? The English colloquial equivalent is "skiving." My compulsive worker forms around a Capricorn ascendant, Scorpio on the midheaven and a Mars-Saturn-Pluto conjunction. It's in contrast to goof-off which forms around Jupiter in Sagittarius, which is the handle to my bucket chart. I'll be slaving away at work and thinking "Why can't I be on the beach somewhere sipping campari and lemon?" But when I do get to the beach, I'm thinking I should have brought my books along to work on things.

Audience: Do you think a strong 5th house can also give play energy?

Howard: Yes, we can add that here. The 5th house likes to play. Also, I've noticed that some people with Venus or Jupiter in the 11th house may fritter away a lot of time in a social whirlpool.

Audience: I have Venus rising in Libra and I like to loll about a lot.

Howard: Yes, certain strong placements of Venus could give a play-type subpersonality.

I try to do time-sharing with these two subpersonalities. When I am working, I tell Goof-off, "Don't worry, you'll get your turn—pretty soon I'll take a week off to do nothing." And when I'm taking time off I say, "Don't worry Compulsive Worker. I haven't forgotten you. Next week I'll work extra hard to get things done."

THE FREEDOM-CLOSENESS DILEMMA

This one is a variation on love-will and change-maintenance and it is very common. Almost everyone I mention it to can relate to these contrasting pulls. One part of the person, or one subpersonality, wants freedom, independence, adventure, experimentation, while another part or subpersonality seeks stability, partnership, closeness and security with another person. Where do you think freedom needs show up?

Audience: It's similar to the change placements. Aries, Gemini, Sagittarius and Aquarius need a lot of space and freedom. Mercury needs variety and Jupiter and Uranus can get restless with what is known.

Howard: Yes, exactly. A lot of fire and air will tend toward this side as well—and maybe a strong 1st or 9th house. The 3rd and 11th need a variety of experiences as well. What placements would you attribute to the need for closeness?

Audience: Taurus and Cancer are the first that come to mind. Also the Moon and Venus.

Howard: Yes, these all have strong urges to relate and be close. Earth and water need that kind of security as well. A strong 4th and 7th house will exhibit closeness needs. Scorpio and the 8th often have a need for intense, consuming relationships. Can you think of any configurations in the chart which would highlight this dilemma?

Audience: Maybe if someone had Venus square Uranus. One part wants to be close and relate, but the Uranus part likes space and independence.

Howard: Yes, any others?

Audience: Something like the Moon in Taurus square Venus in Aquarius. Taurus wants security and Aquarius likes to try different things.

Audience: I have the Sun in Sagittarius inconjunct Moon in Cancer and I feel this conflict strongly. My Sagittarius part wants to be free to travel and my Moon in Cancer likes to be at home with my partner. He's an Aries with Cancer rising so I guess he has the same problem.

Howard: Maybe you should buy a caravan to live in—or a boat. Then you can have your home but move around as well.

Let's examine one of these more fully. Take a woman with Venus inconjunct Uranus. The Venus side wants closeness and relatedness, while the Uranus side may not want to be pinned down in a conventional relationship. Very often it happens that if we have such a conflict, we will side with one end of it and deny the other. So this woman may identify with her need for closeness and intimacy, and deny her Uranian side. Remember what Jung said, however. To paraphrase him, anything we deny in ourselves we attract from the outside and call it fate. So she is identified with her Venus side and denies her Uranian side. What happens?

Audience: She attracts someone who is Uranian and doesn't want to be tied down.

Howard: Yes, she'll consciously or unconsciously choose someone or end up with someone who may walk out on her at some point. Or she may end up with someone who doesn't want something so conventional. In this way, she is forced to come to terms with Uranus. It looks as if it is outside her, but she wouldn't have attracted it unless it was in her. Let's say her Uranian partner does pick up and leave. After this she may go through a hard and lonely period for a while, but then she discovers she likes having her freedom and independence. So she flips into her Uranian side and wants to preserve her individual space and not really get committed. What might happen at that point?

Audience: She meets someone who is all Venusian or Cancerian or something and he just wants to settle down into an enduring partnership and cosy love nest.

Howard: Yes, she has identified with Uranus, so life brings her Venus. Hopefully, over a time, some sort of balance can be reached and she can sort out her own conflict about her needs for both closeness and freedom. This would work best if she met someone who had a similar dilemma. Then in the morning, he could wake up and say, "Alright darling, how do you feel today? Do you feel like being Uranian and independent or do you feel like being held and being close?" It will take a fair degree of maturity on the part of both partners to be able to gracefully accept that there are times when the other person would prefer not to be that close and not throw a tantrum about it.

CRITICS AND SABOTEURS

I wanted to mention a few other common subpersonalities to watch out for. First of all there is the critic or the judge. This can mean you criticising others or yourself. Usually it's yourself. It is related to the Freudian concept of the super-ego: you *should*, you *ought*—those kinds of injunctions. It is like having someone sitting on your shoulders commenting on everything that you do. His favourite phrase is, "I'm sorry, but that is just not good enough." A strong Saturn—Saturn in the 1st house, on the ascendant, on the MC or IC, conjunct the Sun or Moon, etc.—can give rise to a critic subpersonality. Someone with a strong placement in Virgo may also have it, or strong 6th house placements. The critic can team up with the saboteur subpersonality and between the two of them you'll get nowhere. Everytime you start to do something, the saboteur gets the critic going and you are stopped dead in your tracks.

How do you work with the critic? When my critic subpersonality comes in, I acknowledge it and then ask it to go away nicely. I remind it that no one can be perfect right away and that it is a process of creating and adjusting, creating and adjusting, and more creating and adjusting. I do try to determine if the critic has any good advice to offer, but more likely than not, he is just giving me a hard time for the sake of it.

The critic or the judge may be the voice of one or both parents which, as a child, you internalized. The saboteur, however, is something in yourself which likes to pull the rug out from under your feet. The saboteur doesn't like to see you succeed or do anything which makes you feel good about yourself. It is almost as if the saboteur is saying that you don't have a right to be a somebody or to have what you want. The saboteur makes sure that you are at the right place at the right time for the *wrong* thing to happen— *negative synchronicity*. I've seen the saboteur most closely connected with Pisces, Neptune and the 12th house. Isabel Hickey used to say that if you misused a planet in the 12th, it would be the cause of your undoing. I see it another way as well. The whole Piscean principle (along with Neptune and the 12th) has to do with letting go of attachments and giving up your separate-self sense. A distortion of this is, "I can't have anything I want," or, "I must sacrifice what I want." So, whenever you are about to achieve something you want, you undermine yourself and are back to zero again—back to being non-defined again. There is almost a sense of guilt in achieving what you want or doing something which makes you feel special. Another part of you is saying, "Who are you to feel distinct and special, because really your true nature is boundless." (The victim and the martyr subpersonalities are close cousins to the saboteur.)

There is a simple answer to all this and something you might try telling your saboteur if he, she, or it is of this ilk: *Universality does not exclude individuality*. Think about it. On one level we are infinite, unbounded, universal beings, and yet on another level we have a discrete and separate identity. Our individuality needs to be developed and worked on just as much as that part of us which is at one with everything else. The little everyday self has its needs and wants. Too many people try to turn their personality into "the higher Self." Render unto the ego what is the ego's and render unto the higher Self what is the higher Self's.

THE INNER CHILD

We all have child subpersonalities. There may be the hurt child or the frightened child. If you discover a hurt or frightened child in yourself, be sure to take some time to talk to it and give it love. Reassure it. Ask it what it wants and needs. Offer to give it a treat.

Stroke it. As you do that the hurt child will become stronger and more confident and like itself better.

Transactional Analysis talks about the Adapted Child. Remember Good Kathleen—she was an adapted child. She conformed to her view of what her parents needed her to be in order to win love. But there is also the healthy child or the natural child—that part of us which is perpetually childlike, spontaneous, innocent and open to life. We should never get rid of that child.

A Subpersonality Guided Meditation

Let's do an exercise.

1) Close your eyes and go inside to the inner space in you. Use breathing to release any tension inside you. Don't try to force thoughts or feelings away, just let them be.

2) Imagine you are in a summer meadow or field. It may be one you already know or one you just make up. Look around at the details of the field. See the grass, smell the flowers, listen for any sounds. Take half a minute to do this.

3) Now you look out and see a house in the distance. There is a path towards that house. Walk down the pathway leading there. As you get closer you see a sign over the door which says "Subpersonality House."

4) Stand outside the door. Become aware of the outside of the house: what are the doors and windows like? Is it quiet or noisy, in good state or in disrepair? Take a few seconds to notice the house.

5) Now step back a few feet and invite three of your subpersonalities to come out of the house—three aspects of yourself. Have them come out and talk to you. It's okay if they are animals, funny figures, or only shapes.

6) Let them show themselves to you. Watch them for a while—how do these three interact with one another?

7) Focus your attention onto one of these subpersonalities. Go for the one with the most interest for you. Ask the other two to

go back into the house. So just you and this other one are standing together.

8) Have a talk or dialogue with this part of you. Listen to what it has to say to you. Ask it what it needs from you. Ask it what it has to offer you. Is there anything you want to say to it? Tell it how you feel about it. I'll give you a few minutes to do this.

9) Ask yourself how does this part of you manifest in your life? When does it come into being in your life?

10) Now become that part of you—step into it. See what it is like to become that subpersonality. How would it be to live all your life from this one place? When you are in this place, what is it that you really need or have to give? Take a few minutes to explore this.

11) Now step out of this part, back to where you were. See it again in front of you. How do you feel about it now? Is there anything you would like to say to this part?

12) Now bid farewell to it and let it go back into the house. (You can talk to it again at some other time if you wish.)

13) If you were to name this part of you, what might that name be?

14) When ready, slowly and gently bring yourself back to this room and write about what you have experienced.

Now break up into groups of two and discuss your experiences with your partner. It helps to clarify things to talk about it. Be sure to see what parts of your chart this subpersonality and the two others relate to. Does anybody want to share with the group what happened in that exercise?

Audience: I don't know what to do about mine—I had a wild raging wolfman who wanted to kill me. I think he is related to Mars and Pluto in my chart. I've known about this part for a while, but in different forms. It's like a madman who is totally insane and wants to kill for the sake of killing. What should I do with him?

Howard: If a subpersonality comes up in the form of a wild animal, then it usually means that it represents energy in us which is still in a primitive form. First, this wolfman has to be accepted as part of you. Sometimes it helps to draw or paint a subpersonality in order to deepen your relationship to it. If you repress that part, it probably won't become any better. Acceptance allows the healing to work. This doesn't mean to act it out, but to form a relationship with this part of you. Find out what the wolfman is so angry about. You may have to look at that bit of you which is angry enough to kill—a more savage bit. Think of how much energy is locked up in that part of you and what it could do if it were channelled constructively. The wolfman needs some looking after. Give him something soothing to drink. Eventually, he'll calm down if you pay him some attention. Here is another thing that helps—envision yourself climbing up a mountain with your subpersonality. As you get more and more elevated, keep in touch with him. You may see him go through changes or subtle transformations—he may even change into something completely different. When you reach the top, let the sun shine down on the two of you. At this point, let the subpersonality talk some more to you. If you are afraid to go up the mountain alone with it, then bring someone else along whom you trust and who can help you out if you run into difficulty.

Audience: Oh yes—I forgot to mention. I also had a nun subpersonality. The nun had the wolfman on a leash.

Howard: So there are two sides of you, the nun and the wolfman. And she keeps him on a lead. They have an interesting relationship! Well, I would have the nun get her boots on as well and come with you and the wolfman up the mountain. By taking it up the mountain, you are helping to elevate its underlying archetypal drive.

Audience: You know, my first impulse was to try to poison the wolfman.

Howard: I don't think you'll get too far with him that way. Try chicken soup. Or if there is a clear pool halfway up the mountain, pause and take a drink with him. Water can be very cleansing.

That was a meaty image. If you are in therapy with someone, that image could lead on to much productive work. If you are not, it might be good to find someone with whom you could work on that subpersonality. Any of you who had a difficult subpersonality can try this technique of taking it up a mountain with you.

• • •

Subpersonalities are like people: if we accept them, listen to them and treat them with understanding, they will usually open up and give us more of themselves. And, underneath it all, they all have a natural and basic archetypal drive or principle which is part of the great round of life.

In some transpersonal, superconscious realm, there is room in life for all the different archetypes. There is a time to be loving and patient and a time to be wilful and stern. There is a time to make changes and a time to stay where you are. I'm getting biblical! On the level of everyday reality, however, the ego or personality gets confused about whether to be this way or that way at any particular time. Nonetheless, in their pure form, archetypes are all vital and necessary facets of life. The astrological chart is not only helpful in enabling us to diagnose what subpersonalities might be present, but the symbolic language of astrology allows us to glimpse the deeper, underlying archetypal principles involved. To try to ruthlessly eliminate a subpersonality means that we might lose contact with that archetypal principle and with one of the elements which make up the rich fabric of life itself. Accept the subpersonality and see what principle it might be a distortion of. The chart shows the dance the archetypes are doing with one another at birth. Life is all one big dance.

Thanks for coming and be sure to take all your subpersonalities with you when you leave. Remember, you never walk alone!

PART FOUR

PUER AND SENEX

Come away, O human child!
To the waters and the wild
With a faery, hand in hand,
For the world's more full of weeping than you
  can understand.

—William Butler Yeats

THE ARCHETYPAL IMAGE OF THE PUER

I would like to begin today's seminar by considering the image of the *puer aeternus*, the eternal youth, as it appears in myth, and what it might mean both on an inner level in the psychology of the individual and on an outer level in terms of behaviour. Then we can look at the astrology of the puer, and which particular factors in a horoscope might point to this mythic figure as an important theme in the individual's life. Later on in the day we can also examine one or two example charts, so that you can see how this material might work out in practise.

There is a great fascination about the puer, which is evident here today in the fact that this seminar is full with a long waiting list. Obviously the theme of the puer appears to attract a great number of people. This seems to be particularly true in the astrological field, because one of the puer's meanings—one of the things the image symbolises—is a kind of spiritual aspiration, a longing to escape the earth. Naturally we will find the puer more active in an astrology seminar than we might if we were having a conference on interest rates at Lloyds Bank. Another reason why the puer might be particularly relevant at the present moment is that his image personifies new ideas and new potentials which are emerging from the collective unconscious. The puer is the enemy of stagnation, and whenever you hear the word "liberation" you know that he is at work. Anything concerned with the liberation of the spirit and the mind is his domain. Many dimensions of the esoteric field belong to his realm, so you can already begin to get a feeling of what archetypal pattern in life he might represent.

I will try to give you as clear a definition as I can of that word archetype, since the question will inevitably come up later. You should, of course, read Jung on this, particularly *The Archetypes and the Collective Unconscious*.[1] The puer aeternus is an archetypal image. This means that he is an image—spontaneously created by

[1] C.G. Jung, *The Collected Works of C.G. Jung: The Archetypes and the Collective Unconscious, Vol. 9, Part 1* (Princeton, NJ: Bollingen Series, Princeton University Press, 1968; and London: Routledge & Kegan Paul, 1959).

the unconscious, and found in the myths, fairy tales and legends of every nation as well as in the dreams and fantasy products of individuals—of a particular instinct or universal drive, not only in human nature but in life itself. When we consider mythic images such as the earth mother or the heavenly father, these are images of patterns which are inherent in life and which human beings experience as divine because they are compelling, powerful and transpersonal. An archetypal image is a subjective portrait by the psyche of how the psyche experiences these innate and compelling patterns. We associate value and meaning to these instinctual drives, which presumably the animal kingdom cannot, and so the archetypal image for a human being contains a feeling-tone and a value system. It is not merely a flat picture of something going on in the body. Human beings experience their instincts as divine figures with a story, because the instincts have such tremendous power and are beyond or greater than the conscious will; and they also have intent, and are moving toward a goal of some kind. Hence, the story.

So when we consider the puer, one of the things we are look-ing at is an image which encapsulates a spiritual instinct. That may sound like a contradiction in terms, but it would seem that spiri-tual aspiration is as much an innate instinct in us as the urge to reproduce. This has nothing to do with formal religious structures, although the beginnings of all formal religions are marked with some kind of unique and cataclysmic revelation which must be imparted to others. But the puer is more concerned with the aspi-ration toward eternal life, toward some experience of the spirit which will lift man out of the inevitability of mortality, corruption and death and bondage to heredity and fate. James Hillman has expressed this theme of aspiration very nicely in his book, *Puer Papers*:

> The concept 'puer aeternus' refers to that archetypal dominant which personifies the transcendant spiritual powers of the col-lective unconscious.[2]

The puer is a symbol of something which is innate in all of us. He is a dimension of the collective unconscious, not just a particular person's psychological pattern. But it seems—and this is one of

---

[2]James Hillman, *Puer Papers* (Dallas: Spring Publications, 1979), 23.

the areas where depth psychology is supported and enhanced by astrology—that archetypal dominants like the puer may be more active in some individuals than in others, and not just because of environment, parental influence, or cultural attitudes. There may be an innate predisposition to express more of a particular archetypal dominant in an individual life, and that means not only the mythic figure but the story as well. This is perhaps one of the things we mean by destiny.

I would like to spend some time talking about this issue of the spirit, because it is another one of those words, like love, which means different things to different people. When I use it to describe the puer, I am connecting it with an experience of eternity and immortality, with something that does not grow old and die as the body does. The puer struggles against bondage to nature and the inevitable cycle of organic life. So one of his frequent mythic characteristics is that he is immortal, a divine child, or that, if he does die, then he will be resurrected. Fate and corruptibility are connected with the realm of the Great Mother, because it is the world of the body, which springs from the maternal womb and returns to the maternal earth. All things that live on the earth are fated to have their cycle and their season. They are born, they grow, they mature, they begin to wane, they disintegrate and they die. But the puer is that longing in us to be free of these things. He may have incarnated through a corporeal mother in the myths, but he does not feel himself to be a part of her world, for he is engendered by a spiritual father, a god, and therefore embodies the aspiration to transcend the mother's domain. You can see that the image of the puer stands at the core of every religion which concerns itself with a relationship to the eternal and incorruptible spirit. This is obvious when we look at the central motif of Christianity.

Hillman has also written that "puer figures are avatars of the Self's spiritual aspect." So we are here confronting the figure of the messiah or redeemer, the one who carries the message of freedom from earthly bondage, sin, and death. At the dawn of the Christian era, this message broke through into collective consciousness with such immense power that we might consider it one of the most profound examples of how an archetypal dominant can overwhelm an entire society. Here the spirit of the puer proclaimed: "You are not bound by Rome, nor by the world, nor by *rex mundi*, the Lord of the World. You are not bound by death, pain and sin. Here is the vision of the Kingdom of Heaven, which I promise to you." By phrasing the puer's message in this way I am not suggesting anything about the historical Jesus, although one might fruitfully speculate. But I am suggesting that the receptivity to this message on the part of the collective consciousness of the time guaranteed that it would take root, so that the mythic, or archetypal, figure and the historical person crossed paths and resulted in a new religion with a semi-human, semi-divine figure at its core. The experience of the avatar, which is usually projected from the collective unconscious outside onto a human carrier rather than felt as an inner and individual revelation, is very bound up with the figure of the puer. This avatar declares: "I know the secret of immortality, which I will communicate to you provided you make the proper commitment and sacrifice your attachment to the mother's world." The puer is always the son of God the Father, sent down from Heaven to carry the message of the spirit. He is the divine messenger, or, if you want to consider it from another perspective, he is an image of our human longing and our human potential for the experience of meaning and immortality, the guarantee that life is not mere biological existence devoid of purpose.

You can see from what I have said that the puer, in one of his aspects, is the divine intermediary. In this sense, he is connected with our astrological and mythic figure of Hermes-Mercury, who was the messenger between the Olympian world of the sky-father Zeus and the material world of incarnation. Also, Hermes travelled into the underworld and guided the souls of the dead, so that the messages of the eternal spirit could descend even into death itself. Hermes is just one of the mythic characters whom we will meet in connection with the archetypal dominant of the puer. Each of these figures presents a slightly different facet of the puer, as though we were looking at him through a prism, and each facet is mirrored by a different character from myth or fairy tales. The puer is hard to pin down, for the very reason that he does not belong to the world of form. One of his central qualities is his elusiveness, because something so incorporeal cannot be restricted to a constant and consistent physical reality. Spirit means so many things to so many people, and the different experiences of spiritual reality are no doubt why there have always been so many different religions, each of which proclaims itself the only one.

The puer is not a hero figure in the sense that he does not conquer monsters or villains in the world of form in order to rule on that plane. Unlike mythic figures such as Herakles, he is a hero only in the sense that the redeemer is heroic, because he may be subjected to pain, suffering, and sacrifice in order to fulfil his task. But the puer is no conqueror. More often in myth he appears as a victim, as is the case with Jesus, or the Greek Orpheus. The peculiar combination of redeemer, victim and bringer of ecstatic freedom from the bondage of the body is found very particularly in the Greek god Dionysos. Because the puer does not belong to the realm of form, he also does not consider himself bound by its laws, and is therefore beyond or outside the structures of the world. He does not recognise limitation, because his world is boundless and shape-changing—a "higher" law. So he is often "lawless," a criminal in the eyes of the world, or portrayed as mad, which is also the case with Dionysos. You can see how these themes have bearing on many esoteric disciplines where the object is to break the bondage to law, whether this is the law of karma, the law of instinct, or the so-called lower nature. Such teachings are very seductive, because they promise an experience of boundless joy and immortality.

Another dimension of the puer, if we turn the prism around a little, is the image of the divine child. The child embodies potentials which have not yet arrived at maturity and are therefore not yet fixed in time and space. The experience of limitless undeveloped potentials belongs to the puer. Potential does not exist in the world of form; it is something that has not yet incarnated. Once something has been lived out, it succumbs to limits, it has matured, it is now defined as something particular and no longer possesses that elusive "becoming" quality that potential does. So the puer is someone who is still a child, still an adolescent. He has not yet become a man, and never will, because then he would no longer be a puer. He is in the process of development, he is the beginning of something. He embodies that burst of enthusiasm, excitement, and limitless vision that we experience before something has been grounded and subjected to the confines of form. An obvious example of this might be the process of creating any artistic work. When the idea first strikes—and strikes is the operative word, because the puer brings his promise as a sudden revelation from above, not as a carefully worked out plan—it is beautiful and perfect and redolent of immortality. One is on a high. But as the idea is worked upon, in paint or clay or words or whatever, it begins to show flaws, because the created object can never be as perfect as the original vision which came trailing clouds of heavenly glory. The depression which many artists experience when they have finished creating something is perhaps connected with the loss of the puer, who, having brought his idea forth, vanishes when it has become concrete, and leaves the artist bereft and imprisoned in his or her mortality.

So the puer embodies a sense of endless possibilities. This is really what the image of the divine child is about. Even if a potential is grounded and incarnated, the divine child can always produce another potential, for he is immortal, and remains forever in a state of limitless promise. A child might grow up to be anything. Where the puer dominates, the beginning of something is always so much more attractive than the finishing of it. The puer does not stay around to see his idea completed, but has already moved along to the next one. I think you can begin to see something of what we will explore more fully later, which is the behavioural manifestation of the puer in an individual life. The constant enthusiasm of something new, and the dropping of it before completion because another new idea has crowded in, is characteristic of the puer as he works through human behaviour.

Another mythic image which is connected with the archetypal theme of the puer is the complex figure of Eros. Eros appears both as a delightful and mischievous boy who takes great pleasure in shooting his love-arrows into poor unsuspecting mortals, and as a great daemon whose awesome power holds the manifest universe together. Here you can see both the silly and undignified and faintly malicious side of the puer, and the majestic and numinous side of him, embodied by the burning quest for love and union with the divine. In Platonic philosophy, human love and sexual attraction are corporeal reflections of divine love, and we see in the face of our human beloved a glimpse of the god toward whom we aspire. This is a very subtle and important dimension of the puer, for often he is portrayed as a phallic figure, a very sexually active image, yet at the same time his sexuality is not really of the body, but is in some way a ceaseless quest for a divine embrace.

Hermes and Dionysos are both phallic gods, yet they are not truly instinctual like the war-god Ares-Mars, who has no father and emerges wholly from the mother's world. Their sexual curiosity and abandonment contain something strangely cool and detached, as though the real issue is not sensual satisfaction but rather the pursuit of something incorporeal projected upon the desired physical object. Hence we also find literary figures, such as Don Juan, having relevance to the puer, because although Don Juan and his ilk are, on the surface, rampant pursuers of bodily pleasure, it seems, if you look more closely, that they are really being driven by the pursuit of a great love—the nature of which cannot be found in the body. Once again we can see how the puer might manifest in terms of human behaviour. The puer as Don Juan is certainly erotic, in the sense that he is always in pursuit of relationship, and women love him. Yet he is also incapable of relationship, because if ever he fully commits himself to the experience of the body, then he is trapped in the world of form, and the quest for immortality is lost. I think this is why, when the puer dominates in an individual's psychology, there is often a pattern of intense erotic fantasy which results in disappointment when the actual physical partner is obtained. In the end, it is not really sex that the puer pursues.

The puer therefore embodies a kind of magical longing. It is really a mystical longing, but it often expresses as a romantic craving for the One who will give life meaning. These two things are very closely bound together. If you read medieval mystical writers such as St. John of the Cross, or St. Theresa of Avila, both of whom lived in an age when sexual desire was considered sinful, but spiritual desire holy, you will see that the line between erotic fantasy and spiritual aspiration is very blurred indeed. The vocabulary is often the same, and so are the feeling states. The *liebestod*, or "love-death," or erotic "swoon," as Robert Johnson points out in his book, *The Psychology of Romantic Love*,[3] is closely akin to the mystical or peak experience.

At this point I would like to mention two books which are currently available on the theme of the puer, and which I would recommend that you read if you are interested in learning more

---

[3]Robert Johnson, *We: Understanding the Psychology of Romantic Love* (New York: Harper & Row, 1983; and London: Routledge & Kegan Paul, 1984).

about him. One is called *The Puer Aeternus* by Marie-Louise von Franz,[4] and the other is called *Puer Papers*, which I have mentioned previously. This second one is a collection of essays edited by James Hillman, who also wrote the best essays in the collection. Both these books offer valuable psychological insights into the puer. What is also interesting is that one is written by a woman and the other by a man, and I think the essential viewpoints differ because of this. There is a certain tone in von Franz' book which implies that the puer is really a mother-bound boy who has never quite grown up and who is still tied in some way to an incest-fantasy through bonds of fear and fascination. For von Franz, the puer seems to be the image of a particular kind of complex, and you learn a lot from this book about the puer's pathology, and the kinds of problems which he generates when he dominates a man's psyche. The puer emerges here as the mythic son-lover of the Great Mother, and represents a state of adolescent psychology.

Hillman, on the other hand, writes from an altogether different perspective, and for him it seems that the puer is the divine son of God the Father. The most important dimension of the puer in Hillman's view is the relationship between son and father, puer and *senex*, which means "old man." Rather than emphasising the puer's pathology, Hillman is more concerned with the archetypal background to that pathology, and with the puer's creative aspects. Both viewpoints are of course important, perhaps equally so, because while the puer can undoubtedly be looked at from a more creative and positive perspective, he also causes a great deal of trouble and pain in the personal lives of individuals, and stands behind some very characteristic and horribly common relationship and sexual problems. So his pathology, and the darker side of his nature, represented by his ambivalent relationship to the feminine, are also important to consider. Today I will try to explore both. But I have the feeling that the puer is a difficult figure for many women, internally and externally, because for him women are primarily experienced as mother and so his response to the feminine is one of innate rejection of the instinctual side of life. The spiritual dimension of the feminine is acceptable, for this is the soul-mate; but not the corporeal one, for that reeks of entrapment and death. We can see why in Christian myth, Mary had to be pure and

---

[4]Marie-Louise von Franz, *Puer Aeternus* (Boston: Sigo Press, 1981).

immaculate, to be a fitting vessel for the puer's incarnation. The puer has a tendency to fly away from the embrace of the mother, and because mother is a facet of the feminine which exists, to a greater or lesser extent, in all women, the puer poses a great problem in both men and women. The mother feels excluded by the efforts of the puer to reject mortal life and flee upward into the embrace of the spiritual father. The puer's world lacks soul; it is an exclusively male world, although what he seeks seems inevitably to lie in the embrace of women. So if you are a woman with a very powerful maternal dimension to your nature, the puer peeping through an individual man's psychology can prove to be a very hurtful experience. The more a woman tries to bind him, the more he struggles to escape. Although I may be a little unfair to von Franz, I do detect a certain resentful undertone when she writes about the puer. This is probably fully justified, because as an archetypal figure the puer will always resist full relationship with the feminine. On a characterological level, he can manifest some exceedingly unpleasant qualities—immaturity, infantile demands, brutality, complete lack of feeling, even cruelty. But this more pathological dimension of the puer must be considered side by side with his essential meaning, which is the longing for spiritual redemption. In that sense, the puer is an inner figure for a woman as well as for a man, and stands in counterpoint to the maternal world of childbearing and mothering. Equally, one could say that Hillman tries to champion the puer to such an extent that he begins to sound like Mick Jagger writing about David Bowie. I suspect here that it is a case of the puer describing the puer. But since there is no such thing as psychological objectivity, and I am no more capable of it than anyone else, I think you should read both books.

The perspective which Hillman expresses is very important for us to consider, as you will see later when we look at the astrological signatures of the puer, because it concerns the relationship of the puer's youthful spirit to the structured, fixed, formal world of the senex—whom you will of course immediately recognise in myth and in astrology as Kronos-Saturn. These two are indissolubly bound, and you cannot really consider one without the other. Puer and senex embody our human experience of the new versus the old, the future versus the past. Without the earthy dimension of the father which is embodied in the figure of the senex, the puer cannot be truly creative, but degenerates into what von Franz suggests he is—a mother's boy. So we have two dimensions here to look at: the puer's relationship to mother, and his relationship to father. Often the puer qualities can be extremely annoying to a more Saturnian, senex-bound man, because he then becomes just a sort of juvenile delinquent and wastrel who merits contempt and suppression. This is just as great a problem as the more mother-dominated woman treating the puer qualities as immature and effeminate, or trying to eat him up. When we hear these kinds of sentiments being expressed by people about puer characteristics, it is interesting to consider the high emotional charge that often lies underneath. Why should anyone react in such a way to an archetypal figure? No person is an archetype, and therefore no person is "just" a puer. Do any of you have any ideas about this?

Audience: Perhaps all three characters are important in some way in the person's chart. Maybe if a person is manifesting one and is suppressing the others, then he or she experiences what you call an emotional charge.

Liz: Yes, I think that is really the dynamic behind some people's strong reactions to the puer. Where this archetypal dominant is emphasised in a horoscope, then the other two characters in the play—mother and father—are also emphasised, by implication if not directly, because all three go together and make a story. But it is very difficult to hold these figures in consciousness, to recognise them within oneself. We tend to think of ourselves as one thing only. Then you have a drama where the individual will identify with one of the characters, and experience the others outside in life, via other people, because the other characters of the puer myth are unconscious within that individual. The senex-bound person—where Saturn is dominant in the horoscope in some way, either by aspect or by an emphasis in Capricorn—has at the same time an immediate implied issue with the puer, because all the qualities of the senex are mirrored back, upside down, by the puer. One is the dark mirror of the other. You cannot separate them. Where the puer is dominant in the horoscope, then the senex, and the mother too, will also be issues, by implication if not directly, because you cannot consider one without looking at the others.

I think this is one of the most difficult aspects of trying to look at a horoscope from an archetypal perspective. If it were a case of merely "spotting" the puer, that would be simple. But the puer never enters the stage alone. He is not a static figure, but a character in a story, and the action of the story concerns the world he struggles to transcend—the bodily realm of the mother—and the world he is trying to reach—the eternal spirit of the father. Also, to complicate matters even further, the spiritual father toward whom the puer aspires has a dark side, an earthly dimension, which we call the senex. This is the shadow-side of God the Father—*rex mundi*, the Lord of the World—and it is this dimension of the father-principle which the puer must eventually face and acknowledge if he is to be truly united with the spirit. Relationship with the father means embracing both, which the puer is trying to avoid. So puer-spotting is not really the object; we can do that without a horoscope. I think that we need to try to acquire some sense of where and how these eternal figures move within the individual psyche, and what kind of drama they create; where the blocks lie which make relationship between them impossible, and what, if anything, might be a more creative way of approaching the constellation than simply blind, unconscious identification with any particular one of the characters.

Audience: How does the puer feel about the senex? You mentioned that the old man often treats the puer with contempt, as a delinquent.

Liz: The puer will often respond to the senex by treating him as a calcified old dictator who deserves to be overthrown. In the eyes of the puer, the senex becomes the Terrible Father, who imposes a tyrannical authority. You can often hear this in the speech of sons about their fathers: "He tries to obstruct me, he holds me back, he doesn't understand my ideas, all he wants me to do is be successful and make money." The puer will often become the outlaw who tries to destroy the authority of the senex, and once again we can see how this might translate itself in behavioural terms as a grudge against father-symbols in society—anything which is structured, traditional, slow, or demanding of patience and discipline. The revolutionary spirit, directed against the senex projected onto society, is an unmistakeable collective manifestation of the puer. "Down with the old!" is the puer's angry cry against the father whom he feels rejects his vision. What the puer often fails to consider is that the heavenly father whose love he courts, and the earthly father who earns his hatred, are part and parcel of the same archetypal figure. That is why the puer, if he succeeds in overthrowing the old man, will often crystallise into a senex himself, because he is so unconscious of where this dark mirror lies in himself.

Audience: Can the puer manifest in a woman's psychology?

Liz: Certainly. When I refer to the puer, I do not mean men; I speak of an archetypal image which is portrayed by the psyche in myth as masculine because it embodies a spiritual quality. But this figure is also part of the psychology of women. It belongs to the masculine dimension of a woman's psyche, what we call the animus, and it means the same thing as it does in a man—the transcendant instinct of the unconscious toward spiritual redemption. When the puer dominates in a woman's psychology, which happens when the animus—the unconscious—overwhelms a woman's sense of identification with her own female body, then we have what is called in the trade a "puella," an eternal maiden. The word "maiden," of course, ought not to be taken literally. The puella is in love with the spirit, and resents having to incarnate in a woman's body. Many women have an animus who is coloured primarily by the spirit of the puer. But I would repeat the same thing I said earlier—the puer never enters the stage alone. Where a woman is identified unconsciously with this spirit-lover, she will have a dilemma with the mother-principle and also with the senex, the earthly father. The puella, or puer-dominated woman, is driven by the same upward aspiration as the puer-dominated man. But she must repudiate her own physical and sexual identity to do this, and the dilemma is quite different. I would like to save most of this for later, when we concentrate more fully on the expressions through individual psychology.

Audience: I am fascinated by the comparison you made between Hillman and von Franz. I have read von Franz' book and was very impressed by it. She has a sort of basic common sense which I liked. I haven't read the book by Hillman, but it does strike me, from other things of Hillman's that I have read, that there is a kind of ecstasising of the puer.

Liz: Yes, that is what I meant by Mick Jagger writing about David Bowie. I think the puer is very strong in Hillman, and so is the puer's problem with the senex; and he must justify it to someone, probably most of all to himself. But nevertheless many things in the book are quite brilliant and very helpful in understanding the puer. I also like von Franz' book. I think it's impossible to be objective about these issues. Even as I talk today, my own description of the puer is going to be coloured by my own individual response to him, and my response in turn will be connected with where he lies in my own psychology at this point in my life. Von Franz brings a very earthy approach to the puer, which pleases many people but may not please the puer, who feels that he is having his knuckles rapped. On the other hand, sometimes the puer enjoys having his knuckles rapped, because he loves being called a naughty boy. I once gave a talk at an Astrological Association conference a few years ago on the theme of the puer. At that time Hillman's book had not yet come out, and I was very impressed by von Franz' work on the theme; so I quoted her a lot. I talked mostly about the puer's pathology, and brought out some of von Franz' sentiments—that what the puer needs is plain old-fashioned hard work to make a man of him. This comes through strongly in von Franz' book—the puer needs to commit himself to something, to get his hands dirty, to accept mortality. This is saying, in effect, that he must come to terms with the senex, or his creativity is wasted and lost. I was rather amused at the response to this talk. Several young men came up to me afterward—all of them very strongly marked with the puer's psychology—and expressed great delight at what I had said, as though somehow I had become the mother and had rapped their knuckles, and now they felt much better because I had given them an "answer"— hard work—and they could feel suitably pleased with their naughtiness and could go away very happy. Of course nothing would have altered at all in their lives except a new name for their situation. I thought this was fascinating, because somehow a dynamic had been constellated, through quoting so much of von Franz and presenting this particular perspective on the puer. No doubt if I speak more of Hillman's work today, another dynamic will be constellated. It already has been, judging by the last question. I think I am inclined now to try to stand somewhere in the middle, and keep one eye on the puer's corporeal problems and another eye on his creative potential. If I had a third eye I would fix it on the extraordinary range of strong feelings the puer constellates within any group.

Because the puer is an archetypal figure, he is not likely to change just because the ego of a particular person wants him to. He emerges from the collective unconscious and it is an aspect of the collective unconscious that he represents. I think that sometimes he is a kind of fate, and the individual who is bound to him must live his myth. Where we might have some free, conscious choice is in our response to him, and in what qualities the ego might develop to integrate and express him without crushing him. Probably we shall never force the puer into the earth; and even if we could, it would be a complete castration of the spirit, and the death of all joy and play, or sense of spontaneity in life. And he would only rise again even more forcibly. The object of studying the puer is not to put him in chains. He will never serve the senex without great violation to an individual's, or a society's, creativity. This kind of violation is often attempted by people in middle age when they begin to fear growing old and try to become more responsible—without realising what a profound process maturing is—and this creates some pretty dire emotional consequences. One of these consequences is often deep depression, and a loss of meaning and hope. It is the feeling of giving up and preparing to slide into old age and death. Somehow we need to allow the puer his eternal youth, yet also be able to live on the earth and accept our humanity and our human fates. This is the problem of translating vision into actual life. One cannot solve that problem through an eternal adolescence, yet one also cannot solve it through murderous self-discipline. Hillman suggests that the path lies through suffering, although I think we need to be clearer about just what kind of suffering is required. One of the great dilemmas surrounding the puer is the issue of compassion. How does an immortal, disembodied spirit learn compassion for human life? The puer is essentially a cold figure, although he may often be heard making pronouncements about universal love. But love of a person eludes him, because he lacks feeling. His love is of the spirit. The mother cannot offer him a way toward compassion, because her love is mixed with possession. So we are left with the other face of the feminine, the soul, which can somehow embrace the puer without binding him. Perhaps it is only through the alembic of this kind of relationship that the puer can become humanised without losing his essential spirit.

The theme of the puer in a horoscope is sometimes connected with a clearly marked problem around the personal mother. At other times it is combined with a clearly marked problem around the personal father. And it may be that there are many different facets of the puer, and no one individual will evidence or express all those facets. This is why we look at different mythic figures such as Hermes and Dionysos, because they portray subtle differences in the colouration of the puer. Elusiveness is one of the characteristics which I have already mentioned. What Hillman calls "resistance to the imposition of order" is another facet I have already touched upon, and likewise "resistance to the confinement of materiality." There is yet another description from Hillman which I think encapsulates an important dimension of the puer: "He resists the insult of an ordinary fate." It is rather telling that, when one reads about the figure of the puer in myths or fairy tales, one never finds him dying of influenza or old age. The puer always dies in grand style, and he always dies young. He drowns in a fountain because a water-nymph has fastened her arms around his neck; or he falls from heaven into the sea because the wax that holds his wings together melts in the heat of the sun. By his very nature, the puer cannot mature into sedate senility. Life never catches up with him. In the end he escapes it, just as he has managed to escape its responsibilities all along. And often his life is cut off just as his potential is about to be reached. Yet there is a curious rightness about this early tragic death, because the glamour and the beauty and the vision are never destroyed by a paunchy, balding puer with gallstones and prostate trouble. I think you can understand why this motif of the tragic youthful end must necessarily emerge out of the mythic figure of the puer. His death is a natural fulfilment of his life. Although the mother claims his body in the end, still he transcends her because his spirit is immortal and his fate is never ordinary; and his leave-taking is symbolic and breathtaking.

We might consider some of the mythic puer figures from the perspective of their deaths. Attis castrates himself against the trunk of a pine-tree. Adonis is gored by a boar. Icarus falls from heaven into the sea, and Phaeton crashes in flames in his father's fiery sun-chariot. Osiris is torn to pieces by Set in the underworld, while Dionysos is torn to pieces by the Titans. Orpheus is dismembered by the Maenads, and Jesus is crucified. Whatever these figures promise so richly, they die in youth, and although many of them are resurrected—Attis, Adonis, Osiris, Dionysos, Jesus—they never become middle-aged men, or even middle-aged gods. Thus Attis and Adonis and other mythic puer figures are linked with the spirit of vegetation, which rises in the spring with the sap and blooms only for a transient time, destroyed with the onset of winter only to rise again in the spring. Although there is perpetual resurrection, there is no permanence of form.

One can see this motif of the tragic early demise in the world of the arts, where it would seem the puer expresses himself most forcibly in many creative people. We might consider artists such as Nijinsky, the great dancer, who achieved his greatest fame before the age of thirty, and then retreated into catatonic schizophrenia for the remainder of his life and never danced again. This is not an actual physical death, but it is a kind of death nonetheless. Some of you might be familiar with the French symbolist poet Arthur Rimbaud, who wrote all his poetry before he was twenty-one, and then disappeared into Ethiopia to live as a gun-runner until his early death at thirty-seven. Von Franz cites the example of St. Exupery, who wrote *The Little Prince*. Something happens to these people which cuts them off before they have reached maturity and fulfilled the brilliant creative promise of their youth. We might also consider Mozart. Although the creative products of these extraordinary and rather tormented souls may seem legacy enough, one doesn't know what kind of poet Rimbaud might have been at forty, when his style would have matured and his insight deepened. Time is the puer's enemy. Testing his potentials against the world's criticism is too much like compromising with the old senex, and the puer would often rather escape into death than feel that he has used it all up, that there is no further to go.

One of the things which enrages the puer, or enrages those individuals in whom the puer is strongly constellated, is to be treated as though one were a mere ordinary mortal. Because the puer is the divine child, there can only be one of him, which of course is a paradox because this is an archetypal figure and therefore expresses something collective. There is nothing individual about the puer; he is everybody's spiritual longing. But his own perspective on himself is that there is naturally only one of him. I have found that a particularly annoying thing is to tell the individual who is identified with the puer that he or she belongs to a particular type of psychological dynamic. To be a type is a mortal insult to the puer, because the spirit can only incarnate once in a unique and unrepeatable way. It is the puer who, through the client's mouth, asks the astrologer, "Is my chart unique? Have you ever seen one like it before?" It is a great paradox, because on one level the experience of uniquenes, the feeling of being the beloved child of the gods, is a true and valid subjective state. Yet on the other hand, the archetype manifests in a universal way all over the world, and it is possible to line up a thousand individuals who are strongly identified with the puer and their behaviour will be eerily similar.

The feeling that "this can only happen once" is a tremendously inspiring experience. It is the deep inner sense of uniqueness, the possession of a special message or vision, which gives an individual the courage to express himself or herself creatively. Otherwise where would we acquire the nerve to assume that someone might actually want to read what we have written, or look at what we have painted, or listen to what we have composed, when all the world over, people are always producing artistic works? When the senex has crushed the puer, then we have the feeling that one shouldn't waste one's time bothering with creative nonsense because it will probably be no good anyway and besides it won't make any money. So the profound experience of a unique spiritual gift is necessary and valid and one of the most positive dimensions of the puer. He cannot tolerate stagnation or a humdrum life. The divine child is not destined for an existence of drudgery, where one works to eat.

It is interesting to watch the puer at work in politics. Politics is naturally a field where he can express a good deal of his vision, so you find him extremely active, and on both sides of the fence. But his stamp is unmistakeable, because it is both revolutionary, impatient, and impractical all at the same time. Without the puer, nothing would ever change, But his vision is always unworkable in its initial form. The puer loves to tell people what would solve the problems of society, while at the same time disliking direct contact with those very individuals whom he is supposed to be concerned with helping. He is the aristocrat turned socialist, and the working-class man with aristocratic sensibilities. We can see his dark and light faces here, his arrogance and also his great vision.

Audience: Then you would always find him delegating the actual hard work to others to follow up.

Liz: Certainly. The puer is a firebrand, not a worker. He never practises what he preaches, because then he would no longer have the energy or the inspiration to come up with a new vision.

We need to look more closely now at the figure of the senex, which goes hand in hand with the puer. Hillman's writing is again very evocative, although not necessarily practically applicable. He suggests that the puer presides over the blossoming of things, while the senex presides over the harvest. Temporality and eternity are reflected in this pair. A new idea has no newness unless there is an old idea which it can supplant. Eternity has no relevance unless it is measured against the transient. If the puer is seen as a redeemer, then there must be something to be redeemed from. Always we find this shadow standing behind the puer, the shadow of the old man. Because of this indissoluble bond between senex and puer, between order and chaos, old and new, I think that when we consider the astrological significators which might relate to either, we must consider the polarity of puer and senex with each one. For example, Capricorn, which traditionally contains so many of the senex qualities, also possesses a shadow-side which is very adolescent and chaotic and spiritually alive. Gemini, which is a sign that contains many of the puer qualities, also possesses a shadow-side which is very rigid and structured and deeply reflective. Sometimes one face is in the light and the other in the shadow, and one cannot be too certain which face the individual will express at any point in life. All we can say is that the archetypal dilemma of the puer and the senex is part of the individual's journey in life. I have met Capricorns who behave like fake Geminis, and Geminis who behave like fake Capricorns. Sometimes it flips, at different ages and according to different circumstances.

Alchemical symbolism is full of motifs about the sick old king and the young redeemer who is the old king resurrecrted. You can also find this motif in the Grail legends, where the old Fisher King has lost his potency and awaits redemption, and the youthful, brash Parzival, the puer, comes along and inadvertently bumbles into his destiny. These two are always together in myth, and I believe they are also always together in the psyche. Sometimes the puer must battle with the senex, as Theseus must overthrow the rule of King Minos, or Jason must retrieve his rightful throne from wicked King Peleus. With opposites like this, the art is perhaps to live in a way which does not entail that constant splitting and taking sides which is so common a human way of coping with ambivalence. If both are allowed to live, then it is possible to find some kind of relationship between them, not necessarily perfect but at least workable. But if one half of this pair is unconscious, then a good deal of vital energy is wasted in bashing the unconscious side wherever it is met in projection in the world outside, and in suppressing it in oneself.

To live with the ambivalence of senex and puer seems to be a very difficult thing to achieve. Once again I am struck by the difference in tone between von Franz and Hillman. I think that von Franz is implying that the puer should be subdued and made to serve the senex, while Hillman seems to suggest that the senex should ultimately serve the puer and be prepared to give up his throne when required. Perhaps it is quite impossible to achieve anything more than a reasonable compromise where one side will inevitably dominate for a time. In another sense, the puer and the senex seem to embody the polarity of the conscious ego with its structure and control, and the chaotic creative world of the unconscious. The ego is in many ways Saturnian. Freud knew this when he wrote about the ego's natural defensive position, its fearfulness. Consciousness, as well as being solar and light-bringing, can also be very tyrannical, which is why it is difficult to work with the products of the unconscious—dreams, fantasies, strong affects—without always trying to change them to suit one's idea of what a healthy individual should be. The ego has fought very hard for its precarious existence, that little piece of something which can say, "I am myself." It is understandably a little paranoid and reluctant to give the thing up without a struggle. Thus we defend ourselves against the forces of chaos, whether they are experienced within or without. This is the Saturnian dimension of the ego, which has built its sense of identity brick by brick through the long struggle out of childhood, through separations and losses and adaptations and compromises to external life. The puer is an enemy to this Saturnian dimension of the ego, because he personifies flux and

change and the destructive and regenerating power of the unconscious, which can so easily knock down all that hard work without
a moment's hesitation in order to inaugurate a new direction in
life.

You might bear in mind at this point the myth about Kronos-
Saturn, who swallowed his children because an oracle prophesied
that one day his rule would end. To the person who is very
entrenched and defined as a personality in the world, the puer is
quite terrifying. The man or woman who has firmly established a
responsible and successful life—with a house, a mortgage, a car,
a family, a secure job, and social position—will not readily welcome the lightning invasion of the puer, who appears as a subver-
sive and threatens the collapse of all that nice security. This is the
state of mind of the senex. The puer here has much about him
that in astrology we might call Uranian. Often the individual who
has become so entrenched in later life was wild and rebellious in
youth, yet with the onset of middle age the senex is naturally constellated and there is a forgetting and a fear of what it was like to
be young. Naturally such a person will not welcome the puer's
wonderful new potential. The reaction is, more usually, "Kill him."

So where the puer fears law and structure, the senex fears
disintegration and chaos. The great strength of the senex lies in
his profound integrity and respect for time and experience. We can
also look at this polarity of puer and senex in terms of the progress
of a relationship. At the beginning of many love affairs, the excitement of the puer is dominant, and his intense eroticism and sense
of boundless potentials can be quite overwhelming and ecstatic.
The puer seems to have a great deal to do with what we call "falling in love." Here we are back to Plato's vision of the great daemon
Eros, whose longing drives individuals into seeking their source
through the experience of a human lover. The puer can express
himself most beautifully through a new love affair, or an unobtainable one. But the moment a love affair becomes a marriage, or a
living-in arrangement with a commitment and a promise of consis-
tency through time, then the senex is constellated. Without the
senex, no one would be able to cope with the hard work necessary
to sort through the inevitable adjustments and compromises of a
relationship; nor would one be able to give appropriate value to
the kind of love which grows through time and the familiarity of
shared experiences. But the moment the senex is constellated,

then he and the puer begin to quarrel. The senex fears the puer's instability, and the issue of how much freedom must be included in the marriage inevitably arises. Often this polarity is expressed in a relationship through one person playing the role of the senex, and the other the puer. We have a model of this kind of marriage in myth, with the union of Zeus and Hera. Zeus is always running off to seek new conquests, and Hera is always reminding him of his marriage vows and the sanctity of home and hearth.

One partner may be overwhelmed by the puer, and begins to feel suffocated and claustrophobic in the relationship. The other partner may then polarise and try to restrain the puer, full of fear and insecurity. But what I have found, and what the two horoscopes will usually show, is that both people generally have a puer-senex dilemma. What is unconscious in one becomes manifest behaviour in the other. If they split up, then very often the person who acted out the puer in the former relationship will become the senex in a new relationship. We will look more closely at the astrological factors which might suggest this kind of dynamic a little later.

We might also look at creative work from the perspective of puer and senex. I think I have already touched on this. The puer expresses himself through initial inspiration: I am going to write a book, I have a wonderful idea, I am going to start art classes, I am going to study astrology. The sense of excitement and potential is wonderful. But as time passes, it becomes apparent that a lot of hard work will be involved if the end product is going to look anything like the initial vision. The puer does not want to have to do ten rewrites of his novel, or practise sketching flower petals for six months, or learn the mathematical calculations necessary to draw up a horoscope. Once the creative work is grounded in form, it comes under the domain of the senex. Often there is a sense of loss and depression until the puer returns with another inspiration. You can see that puer and senex are not just descriptions of psychological attitudes. They are great archetypal principles which occur in every dimension of life, human and otherwise.

There is another facet of the mythic image of the puer which I would like to mention now, and that is the fact that he is often portrayed as crippled, or lame. Or he may be wounded in the hands. Because myth has an eerie way of enacting itself through people's lives, sometimes this situation is reflected in actuality, and the individual who is strongly dominated by the archetype of the puer may be literally damaged in some way in the hands or feet. The symbolic meaning behind this seems to be that the puer is injured through his contact with earthly reality. In flight he is strong, because the heights are his domain. But when forced to the earth, he is frail, or damaged through collision with the rocklike Saturnian structures of the world. On an inner level, we might describe this damage as bitterness, or a sense of alienation. The injured hands likewise continue this theme, because we make things with our hands. Hands are very profound symbols, because animals do not possess them. It is through the hands that we actualise our creative visions. This is why mythic figures such as Prometheus or Athene are always portrayed as teaching mankind how to make things—weaving, shipbuilding and so on—because the gift of the hands is our great human blessing, and our knowledge of how to use them is a boon from the gods. So if the puer has maimed hands, then he is unable to actualise his vision, or he is hurt through the process of actualisation. It causes him pain to make his ideas real.

One of the most characteristic myths of this kind is that of Icarus, who flew too high and whose wings came apart when the heat of the sun melted the wax that held them together; so he plummeted to earth and drowned in the sea. Also relevant is the story of Hephaistos, who was thrown out of heaven by his father Zeus, and who was forever after crippled and had to walk about with golden crutches. Hephaistos is the divine artisan, a figure who can actualise his creative vision; but he has paid for this gift with wounded feet. The puer in him has been damaged. Of course we can also look at the figure of Jesus, who is crucified with nails through his hands and feet. For the puer, living on earth is a kind of crucifixion. When the puer enters the senex world, Saturn crucifies him on the cross of matter. It is an experience of the suffering spirit which longs to fly home but which is nailed to earthly incarnation.

Audience: I was thinking of Lord Byron, with his club foot. He was certainly an embodiment of the puer myth.

Liz: Yes, he was an excellent example of the way in which a myth can apparently possess an individual's life in almost every particular. Byron also enacted the puer's pursuit of the unattainable, and

the early and dramatic death. There is a very strange fairy tale
which I want to mention, called "The Girl with No Hands." In this
story, a miller sells his daughter to the devil for gold, but the girl
weeps tears over her hands and the devil cannot have her. So the
devil demands that the miller cut off his daughter's hands. He
does so, but the girl then weeps over the stumps, and the devil
is cheated of his prize. She wanders off and goes through many
adventures, but only after long, lonely efforts do her hands grow
back again. There is something in this fairy tale which can tell us
a lot about the way in which the puer works in women. Here the
girl must suffer because of her father's meanness of soul; she is
the sacrifice to his greed and his devaluation of the feminine. She
only escapes being corrupted herself by sacrificing her hands, and
thus she is a kind of puella—a girl who fears life. She cannot incarnate as a woman and cannot actualise her potential because of the
wound inflicted on her by her father. I think that very often a
woman will identify with the puer—the spirit-animus—and
remain somehow dissociated from life and unable to let life pene-
trate her, because the experience of the father has been so terrible
and destructive. The puer then becomes the spiritual redeemer
who will lift her out of the terrible pathos of the world, where
people cheat and lie and betray. In wedding herself to the spirit in
this way, she denies any human love entering her life, and it is
only through time and effort that her hands can grow again and
she can grasp life as a real person.

We might begin to look more closely at the way in which the
puer manifests through human behaviour. The elusiveness of the
puer is certainly one of his facets which is immediately apparent
in those individuals who are dominated by him. Yet there is a paradox in this too, because at the same time that the puer wishes to
remain elusive and uncontained, he also loves to exhibit himself.
There is a curious mixture of narcissism and evasiveness about
him. His divine uniqueness must be displayed, yet he does not
wish it to be pinned down in a particular structure. Another characteristic, which follows on from this, is the puer's tendency to live
a provisional life. This is quality of living in the future rather than
in the present. That is understandable if we remember that the
puer's world is the world of potential, which is always in the
future. "Now" means the death of future potential, because the
present destroys the sense of unfolding possibilities that are still

vague and far away. For the puer, whatever is happening in the present is not the real thing. It is a kind of trial run, and therefore does not have to be taken seriously. One's job isn't the real vocation, so what is the point of committing oneself to it? That might mean that one cannot go any further, and to the puer that is death. One's home is only a temporary stopping-place, so why bother to fix it up and put down roots when one will only move again soon? One's country is only a place one is passing through, because the faraway land with better and more romantic opportunities is just around the corner, so why establish oneself? One's lover isn't the One; he or she is just a passing experience, however pleasant, and the Great Love has not yet come along, so why suffer and commit oneself and endure compromises and limitations? For the puer, the Real Thing never arrives. It is always just around the corner. The Real Thing must be perfect, because the future vision is perfect, and an actual job, home, or partner is inevitably flawed and therefore can't be the Real Thing. The puer is not driven by ambition in the ordinary sense, although it may look that way to the outside observer. It is the incessant dream of more and better possibilities that makes the puer seem such an opportunist. It is a craving for a "peak" experience which will transcend all others, and when one looks for such a thing in the situations of earthly life, one will of course be disappointed. Certainly in behavioural terms the puer's nature can seem cold, callous, manipulative and opportunistic, because once it has occurred to him that something is not the Real Thing, he is quite capable of turning around and vanishing without the least indication of real regret or sorrow. But I don't think this is opportunism in the calculating, Saturnian sense. The puer's eye is always fixed on that elusive vision, which is ultimately his Great Love. The events and people in his immediate life are simply not that real to him.

Amorality is another attribute of the puer. This is also in keeping with the archetypal image, because morality has a great deal to do with the realm of Saturn on the one hand, and with the feeling world of the feminine on the other. Since the puer is dissociated from both, he can hardly be expected to share the values of either. The puer's morals are highly questionable, at least in collective terms. Social definitions of right and wrong are not really relevant to him, since pursuit of the vision is all, and moral demands imposed upon him from without are felt as an obstruction to that pursuit. Morality always implies choosing one thing and sacrificing another, and the puer resents being forced to make choices. He wants to have his cake and eat it too, because choice limits possibilities. Also, the rebellion against the mother and against the senex can mean that the puer will deliberately flout moral values which he perceives as "parental," because they seem an affront to the freedom of his own spirit. Naturally this is a questionable freedom, because behaviour which is determined by a compulsion to rebel is no freer than behaviour which is determined by blind obedience. But despite the puer's rejection of collective morality, he has his own morality, his own worship of the truth as he understands it. He may betray a lover, but he is loyal to his vision of the beloved. His is an experimental spirit too, and things should be tried out, rather than feared or avoided.

This particular issue of experimentation and amorality can provoke some very strong responses in people, for obvious reasons. The puer delights in being an *agent provocateur*, mischievously stirring the pot and deliberately treading on the corns of people's rigidity and defensiveness. He loves to taunt the senex. He works to undermine too much calcification in a person, and always attempts to open things up. At the same time, this very creative stirring of the pot can carry a great deal of cruelty with it, rather like a child who pulls apart an insect to see what it will do without wings. The spirit is not related to feeling values, so the puer is not really concerned with whether or not someone has been hurt. He is only interested in whether or not someone is growing. As soon as the puer is reminded that he is being hurtful, he will become resentful and fly away, because he does not wish to carry any of the responsibility for another person's happiness. If you get hurt, then that is your problem.

We can also take the image of lameness or crippledness and look at this in terms of behavioural patterns. The puer is crippled and therefore feeble on the earth, whereas he is strong when he is in flight. This often manifests as a quality of feebleness or helplessness in the face of practical demands. The puer seems to carry a message of: "I really am much too sensitive and special to cope with these abrasive mundane tasks, so can you please do them for me while I get on with my more important vision?" This weakness and helplessness is exceedingly attractive to more maternal women and more paternal men, and will often exist side by side with an incredible confidence or sense of superiority. The puer collapses like an infant when he is expected to walk on the earth. This is the area of his wound, which he will both hide and yet display in a most tantalising way. Yet there is also truth and value in his fragility, for the aesthetic and spiritual sensitivity of the puer are precious in the best as well as the worst sense of the word, and too much heavy clay without hyacinths for the soul will destroy his vision and all the creative inspiration which he can contribute to life.

We might here consider the mythic figure of Achilles, the hero of the Trojan War, who was invulnerable save for his heel—the part of him which his mother was holding when she dipped him, as an infant, into the waters of Styx to make him immortal. The earthly plane is the puer's Achilles heel. This is the one area where he suffers. This motif of invulnerability save for one special part of the body is a common mythic motif. Another figure who embodies it is Siegfried, who cannot be destroyed save through his back, which is vulnerable. So we can see that the puer feels tremendous anxiety around the issue of coping with ordinary life. Sordidness, banality, and ugliness threaten to destroy him. This anxiety lies behind his apparent arrogant contempt for mundane things.

Audience: It seems that the puer's behaviour is really quite normal for an adolescent.

Liz: It is. The puer is the archetypal image of adolescence. It is natural to be dominated by him during our teens and early twenties. Like all archetypal images, the puer describes both a pattern of organic life and a psychological dynamic. The former is bound up with the body, and therefore the adjustment of puer to senex is also an image for the process of ageing. The senex is the archetypal image of old age. But within this great collective pattern we also have individual natures and individual horoscopes, and this sometimes conflicts with the states of consciousness which we would expect for particular stages of life. One can sometimes meet very Saturnian people who were little old men or women when they were young, people who never experienced the irresponsible bliss of being children. In the same way, one can meet very Mercurial people who are still children at seventy, who continue to view and experience life through adolescent eyes. But in general, we are all under the governance of the puer when we are eighteen, and under the governance of the senex when we are sixty. Physiologically, that is our fate. This does not preclude a sense of responsibility at eighteen and a sense of play at sixty. Many older people do crystallise and lose their creative spirit; they stagnate and talk about the past all the time, as though the future were worth nothing. They then become very intolerant of youthful escapades which they themselves were culpable of a long time ago. It would be nice to feel that one was not irrevocably bound, at least on an inner level, to the cycles of the body. Physically, we are bound. Face lifts and jogging notwithstanding, we all grow old. And parents usually get the projection of the senex from their children, just as children get the projection of the puer from their ageing parents.

Audience: Do they always sit together within the individual? Can't someone just be one or the other?

Liz: Life would be very simple if that were the case. But I have never seen one end of a polarity strong in the psyche of an individual without the other end being present in equal strength. It seems that life expresses through polarities. It is very hard for some people to think double in this way, but I fear we must learn to perceive in opposites if we are to understand human beings, not to mention astrology. I think this is where so much astrological thinking becomes sterile and two-dimensional. For example, when we see a Saturn transit coming along, the usual interpretation is that it means a period of restriction, hard work, depression, withdrawal, and perhaps the satisfaction of achievement in worldly terms. But it's never that simple, because if Saturn meant just the senex—which is what these experiences describe—then we could just put up with it, talk ourselves into a senex frame of mind, and wait for a more pleasurable time to follow. But what makes Saturn transits so difficult is that both the senex and the puer are constellated at once. The moment we are subjected to one end of that puer-senex polarity, it stirs up its opposite within us. On the one hand, Old Cheesefoot usually brings with him the necessity of accepting limits of some kind—internal or external—and facing those things which must be faced as the reality behind the romantic illusions and fantasies. One must wait patiently, applying oneself without any apparent movement or gain, and learn to cope with aloneness and self-sufficiency. But on the other hand, this very pressure provokes a devilish restlessness that erupts at the same time, which might not have been there before. Suddenly the puer bursts onto the stage, and we feel we will suffocate if we cannot move and change and break free. The moment that the issue of commitment appears as a challenge in life, the thing that doesn't want to commit itself also appears. This is why Saturn transits are never just hard work. They are a soul-wringing collision of opposites, and if we are wise and honest with ourselves we can get a much deeper glimpse of our own contradictions and complexity at such times.

This same simultaneity occurs in relationships. A person can be getting along quite well, without an apparent problem with the puer-senex polarity. Then he or she falls in love, and immediately both are constellated, and usually the couple will make a kind of unconscious bargain or deal to divide the polarity between them. It is a little like, "You be the doctor and I'll be the nurse," except that here it is, "You be the puer and I'll be the senex." Or a person may work out this dilemma through having two lovers, or a husband and a boyfriend, or a wife and a mistress. The husband or wife gets to play the senex, providing security and constancy, whom the individual loves and doesn't wish to hurt—but all the romance and excitement are gone. The boyfriend or mistress or other lover gets to carry the meaning of the puer, who brings a sense of excitement and great possibilities opening up in life—but also a great instability. Here I am not talking about the feeling level of such relationships, but what they might mean in terms of symbols in the person's life. Wherever one end of the puer-senex polarity is strong and activated, inwardly or outwardly, the other end is never far away.

The puer-senex constellation is not necessarily every person's dominant mythic theme in life. For many people there is quite a good integration between the two, and life carries other challenges. But there are certain indications in a birth chart which can suggest that the puer-senex story is one of the core themes of the individual's journey through life. Also, the pair do not always manifest in the same way for everyone. For one person they may enact their dynamic in the sphere of relationships; for another person, the issue may lie in a work or creative expression.

Audience: I had a client recently who seems to have embodied many of these puer characteristics. His two passions were skiing and rock climbing. He hated to walk so much that when he lost his driving license because of drunken driving, he bought a bike, because he simply refused to go anywhere on foot.

Liz: Thank you, your remark reminds me of something I have forgotten to mention—the puer's love of dangerous activities. There seems to be a constant flirtation with death, which drives the puer into all kinds of hair-raising gymnastics which saner individuals would never go near. Part of this is perhaps the sense of defeating the senex again and again by proving his immortality. At some time you should read Mary Renault's novels about Alexander the Great, *Fire from Heaven* and *The Persian Boy*.[5] She describes very beautifully this burning, audacious spirit that compels Alexander—who believed himself to be god-begotten—to flirt with death over and over, pitting himself against his own mortality. Each time the puer succeeds in staying alive, he has won again. But at the same time there also seems to be a sort of unconscious death-wish embedded in these flirtations with death. Perhaps it is the longing for the mother whom he has rejected and left behind.

Audience: A lot of pop stars and film actors have died through that kind of recklessness. I was thinking of James Dean and Eddie Cochran.

Liz: Yes, they are good examples of that strange bravado and courting of death that the puer can sometimes manifest. We might also look at people like Janis Joplin and Jimi Hendrix and Brian Jones, and other singers who performed the same flirtation with drugs rather than fast cars. The death-wish of the puer is a common dream motif. Often, in individuals who have a problem containing the puer and integrating him in their lives, a dream will appear where a beautiful young man or woman is sacrificed or voluntarily commits suicide. These are often quite painful dreams, because the puer figure is usually very lovely and often very spiritual. Yet such a dream may suggest that the puer needs to die, so that he may be transformed into something more whole, more related to

---

[5]Mary Renault, *Fire from Heaven* (New York: Random House, 1977; and London: Penguin Books, 1972) and *The Persian Boy* (New York: Pantheon, 1972; and London: Penguin Books, 1974).

life. This kind of dream may mark the beginning of a depression, where the senex begins to make himself known and one thinks a lot about time and dying and what one has really accomplished with one's life.

Audience: What does the puer look like as a puella?

Liz: Fairy tales offer us some very explicit images of the puella. I mentioned "The Girl with No Hands." The lovely princess who is locked up high in a tower, and who insists on putting all the suitors through terrible tests to prove themselves, is a puella image. You might also read "King Thrushbeard," where the princess is so superior and arrogant that no man is good enough, and she must undergo great suffering before she can accept human love. Often in the tales the princess is not herself arrogant, but is imprisoned by her wicked sorcerer-father. That dynamic is often active in an actual woman's psychology—the father-animus tells her that every man is a beast, that no one is good enough, and that she must not leave him to enter life. The princess is bound to a fantasy-marriage with a beloved, spiritualised father-lover, and does not see that the dark face of this father keeps her imprisoned and virginal. We might also look at the figure of Brunhilde in Wagner's *Ring*. Brunhilde is the spiritual anima of her father Wotan. She has no will but his, until she begins to feel love and compassion for the plight of Siegmund and Sieglinde. Then she defies her father, and in doing so sacrifices her eternal maidenhood. Wotan punishes her by putting her into an enchanted sleep surrounded by a wall of fire, and rules that the first man who is brave enough to pass through the fire may claim her. The thing which awakens Brunhilde is passion. This is often the experience which brings the puella down to earth and into the body. Often the body, which belongs to the realm of the Great Mother, will pull the puella down through an "accidental" pregnancy. But the dynamic at work within the puella is essentially the same as her male counterpart. She is the daughter-bride of the heavenly father, and tries to fly away both from the maternal realm of the instincts and from the worldly and realistic domain of the senex. It is a state of eternal virginity, although on a literal level we often find quite the opposite. The puella often carries a seedy air of having had a lot of sexual experience, sometimes heterosexual and sometimes homosexual, yet she is curiously innocent of real passion and often in need of protection despite her apparent callousness. She is seductive toward the father, but her sexuality is really unformed, because she does not yet have a relationship with her own body. There are many fairy tale figures who imply different facets of the puella. Rapunzel is one of them, and so is Little Briar Rose or Sleeping Beauty, who exists in an enchanted sleep until that old devil sexual passion awakens her. The puella often carries with her an air of living in an enchanted world, untouchable and unobtainable. To come down to earth means giving up the spiritual union with the father. This is a great sacrifice, because it means becoming mortal.

Audience: Do you think that post-natal depression could have some connection with this problem?

Liz: I suspect that in many instances it does. The birth of a child always constellates the sense of mortality, because one is no longer an eternal girl. One is now a mother, and placed firmly in the continuity of time. A depression may often follow confrontation with this situation. Sometimes the new mother may find it impossible to relinquish her marriage to the father-spirit, and so projects upon the baby the fantasy of the divine child. Then the real father is pushed away, and the mother tries to claim the child as though it were divinely fathered, a vessel for her own fantasies of immortality and greatness. In this sense the puella can be a very destructive mother, if pregnancy and motherhood have not successfully helped her to get in touch with the principle of the Great Mother working through her body.

There are many fascinating mythic motifs about the problem of the spirit entangled in worldly reality. In the Old Testament we find the image of the angels of God mating with the daughters of men. Something heavenly and uncorrupted gets seduced and pulled down into the dark world of matter. There is an implication of sin and contamination around these images of the puer being seduced and dragged down to earth. I think this mythic dimension is also experienced in psychological terms, as a deep sense of guilt and sin about the body. Despite the puer's apparent rampant eroticism, paradoxically he may be ashamed of his body, and secretly believes it to be dirty. The puer's horror of being trapped in matter is not only a horror at the loss of freedom. It is also a dread of contamination, of being tainted and losing his spiritual purity. The dark background of the Great Mother both attracts and repels the puer, because it is incestuous, dirty, forbidden and a place of bodily ecstasy that leads to death.

Audience: I am having some difficulty in understanding the image you gave us of the princess locked up in the tower. When you describe the puer, he seems to contain so much movement and vitality. But the princess is a static figure. She doesn't go anywhere or do anything. What is the connection?

Liz: The puer himself has movement and vitality, but he is the spiritual dimension of a woman; and the woman herself, her femininity, is frozen and static when the puer dominates her. But I can see why you might be confused by the image. Perhaps we might think of these princesses as a more introverted expression of the redemptive urge. The puer himself can also appear as still and quiet and withdrawn, and this image also appears in myths and fairy tales. Narcissus is one of these static puer figures, frozen in the act of contemplating his own reflection. And there are puellas in myth, like Atalanta the huntress, who fly from penetration by life but who are full of movement and vitality as you describe. But I think the reason we have so many static princesses is that the energy of the puer, working on the spiritual plane, abstracts a woman from life, and from the point of view of feeling and instinct, she becomes frozen. Whether the puer is expressing in an introverted or an extraverted way, he still embodies our aspiration toward the pure, abstract world of the spirit, and the fear and repudiation of everything in incarnation. The image of the princess often describes in very precise imagery the inner problem of a woman who might, on a personality level, be very animated and lively. She may fly through life, apparently uncommitted and having a wonderful time, but on some level she has never passed through puberty and still lives frozen and unawakened in her tower. I know it is difficult to see how the exciting, romantic puer and the frozen princess might relate to the same dilemma; but it is the feeling-tone in both that is the same, and these apparently different facets really spring from the same archetypal dominant.

For the princess in the tower, no mortal man is good enough. We are again looking at the puer's propensity for the provisional life. "One day my prince will come" describes it nicely. The incurable romanticism and perfectionism of the puella seem to point toward trying to find the right man. But there is not and never will be any right man, because she is secretly married to God. Her father-lover belongs to the realm of the spirit. No mortal can match up to that. Often this inner dilemma is projected in the form of a puer-animus, so that a woman bound by such an inner constellation will constantly fall in love with rather spiritual or unobtainable types of men. The woman who has a pattern of throwing her passions away—on married men, homosexual men, men who live four thousand miles away, spiritually evolved men who reject her body—is really secretly entangled with a puer-animus who keeps her from life. And all the time she may tell herself consciously that she really does seek a deep commitment, but that the men are always wrong. This is projection of the puer onto men, and the woman herself may not seem to be a puella type. But inwardly it is the same thing. Inside, this woman is locked up in a tower by her own aspiration toward perfection, and none of the suitors are good enough because she does not intend them to be.

The puer's fear and disgust at the realm of the body often emerge in women as a disgust with their own bodies. The puer-animus then constantly holds up to them an image of incorporeal perfection, against which things like periods and vaginal odours and body hair seem very horrific indeed. I think you can see where the puer might be at work in problems such as anorexia, bulimia and compulsive eating. If this puer-animus with his demands for perfection is projected onto men, then the woman can always find a man to blame for rejecting her body. But although there are undoubtedly men who have problems with women's bodies, and although there is, as the women's movement claims, an enormous pressure to live up to certain unrealistic standards of beauty and glamour, nevertheless when a woman has a pattern of relationships where she feels her body to be rejected, then I think we can assume that there is someone inside her, a puer-animus, who treats her body with the contempt and fear which she seems to experience from men outside. This is a very difficult issue, because we create our outer realities from our inner complexes. The old sorcerer-father who imprisons the princess often does it through denigrating her instincts, and frequently this is in reality the problem which the actual father has with his growing daughter's erotic feelings. Then the body is just flesh, dirty and bad and banal compared with the spiritual realm.

Audience: Can you say a little more about the puer's relationship with the mother?

Liz: The puer forms a polarity with the mother just as he does with the senex. But in the mythic son-lover relationship, what seems to be embodied is the issue of spirit versus instinct, or spirit versus nature. The mother is possessive of the puer, and tries to bind him to her and keep him in adolescence, because from her perspective he is an extension of her, the creative potency of nature and of the feminine, and he has no right to become arrogant and assume he is entitled to a separate existence. In other words, the mother will step between puer and senex, because if these two are reconciled, then she has lost him. You can see this dynamic in many families, where the mother—who is usually full of resentment against her husband—will appropriate the son and make him her own, coming between him and his father until he begins to believe that his father is really as terrible as she has taught him. There is a tremendous attraction between the puer and the mother. The puer represents all the potentials of new creative life, and he fertilises the mother, who can live her masculine spirit out through him. He is her redeemer. She in turn represents roots and embodiment to him, and pleasure in the body. She offers to help him to manifest his potential, always providing he offers it on her altar. But what he really needs is a father, because this gift of the mother always comes with strings attached. She is so much more powerful than he is, because she has given birth to him, and can claim his body through death. Until he can incorporate some of the strength and self-sufficiency of the senex, he will always be impotent in the face of her power, which is why he perpetually tries to free himself from her attraction. In human terms, it seems a difficult issue for the puer to come to terms with lonely survival without the mother. Although he struggles against her, he keeps flying back to her, secretly asking for the very thing he fears. Behind every dominant mother there is also a dependent son. The mother seduces the puer through the senses and through his need of her. But it is a terrifically ambivalent relationship. It can become very negative and destructive in personal terms. The puer ultimately needs to be about his father's business. He cannot make a true relationship with the feminine realm without a sense of manly potency, because otherwise the feminine always appears as the powerful and, threatening mother.

The Great Mother is also the great comforter, the one who will heal the damaged hands and feet and numb the pain of lonely earthly existence. She is also very seductive in this way. She makes his pain less, and therefore allows him to go on, but at the same time she keeps him infantile, because she will never allow him to carry his own pain. I think that different individuals need to explore different facets of this triangular story. For some, the problem of dependency upon the mother must be faced before there can be any reconciliation with the father. For others, the problem of relating to the father must be faced before there can be any reconciliation with the mother.

In myth we can see this difference in emphasis reflected in the stories. Some heroes, such as Perseus and even Parzival, must battle with the seductiveness and terror of the mother before they can be reconciled with the father. Perseus must slay the Gorgon Medusa before he can rescue his princess from the wicked king of Ethiopia and take his place as a king himself. Parzival must resist Kundry's seductive wiles before he can win the Holy Grail or, in Wagner's opera, the Spear. But other heroes, such as Theseus, must cope with the father-problem, in the form of an evil king or male monster such as the Minotaur, before they can resolve the issue with the feminine. The puer seeks at-onement with the father, and to accomplish this he must accept the earthly side of the father-principle—in other words, his own male body. The mother interferes with that process, because she wants to possess his body for herself. He must leave her not only for his own redemption, but also for hers. But ultimately he must make peace with her, as a man, or he will forfeit human love and warmth and compassion.

The onus falls upon the puer to leave the mother. Many men of course cannot do this, but remain in puer-mother marriages and hope that someone or something will come along to get them out. The mother will often not facilitate the separation herself, because it will hurt her; but at the same time she may push him out covertly and indirectly, because her own evolution also depends upon his leaving. You can see this pattern at work in many broken marriages. A man leaves a woman, claiming that she stifles him, and the woman undergoes great grief and anger and blames him.

But secretly she was driving him away, because in some way this separation was necessary for both of them. But it is the puer who acts it out.

The puer may often be heard to blame the mother for his ills. But both are in collusion to keep him bound, and although mother-bashing is a popular puer pastime, it is also the puer who continues to cling to the mother and does not allow her to also be a hetaira, an erotic companion and soul-mate. I have known men caught in this dynamic who complain endlessly about how possessive their women are, and how they cannot tolerate the restraints and jealous scenes and so on. Yet one wonders why they should expect unconditional acceptance for everything they do; and on closer inspection, one can see that their own rejection has as much to do with the woman's possessiveness as her nature does. The puer will go back to the mother again and again, demanding that she accept everything about him without any feelings of her own, all the time needing her love and support, yet reluctant to allow her to become anything other than a mother. Naturally this kind of dynamic just gets worse and worse, with recriminations on both sides. Usually the problem lies in both people, just as the puer-senex problem does. The puer is truly the mother's redeemer, because it is through him that she becomes something other than just blind instinct, and develops an individual feminine soul. That is the creative potential between them. But of course both will resist such a transformation.

The Great Mother is an image of instinctual life, collective and compulsive, which naturally resents the evolution that the spirit demands. The instincts are very conservative. They have not changed at all in several billion years. So the puer is the avatar of change and transformation, and is therefore threatening to the mother. Very often this problem expresses itself in the area of creative work. There is often a sense of guilt which accompanies any individual creative withdrawal into the imagination, because this means canalising libido and transforming it into individual symbols, and that is tantamount to leaving the mother behind. It is like stealing sacred fire from the gods. You can see that there is a much deeper side to this issue of the puer and the mother, beyond the problem of possessiveness and fear of the instincts. When we consider the whole issue of the redeemer, which is the puer's essential role, it is she whom he redeems. This is what we understand as the evolutionary spirit in man, which slowly, over millennia, raises life from blind instinctual unconsciousness. Often the puer can redeem the mother only by abandoning her. It seems that some women only begin to grow when they have been betrayed. This sounds harsh and cynical, but I have seen it so often that it strikes me as an archetypal pattern. When a woman is completely identified with the Great Mother and possesses no individual feminine spirit of her own, then often she is shaken awake only through betrayal. It is only when the Great Mother (whose inertia embodies the immovable darkness of nature itself) is abandoned that a different and more individual dimension of the feminine can emerge. Of course this is the worst thing the puer can do in terms of his own feeling, because he needs her love and support, and fears her hatred and vengeance. But often this act is his initiation into the world of the senex, who is realistic enough to know what must be done.

THE ASTROLOGY OF THE PUER

I would like to look now at some of the astrological configurations which might give a "home" to the puer in the birth horoscope. No doubt many of these will have already occurred to you, because some of them are rather obvious. One of the most obvious pointers to the puer as a dominant theme in the individual's life is the absence or weakness of the element of earth in the birth chart. Lack of earth seems to suggest that there is a predisposition toward a certain kind of lopsided adaptation to life. The life of the intuition, the imagination and the spirit are often very strong in such a person, and the sensation function—the relationship to material reality—is often weak and undifferentiated. Since no one person can be all things, this is not a statement of pathology, but simply one kind of human being. The puer is particularly at home in a horoscope without much earth, particularly if air or fire are strongly emphasised. It is almost as though this particular archetypal figure feels comfortable expressing through such a temperament, and will manifest both the intensely creative dimension and also the more problematic one. The dilemma of the puer, and his difficulties with the senex world of earth, are very often a major theme running through the life of someone who lacks earth in the horoscope.

Depending upon which sex the individual happens to be, I think this lack of earth will manifest quite differently. In a man's chart, the mother-anima may appear as a very seductive Earth Mother, while the senex becomes the obstruction in the world outside. In a woman's chart the father-animus who will provide for her and take care of her becomes the attractive figure, while the Earth Mother with her instinctual needs becomes the enemy. But these are very general statements, and we must look at everything in an individual chart to see where and in what way the puer and his story may be expressed.

Audience: What if there is no earth, but the earthy houses are tenanted? Does that compensate?

Liz: Someone always asks that question. I think there is a great difference between planets in an earthy sign and planets in an earthy house. The sign seems to describe the substance of which we are made, while the house seems to describe our destiny—in other words, through which sphere of life we will encounter, express and develop the stuff of which we are made. A strong emphasis in earthy houses will not make a person earthy in nature. But it might mean that the individual has a destiny which involves coming to terms with different facets of the mundane world, whether or not he or she is temperamentally suited to such a task. Naturally if one is a more intuitive temperament yet has planets in the 2nd, 6th or 10th houses, then one will have to work much harder to cope with and express creatively in these spheres of life than the person who has many planets in earth and the same kind of challenge shown through house placements. But on the other hand it may be much more rewarding, even though it is more difficult.

Strong aspects from Saturn do seem to provide a kind of earthing, even when the earthy signs are weakly represented. But here it is the senex alone who dominates, and the other aspects of earth—the sensuality and joy in beauty of Taurus, and the clever dexterity and intellectual playfulness of Virgo—are not present. There is a different feeling, for example, about a Sun-Saturn conjunction in Leo versus the Sun in Capricorn. The Sun-Saturn person may be compulsively practical, or bitterly realistic, but there will also be great internal tension because the fiery sun is forced to accommodate the senex. The Sun in Capricorn is usually a little more relaxed about it. When the puer expresses through an unearthed chart but is fated to keep meeting material challenges through the earthy houses, then sooner or later—usually later— he will begin to come to terms with this dimension of life. But he does it unwillingly at the beginning. This suggests a story where the puer can eventually become grounded in reality, but must learn to live with his injured feet.

The shadowy senex is always present when a chart lacks earth, although often he is experienced in projection, at least in the first half of life. There is frequently a very concrete and materialistic streak in people who lack earth, although usually they do not consider themselves to be like that at all. This is the dilemma of the extremely intuitive temperament who professes not to be tied to material objects, and who fears the banality and boredom of ordinary daily life, yet who is secretly very dependent on the material world for his or her security. Often such people need an earthy partner—whom they can then complain about for being too boring and stifling—who actually provides the ballast and sense of security in the relationship. Another manifestation of this senex-shadow is a queer sort of Saturnian morality which emerges out of the unconscious. It is often quite archaic and Biblical in nature, straight out of Yahveh's mouth and often very out of keeping with the consciously enlightened and liberated vision of the puer. On a conscious level, a person without much earth will often profess to be free in his or her ideas, and also free with the body—or, at least, apparently free. But often the dream-life is full of images of tremendous inhibition and a sense of sin. Matters of money and sex are characteristic areas where the shadowy senex will show himself, along with the problem of status and the opinions of society—to the horror of the puer who is apparently having so much fun playing about in an unearthed chart.

Just as the element of earth strongly tenanted suggests a good relationship with the positive side of the senex, so a weakness in earth implies a difficult relationship with him. Likewise, a preponderance in the element of fire suggests the same thing, and emphasises certain aspects of the puer. When earth and fire are both strong in a horoscope, the puer-senex problem often expresses itself quite clearly. All three fiery signs have something of the puer about them. Sagittarius is the most obvious, because of its mutability. The spontaneity, exhibitionism, love of the provisional life, and strong spirituality of Sagittarius are very close to our description of the puer. I think you all know the classical descriptions of the Sagittarian temperament, and you can see how much of the archetypal figure of the puer this sign carries. Understanding the puer can help us to understand the deeper motivation in Sagittarius much better, not to mention the peculiar behaviour of the sign. Naturally I hope you do not take this to mean that every Sagittarian is a puer. But where there is a powerful emphasis in this sign, then often the myth of the puer is a strong thread in the fabric of the individual's life, inwardly or lived through others. Likewise I hope you do not take my statement about fire as a blanket assumption that every fire sign is a puer. There are many attributes of the fire signs which do not belong to the puer at all, and when I suggest that a preponderance of fire makes a good home for the puer, I think other factors need to be present in the chart as well. For example, the fearlessness and aggression of Aries are not very close to the figure of the puer, who is not really a fighter, and is rarely to be seen as "macho." Leo's qualities of loyalty and honour are also not really in keeping with the puer, although the more childlike and playful side of Leo, and its strong spiritual sense, do accord with the figure of the eternal youth. But of all the elements, fire probably provides him with the most congenial home.

Jupiter, as chief representative of the fiery trigon, probably personifies him best. Zeus-Jupiter in myth is a characteristic puer figure in many ways. But Zeus is also the Great Father, and contains other attributes as well; and Sagittarius can also show a paternal and wise face which is quite different from our blithe spirit. The Indo-European root for the Greek name Zeus means "enlightener," the one who brings illumination. This is the role of the puer. This is also what Sagittarius loves to do most—bring enthusiasm and enlightenment to others. That is why the sign is always associated with teaching, although it is not teaching in the sense of imparting practical information. Jupiter and Sagittarius are prone to sudden insights and revelations straight from the "transcendent" dimension of the unconscious. This again reflects the puer, who can never prove his statements—he just "knows" that something is true—because he has experienced a kind of illumination. He certainly didn't get it by doing careful statistical research; he got it from heaven.

Audience: That sounds more like Uranus.

Liz: Yes, there are many affinities between Uranus and the puer. But the inspiration of Uranus is quite different from that of Jupiter. The revelations of Uranus have to do with a glimpse of a vast cosmic plan, a perception of the machinery and how it works. There is a dimension of cool logic and authority in Uranus, whereas Jupiter operates by pure intuition and an innate feeling for the symbolic realm. This cool logic does not really belong to the puer's intuitive, romantic, inspirational nature. Uranus is certainly another astrological factor that I would consider to provide a good home for the puer. But in talking about the quality of illumination and intuitive insight, I think I am describing Jupiter rather than Uranus. It is the difference between Sagittarius and Aquarius: Although both are visionary and future-inclined, the former seeks and is most receptive to the feeling of meaning in life and the power of symbols, while the latter is most receptive to the orderly workings of the plan behind concrete manifestation. Although many of you might argue with me, I would not call Uranus intuitive, not in the sense that intuition is a function of perception via the unconscious.

Jupiter is also characteristic of the puer because of the eternally youthful quality of the god and his irrepressible promiscuity. The marriage of Zeus and Hera, which I have already mentioned, seems to personify many of the dilemmas of the puer wedded to the Earth Mother, who, despite her sex, contains many of the senex attributes because of her insistence on law and form. Zeus in the myth has managed to overthrow his father Kronos, but then he is saddled with Hera instead.

Audience: It sounds as though the puer can easily marry a woman who is really a father-figure rather than a mother-figure.

Liz: I think he often does. The line is quite blurred between the senex and the Earth Mother, both of whom preside over the same realm. But the Earth Father is really a representation of law, the law at work in society and in material life, while the Earth Mother is a representation of nature and instinctual patterning. But you are right. I have known many men in whom the puer is strongly constellated who pair off with very Saturnian women. These Saturnian partners do not so much embody the seductive sensuality of the Great Mother as they do the structures and responsibilities of the senex. Such women seem to carry the issue of the father-principle for their men.

When Jupiter is emphasised in a horoscope, either through his sign Sagittarius, or through strong aspects such as Sun-Jupiter conjunctions and oppositions, then I think it is worth considering the possibility that some issue around the story of the puer will be dominant in the person's life. If the chart is very earthy but the Sun and Jupiter are strongly aspected, then the strong spirit of the puer will often be unconscious, or at odds with the structured and realistic nature of the earth. I have seen this kind of juxtaposition quite a lot in many women's charts, where there are strong Sun-Jupiter contacts but the element balance of the chart is not fiery. Then the puer is acted out through the father, who is often an overgrown boy, and through male partners. The traveller is another dimension of the puer, who is essentially a wanderer without roots. So the travelling instinct of Jupiter is also in keeping with the puer's nature.

The difficult issue with configurations involving Jupiter and Sagittarius is to be able to ground the immense creative potency of the puer without crushing him with too much responsibility. It seems that one of two expressions of dissatisfaction are often heard with this kind of chart emphasis: either the individual has too many talents and too many possibilities and does not know how to actualise them, or he/she is frustrated, bored and unable to release the creative imagination, and is often entangled with a partner who is uncommitted, promiscuous or unreliable. There is a great challenge to contain the fiery spirit in some kind of actuality without suffocating it. I have done quite a few charts for Jupiterian people in middle age, who are tormented by the feeling that they have not really done anything productive with their talents and ideas. This is a very painful experience, and the task seems to be to anchor the imagination without crucifying it. But there is a problem with this very good advice, which is that the puer naturally resists any efforts at any sort of change. He is as rigid in his own way as the senex is. Trying to deal with the difficulties of too much fire in a psychological way rather than a "go out and get a proper job" way can be just as irritating to the puer, who dislikes personal confrontation and would rather not consider that he might have a problem. There is a certain amount of suffering entailed in anchoring even a little of the Jupiterian spirit, because it means giving up youthful possibilities and committing oneself to a choice.

Whenever people come for a chart where this issue is disturbing them—the problem of actualising creative potential—then I will always try to look at the transits and progressions at work at the time, because these can suggest what the psyche is up to in terms of stages of development. Very often, in fiery or unearthed charts, the transits of Saturn are the most critical times in life, because this is when the issue of the senex will be brought home most forcibly, and when there is a real opportunity of bringing a more creative relationship into being between the spirit and the senses.

Paradoxically, the same situation in mirror-image reverse can be seen in a Saturn-dominated chart, or a chart with no fire. Here the puer may be the unconscious shadow-side, but often this rises up and claims the ego, so that the earthy individual appears to be fiery, and the Saturnian whom one might expect to behave like a senex, instead displays the longest adolescence in history. I think if you have understood what I was saying earlier about the way these things mirror each other and flip back and forth, then you will not be surprised. But I think it is sometimes useful to think in terms of a "real" puer and a "fake" puer, although that may sound like a gross insult to the archetypal realm.

Now we have looked briefly at one line of astrological significators which might pertain to the puer—earth and fire, Jupiter and Saturn. I would like to consider a rather different line, and that is the issue of air and water. When the element of water is missing or weak in a chart, we may also find that the puer has made his home. This is a rather different facet of him from the earth-fire, Jupiter-Saturn dilemma. I think what we are looking at in the air-water polarity has more relationship with the puer-mother constellation. Water is the primary element of the Great Mother—as the Koran tells us, out of water all life comes. Lack of earth poses the problem of actualising creative potential in form, and also the problem of incarnating in a physical body. Lack of water poses the problem of feeling and attachment, and the fear of emotional dependency. Feeling binds the puer to the world through his emotional needs, his dependency upon and care for others. Attachment to other human beings, as Indian philosophy tells us, binds the individual to the wheel of incarnation. When the puer begins to feel compassion and love for another individual, then he is no longer a puer, for he has been humanised. The puer fears emotional ensnarement, because it will tie him to the human world and block his flight into heaven. I am thinking of *The Valkyrie* in Wagner's *Ring* cycle, where the hero Siegmund faces his difficult choice between abandoning his lover-sister Sieglinde and entering Valhalla, the abode of the gods where his father Wotan rules, or remaining with his love and facing probable death and abandonment of all hope of heaven. While Eros, the great daemon, in many ways embodies the figure of the puer with his romantic longing, human love transforms the purity of the puer's spirit, and he is no longer free. He is vulnerable, he can be hurt. Lack of water may not impair a person's creative capacities, but it will often generate a tremendous fear of the power of the emotions, which are frequently projected upon a "too emotional" partner. Thus we see that facet of the puer who is the mother's son, fleeing from her too powerful embrace yet longing for her unconditional love.

Here we may return to Uranus, which is the airiest of the airy planets. Venus and Mercury both rule earthy signs as well as airy ones, and although, as we will see later, they too have a relationship to the puer, Uranus is really pure air. If we look at the figure of Ouranos in myth, we have very little real characterisation of him as we do with Zeus or Kronos. But there is the story about Kronos' castration of his father Ouranos which is perhaps relevant. Here the old senex castrates the Uranian world of grand, disembodied cosmic vision. Even more relevant is the story of Ouranos' dealings with his children. When they are born to Gaia the earth mother, he is disgusted by them because they are made of earth and are flawed and ugly to behold; so he casts them down into Tartarus, the bowels of the underworld. The Uranian spirit of perfection, which demands that everything fit neatly into the grand plan, repudiates the messiness of incarnation, and has a strong flavour of the puer's intense spirituality and search for purity. Poor Aquarius has both Saturn and Uranus as rulers, so we might consider that when Aquarius is strongly tenanted in a chart then this dilemma between the perfect world of mind and spirit, and the highly imperfect world of matter, will be an important issue in the person's life. Likewise, if Uranus is strongly aspected—conjuncting, or opposing, or squaring the Sun, Moon or Venus, for example—then we might expect that the perfectionist vision of the puer, and his dislike of the flawedness of form, will express quite powerfully in life.

Gemini is another sign which embodies many of the facets of the puer, and like Sagittarius, it is one of his favorite abodes. The youthfulness and ambiguity and elusiveness of Hermes, his rulership over the traveller and the thief, and his amorality all mark him as one of our most powerful mythic puer figures. But Gemini's dilemma is not the same as Sagittarius'. Here we are back to the issue between air and water, because Gemini is much more frightened of emotional depth and bondage than it is of concretisation of the spirit.

Audience: What about Neptune? That seems to me to represent a lot of the figure of the puer. You mentioned Jesus several times, and the whole myth of the Piscean Age seems to be full of the issues of the puer.

Liz: Yes, Neptune is also important to consider, although it is a watery planet. But like Saturn, Neptune seems to contain an enormous paradox. I mentioned earlier that wherever Saturn is heavyfooted in the chart, the puer will spring into being simultaneously, as his opposite. Where Neptune is heavy-footed in the chart the Great Mother is constellated, and the puer as her redeemer will also spring into being simultaneously. There are elements in Neptune which seem to be connected with the god Dionysos, whom I spoke about before—the theme of the redeemer who carries the mystical longing of the collective and is sacrificed to absolve collective sin. Dionysos and Jesus are very similar figures, and it will no doubt horrify the more orthodox Christian to consider that before the Emperor Constantine elected Christianity for the official religion of the Roman Empire, it was really a toss-up between Jesus and Dionysos, whose cult was steadily gaining in strength. Had Constantine not been swayed in the direction he was for largely political reasons, it is interesting to imagine what sort of world we might live in now. Anyway, both Jesus and Dionysos are born of virgins; both die and are resurrected; both are the sons of God the Father. Neptune bears many of the puer's characteristics, particularly the bittersweet longing to abandon the darkness of incarnation and return to the spiritual source.

But Neptune bears a double face, just like Saturn with his old man masking the goatish youth. In the mythology that surrounds the constellation of Pisces, you will find a classic puer myth. In the Phoenician version of this myth, which predates the Greek, the big fish in the constellation of Pisces is the great goddess Atargatis, who bears a fish's tail. She is an embodiment of the chaos of the senses, symbolised by the voracious appetite of the fish which will eat anything. Here we see the element of water as the source of life, both creative and devouring, life-giving and also representing the hell of the passions. The little fish is her son, Ichthys, which in Greek simply means "fish." He is a puer figure—young, beautiful, and doomed to early death and subsequent resurrection. His mother simply swallows him, and then he is born again from her mouth. He is the redeemer, the carrier of the spiritual vision, and the thing which he attempts to redeem is, of course, his mother, who personifies the voracious and sinful appetites of the world. So in response to your question, yes, Neptune may personify the puer; but Neptune also personifies the Great Mother to whom he is eternally bound. This myth is fascinating because of the way in which nature mirrors the archetypal world and vice versa. If you have ever kept tropical fish, you will know that you must be very careful about feeding them, because unlike cats or dogs they do not stop when they are full. They simply go on eating until they get very sick. There is no sense of boundary. You can see why the fish became attached to the cult of the Great Mother, who devours all life, spawning indiscriminately and then eating her own progeny. But the fish is also that quicksilver flash of light in the murky depths of the water, so it is also the elusive redeemer, the flash of the spirit's promise lighting up the darkness of the unconscious.

When the puer looks down into this bottomless pool of emotional life, naturally he fears drowning or dismemberment. Neptune's sign Pisces, which is co-ruled by Jupiter, carries this facet of the puer's dilemma. A strong component of Pisces in the chart may suggest that the oceanic depths of the Great Mother are powerful in the psyche, and that the puer will constellate in counterpoint to her. Very often a woman with a strong Piscean or Neptunian component will play out the role of the Great Mother, and the spiritual redeemer formulates as the animus, projected upon somebody else. In a man with the same constellation, the identification may be with the puer-redeemer, and the Great Mother appears with the face of the female partner. It is the same dynamic that we find with a strong Saturn or dominant Capricorn—very often the opposite of what we might expect appears in conscious behaviour, and the other formulates in the unconscious.

This business of opposites and paradoxes is very difficult for an astrologer who needs to think in a very linear and concrete way. But every astrological factor needs to be considered in relation to the opposite which is secretly contained within it, and every psychic factor needs to be considered likewise. Whenever we speak of the puer, we are faced not only with his elusiveness, but also with his secret earthiness and rigidity. It would make life for astrologers so much simpler if every Capricorn client behaved like a Capricorn, and every Piscean like a Piscean. But then someone turns up who is a Capricorn disguised as a Sagittarian, or a Scorpio disguised as a Gemini, or a Piscean who appears to be an Aquarian—not necessarily because those signs appear prominent in the chart, but because the puer constellates as a counterpoint to the dominant theme of senex or mother. This is why I keep asking you to try to think double and to not be too literal—despite the fact that the puer is in his own way a very clear and distinctive and unmistakeable figure who can be spotted easily anywhere in a crowd.

I would like to go back to the element of air for a moment, because I got sidetracked by Neptune. Neptune of course has a way of doing that. Air contains many of the puer characteristics—the detachment and idealism, and the dislike of emotional entanglement. Also, air is the great generaliser—which is why it has such an affinity with subjects like astrology. Air loves maps, because maps make the general messiness of life more orderly and keep threatening personal feelings at a distance. This is perhaps one of the reasons why people keep insisting that Uranus rules astrology, although there are so many facets to astrology that one planet surely cannot cover them all. But identifying something in a horoscope, as we are doing right now, is extremely satisfying, not only to the intellect, but also to the puer, who can then remove himself from direct collision with an emotional experience and can lift it up to the cooler, calmer and more meaningful level of a concept. The creative dimension of this should be obvious, because this is where the puer can bring clarity and light into the apparently random vicissitudes of life. He conceptualises and turns experiences into patterns which are elusive, beautiful and full of meaning. In alchemical language this is called *sublimatio*, which is that stage of the alchemical process in which the essence rises in a vapour from the base matter cooking below. What Freud meant by sublimation is quite close to this, although the implication in Freud's work is that we sublimate to escape from the terrifying compulsion of the instincts. But the puer sublimates not only as an escape from the mother, but also because that is what he is—an instinct to transform instinct into symbol and experience it at a higher level. The difficulties of life are consequently less hurtful and disintegrating, and the sense of a meaningful pattern emerges.

Naturally the negative side of this sublimation needs to be considered, because the puer threatens to do so much of it that he ceases to experience anything at all. Then he is unreal, and life is unreal to him in turn. Everything is conceptualised, which is what many people try to do with astrology. That is in part why I mentioned in the beginning that the puer is very active in the astrological world. Astrology is a wonderful vehicle for both the creative and the pathological dimensions of the puer. He is also very active in the prognosticative dimension of astrology. To foresee the pattern of the future pleases the puer, both because of his fascination with the beauty of the design and because of his desire to avoid the traps which fate, or the Great Mother, lay for all mortal creatures. Inevitably the planets which have the most to do with fate—Saturn and Pluto, the chief significators for the senex-world of the father and the instinctual depths of the mother—catch him up.

No amount of either astrological theorising or psychological insight can forestall the experiences that Saturn and Pluto bring. Although insight and understanding can help us to make more creative use of them, and can also sometimes help us to avoid acting things out in too blind a way, the nature of the experiences themselves is unavoidable. Saturn always reveals the weak foundations in the ego structure, and Pluto always brings with it a feeling of fatality and transpersonal power at work in one's life. Both planets bring suffering to the puer, although they do not have to crush him. He can still offer his gift of meaning and revelation to these planets. But they humanise him.

It is sometimes difficult for a person with a predominantly watery chart to allow the puer into his or her life, in his positive as well as his negative forms. In part, this is because the puer within us often leads us into an isolation of the spirit, and away from human relationship. When one is inspired by something, a new study or a new creative project, the puer carries one off, and it is rather like a love affair, although there is no corporeal lover. Sometimes this means leaving other people behind, and the watery individual often finds that extremely painful. There is the fear of losing the other person, and also a kind of psychic vertigo, a terror of going up too high. The puer fears deep water; but the watery nature fears heights. Claustrophobia and agoraphobia are also psychological experiences which I connect with the puer, because he fears being enclosed just as he fears drowning in the depths. Claustrophobia is a fear of enclosed spaces, while agoraphobia is a fear of open ones. But they are a little like anorexia and compulsive eating; they are opposite symptoms which spring from the same archetypal core. They both reflect the fear of something terrible which will catch the individual in a place where he or she cannot escape. If one is trapped in a lift or a closet, then the thing might get one because there is nowhere to run. If one is trapped out in the open, in an unprotected place, then the thing might get one because one can be seen and there is nowhere to hide. Phobias are displacements of a fear of something in the psyche onto outer objects which carry a symbolic meaning. And the puer is definitely phobic, because he is half of something, and therefore vulnerable to the unconscious opposite. So the opposite will always constellate fear for the puer, and this opposite—whether it is the concrete limitations of earth or the amorphous depths of water—may displace itself onto all sorts of things. Spiders, snakes, depths, various animals, germs, infection—all these are typical phobic images of the Great Mother; while earth, prison, walls, body odours and secretions, shit and money are typical phobic images of the senex.

Audience: I have the feeling that my mother has this kind of split in her, and that she has never looked at it. And I feel I am acting out the same puer-senex conflict. Do you think that children can act out this kind of thing for the parent?

Liz: Yes, certainly, that is what much of family therapy is about. But I think there must also be something in your own chart which picks up the theme, so that it is your own conflict as well as something inherited. Otherwise there would be no soil for it to have taken root in. But if the conflict is a bad one in the parent, then it is made much worse for the child than it might ordinarily have been. If you have a parent who identifies very much with the senex, then even a child with a fair balance of water and earth in the chart, and a reasonable potential for relationship with the concrete and instinctual worlds, can be pushed into puer behaviour because the child is carrying the unlived life of the parent. Sometimes you can see this quite strongly when you look at family charts as a group. The individual's chart may not really suggest the puer themes we have been talking about, yet he or she may be cornered into one particular configuration in the chart, because of having to carry the burden of the parental shadow.

One can also find the opposite—where, for example, the father is very much a puer type, an eternal adolescent posing as a responsible husband and father, and perpetually wishing he were somewhere else. Often the sons of these fathers feel responsible for the family, and obligated to take the father's place as guardian of the mother, especially if they have a little Capricorn in the chart, or a strong Saturn. They become mature and controlled at a ridiculously young age, as though they must redeem the irresponsible father. I have met women who have had to carry the senex, too, where the father has been a boy and the daughter must be the man in the family, even if she is only a child.

We should look now at some of the planetary aspects in a chart which might suggest a home for the puer, or a reflection of the puer-senex conflict, or the puer-mother conflict. A single aspect can embody these archetypal themes and can sometimes dominate the entire chart, and it then becomes important for the person to become conscious of other factors in the horoscope to help balance the puer dilemma so that it can be contained and integrated in a more creative fashion. One character in a play who tyrannises the stage so that all the other actors are locked in the green room is not really a very helpful way to live one's life, because the locked-up characters eventually burn the theatre down.

Aspects to Saturn are of course important to consider in relation to the puer-senex polarity, especially the squares, oppositions, and conjunctions of Saturn to brighter planets, such as Sun and

Jupiter. Sun-Saturn contacts are often related to the dilemma between the eternal youth and the old man. The Sun and Leo (and also the 5th house) carry some of the themes of the puer, in particular the experience of the divine child and the whole issue of creative play. Also, the Sun is connected with the mythic figure of Parzival, the young redeemer who seeks the Holy Grail and must heal the sick old Grail King. The solar quest for meaning and reconnection with the spiritual source—God the Father—is a part of the puer's identity. So you can see that a difficult aspect between the Sun and Saturn will reflect a mythic conflict between the divine child and the old man. You can also find this same mythic theme reflected, although not quite so energetically, in configurations such as the Sun in Capricorn and Saturn in Leo, or Saturn in the 5th house, or the Sun in Leo combined with Capricorn rising, and other variations on Sun and Saturn through house and sign. Often the individual will identify with one and pit himself or herself against the other. Whenever the sun tries to be joyful and spontaneous and self-expressive, Old Cheesefoot begins to list all the rules and regulations which must be followed in order to be a proper member of society and the Right Sort of Person. Rebellion of the Sun against Saturn means that authority figures in the world become enemies, and all the father-institutions and organisations in the world cannot be valued or appreciated, but become merely stifling and soul-destroying. Naturally if one has this kind of chip on one's shoulder, then the father in the world retaliates by not valuing what one has produced, and then that characteristic insecurity and fear of rejection which plagues the Sun-Saturn individual will inevitably develop.

Feelings of guilt are also part of this constellation, because one has sinned in the eyes of the father. Freud used the term superego to describe the Saturnian voice of the great They, the parent who perpetually dictates from within the psyche what one must and mustn't do in order to be acceptable to Them. This is not an individual parent, but an archetypal council of elders, dictating limits to the divine child who might be a little too rambunctious and rebellious to please them. Very often the actual parent has some of this ingredient, and is a good hook upon which to project the superego. But it is perhaps more accurate to say that the parent in question has probably been enslaved by the same collective voice and can do nothing other than pass it down to the child. This is a truer way of looking than simply blaming the parent as the origin of something so archetypal.

Audience: I have always felt that there was something more than just a socially timid parent behind that very powerful voice.

Liz: There is. It's the senex. He is an archetypal dominant just as the puer is. Obviously social mores change according to culture and time in history, but the voice of the elders, rooted in tradition and hierarchy and resistant to change, is a constant, although the actual precepts might vary.

Another configuration we might look at is Jupiter and Saturn in difficult aspect, or in conjunction. Also, we can include under this general heading placements such as Saturn in Sagittarius and Saturn in the 9th house. These are very specific configurations, and they do not make a person a puer. Here the senex takes the form, not of material restrictions, but of the voice of conscience. When I find Saturn in Sagittarius or in the 9th, particularly the latter, I will often ask the client what the family religious background is like, because there is frequently a correspondence between the Old Testament outlook of a 9th house Saturn and the actual religious attitudes within the family. The Old Testament outlook may of course be quite unconscious, but working very powerfully within the individual anyway. Sometimes the parents themselves may not be particularly religious, but the grandparents have been, and the parents may themselves have tried to rebel and have apparently thrown out the old restrictive teachings. But they remain in the unconscious and infect the next generation. I have found many people with backgrounds such as orthodox Judaism, or strict Roman Catholicism, or Plymouth Brethren, or Seventh Day Adventists, or Southern Baptists, where Saturn is in the 9th house. Obviously not everyone with a 9th house Saturn was raised as a Jehovah's Witness, any more than every Roman Catholic has a 9th house Saturn. But the nature of God, when Saturn appears in connection with Jupiter's realm, is often not that of love, but rather sternness and rigidity—a God who embodies unbreachable Law and demands absolute obedience lest some dire punishment befall the transgressor.

Audience: I have Saturn in the 9th house, and I was brought up a complete atheist. This was imposed on me very strongly. It wasn't just a lack of interest in religion. It was a flat statement: "There is no God, God does not exist." It was just another kind of dogma.

Liz: I have seen that manifestation of the senex before. Here he crushes the sense of the living godhead which the puer embodies. This is a purely materialistic view of the universe, and it belongs very much to the realm of the senex, just as the more concrete religious dogmas do. But I wonder what your parents were fighting when they adopted such a militantly atheistic viewpoint. Perhaps it was a rebellion against something in their own parents, too rigid a religious outlook. Rigourous atheism, which is a senex expression—unlike agnosticism, which allows room for doubt and question—is often a reaction to too stern a God, which is also a senex expression. Often the individual does not realise that in fighting the old man, he or she has simply become another form of the old man. Morality is often very black and white with a 9th house Saturn, or with Saturn and Jupiter colliding. The sense of guilt can be enormous.

Audience: What about Jupiter in Capricorn?

Liz: To a lesser extent, the same flavour is present. Often the sense of a quest for meaning, which is related to Jupiter, is confined to material success, and there is a kind of senex-like cynicism about life. But I don't think that Jupiter in Capricorn is quite as typical of what I was describing as Saturn-Jupiter contacts or Saturn in Jupiter's house. One can also find this dilemma with a combination of Sagittarius and Capricorn in the birth chart. The deep questioning and philosophical searching of these combinations can be very creative, and so can the unique capacity to express one's vision in a solid and socially helpful way. The darker side of this dilemma is the loss of real faith, that childlike and spontaneous faith that can outlive material difficulties. Jupiter-Saturn is often deeply philosophical, but also prone to depression if life goes wrong occasionally. The faith does not stand up to the test, or there is the feeling that God is a little nasty after all and one had better be careful.

Audience: I am feeling increasingly angry with the puer and want to hear more about the positive side of the senex. I don't know whether that is just my reaction, but I feel the senex is being treated unfairly.

Liz: Well, you could start a Senex Liberation Movement, but then you would be in the hands of the puer. I will try to speak more kindly of the senex, although I don't think I was really insulting him—at least, not inordinately. One way of understanding the senex is that he is the embodiment of law. I think one needs to think of the law which binds the motion of the cosmos, an orderly system where everything has its appropriate place and nothing is permitted to transgress its limits. That is the senex. Without this law, the cosmos would fall into chaos. Law is also a principle in nature, and is bound up with time and cycles. Everything must have its cycle, everything reaches fruition and must give way to the next phase. Nothing is timeless, or free to escape those limits. Life from the senex perspective is beautiful in its profound and impeccable order, for there is a deep connection with cyclical motion and law. Law is the restrainer and container of hubris, arrogance and chaos. Death is therefore not a terror or a humilia-tion to the senex, but the inevitable ending to a natural cycle. The senex does not fear life on earth, because he does not fear death. He can therefore savour the moment, because each moment con-tains its own pleasure and meaning. He does not need to peer into the future or live provisionally to find meaning and joy in life. Where the gifts of the puer lie in inspiration and movement, the gifts of the senex are encapsulated by a quality of serenity.

The senex can endure the changes and difficulties of life with-out breaking apart. This kind of inner strength is a quality which the puer lacks—hence the puer is lame when he walks on earth. He is weak and helpless where the senex is strong and enduring. The senex also appreciates the value of time, and understands how to wait. If one waits long enough, everything will come round full circle again. He can wait forever for something to ripen, and is not averse to the hard work along the way, and therefore he can finish what he has begun and can actualise the children of his imagination. The puer is always in a hurry, and becomes bored when the inspiration gives way to prolonged labour or waiting. If he cannot have it now, then it is not worth waiting for. Also, the senex is not shocked or repelled by the flaws and imperfections in life. He accepts these because it is the nature of reality, and uses what comes to hand, rather than perpetually wishing it could be more perfect. These are some of the more creative or positive facets of the senex, and obviously if one can combine some of these qualities with the spirit of the puer then one has a whole.

You can also see that all the earthy signs contain one or another of these qualities and capacities, just as all the fiery signs contain one or another of the characteristics of the puer. Earthy charts offer the senex a comfortable home, just as fiery ones offer the puer a home. For the element of earth, life is a serious business. Even pleasures are taken seriously, so that they can be savoured to the last drop. One isn't here to indulge in shallow play and gadding about. One is here to work, and if there is a strong spiritual inclination along with an earthy bias, then one is here to serve. You will rarely hear the puer talking about service, except as a kind of abstract idea to save humanity. Service as a concept appeals to the puer, but service that requires real commitment and not a lot of flamboyant thanks is anathema to him. I have noticed this frequently in various esoteric groups—everyone talks about service, but it is usually the Taurus or the Virgo or the Capricorn, considered uninspired by the rest, who does all the hard work of typing envelopes and collecting money and washing the coffee cups. That kind of service is not glamourous, and therefore to be avoided by the puer.

Now I would like to pose a question to all of you. Many of you are practising astrologers who see clients. I think you have now got a fair picture of the puer, and the peculiarly electric and enchanting and often irritating qualities which communicate themselves when a person is closely identified with this archetypal figure. What do you feel when you meet him in the consulting room? How do you respond to the client?

Audience: I want to bring him down to earth. I feel I have to provide some sort of balance to him, to show the person that there is an earth to come down to that isn't so bad.

Audience: I have exactly the same reaction. I find myself giving a more practical chart reading, with advice about jobs and so on. Normally I wouldn't do that.

Audience: I have a woman friend who expresses many of the puer or puella characteristics, and I get very irritated with her. I find myself saying, "Oh, you could be really fantastic at doing this *if only* you'd get it together."

Audience: I saw a client about ten days ago, a woman in her late seventies. She was talking about her mother, and I said something in which the word "woman" figured. My client pulled a face and said, "I don't like the word 'woman.'" I said, "What do you like?" and she said, "Girl." Her mother is ninety-five or older, and she felt uneasy because I referred to the mother as a woman.

Liz: There is an interesting issue around that. I don't know whether it applies specifically to your client, but it certainly applies to the puer. The cult of youth and beauty belongs to the puer, because he is the eternal youth—or, in the case of the puella, the eternal maiden. I have met a number of people who think of themselves as a boy or a girl, or who refer to women, irrespective of age, as girls. Ageing is a frightening issue for the puer, because it sounds the bell of doom. The puer is the spirit of eternity, and the ageing of the body, which belongs to the realm of the senex, is a profoundly disturbing issue. There are certain cultural pockets, like, for example, Los Angeles, where it seems the archetype of the puer dominates in both the most creative and also the most destructive ways, where the cosmetic surgery trade is one of the most lucrative and thriving of professions. The puer is very active in the entertainment field, as we have seen, and one can witness his tremendous creative life and also his transience, and his terror of the flaws and imperfections of the body. It is a very paradoxical world. On the one hand there is so much callousness and unrelatedness in the entertainment field, and that reflects the negative side of the puer. On the other hand, it is the most exciting medium in the world, and even the most scathing critic of the puer and his domain will still, sooner or later, be caught by the enchantment of a good film. Health and fitness are in some ways related to the senex—common sense about the body—but in other ways they reflect the puer, particularly when they emerge as an obsession to conquer the body at all costs and make it eternal. But there is so much benefit arising from the obsession with fitness that even if there are some very narcissistic roots to it, the puer has indeed shown us that we can prolong youth and vigour and beauty. The puer's spirit brings us the idea that the body could be made better, reshaped, healthier, more beautiful. One can see the ambivalence in this issue.

The responses you have given are very interesting, and I think also very characteristic. When we contact archetypal material, then a high emotional charge is provoked, and the opposite is constellated in our own unconscious. The puer is not just an interesting theory. He is either infuriating or fascinating, or both at once. When a situation develops between two people where the puer-senex issue is constellated, then often one can hear very heated arguments of a very characteristic kind. It is as though one's own voice vanishes, and the ancient lines begin to be spoken. There is a strong senex component in astrology, which is connected with Saturn as symbol of the law. Before the discovery of Uranus, astrology was traditionally ruled by Saturn as lord of boundaries, because the birth horoscope was said to describe one's fate, one's mortal limits. I think this dimension of astrology is provoked when the puer speaks through the client's mouth. One begins to feel that one must emphasise the limitations of the personality, the necessity of channelling energies, the need to produce something with one's potentials. The puer will often bring the Saturnian side of the astrologer into play. Alternatively, the senex tends to constellate the more Uranian side of astrology, or the Jupiterian, both of which are the domain of the puer—the sense of meaning and potential, and the idea that one can transform one's fate with knowledge. When a client comes who is very identified with the senex, very entrenched and earthbound, then the puer in the astrologer is constellated, and the issue of taking risks and making changes becomes very important. I think these responses are natural when we come into the presence of one end of an archetypal polarity. Not every client is so strongly polarized. But when they are, the opposite end is stirred up within us. There is nothing wrong with this, and also even if there were it is probably inevitable anyway. But perhaps this kind of response is what is needed; otherwise it would not happen so obviously and so frequently. The client calls it out. As long as it does not result in an unconscious falling into the split, with an angry stalemate, then a good middle perspective can come out of such a confrontation. But one must try to be conscious, because otherwise the archetype takes over and one is caught in a compulsive dialogue with autonomous feelings that run away on their own locomotive power. Obviously one is no use as an astrologer or a counsellor in such a state.

This is true not only of the puer-senex polarity, but of any pair of archetypal opposites where an individual has pulled violently to one extreme and has generated a split in the psyche. The astrologer must then carry the unconscious side of the client. Analysts know all about this kind of dynamic, for which they give the term transference-countertransference. This is not just about parental material, as Freud originally believed it to be, but also about archetypal content, which is often mixed in with the personal unconscious material. But because many astrologers have no experience of analysis or of the unconscious, they do not know what is happening when these polarities are activated. And the puer is one of the most potent of activators, partly because it is his nature to stir the pot and generate change.

One of the themes on which Hillman spends some time in the *Puer Papers* is the fact that there is not only a puer-senex polarity; there is also a polarity within each end of this axis, a positive and negative puer and in turn a positive and negative senex. Astrologically we would of course understand this about any planet or sign—there is a positive and a negative dimension to Saturn, as there is to everything in the chart. So a more subtle polarity arises here, where the more one identifies with the wholly "good" side of the puer—the divine child, the redeemer, the bright creative spirit—the more the "bad" side of the senex is constellated in the form of the Terrible Father who stifles and crushes potential and destroys the spirit of change. In other words, if all one can see is the beauty of the puer, without his pathology, then all one can see is the ugliness of the senex, without his creative contribution. It works the same the other way around. If all one identifies with is the "good" senex, with his wisdom and patience and serenity and inner authority, then all one will experience of the puer is the callous, shallow, irresponsible, heartless and inconstant little bastard. We cannot help but react to someone where there is a big charge in the unconscious, and our value judgements are often brought out of us violently, unwillingly, and quite out of character when the client has polarised in these "good" and "bad" facets of the polarity. But we can make the effort to be aware of what is being constellated in ourselves, which in turn can help us to understand better the split in the client.

Audience: I am wondering whether the puer has anything to do with what psychiatry labels manic depression. I was thinking about a patient with whom I worked in a psychiatric hospital. He was absolutely delightful in many ways, and seems to reflect your description of the puer. But I always felt I had to restrain his thinking in some way, and inevitably I came away from all my meetings with him feeling very depressed.

Liz: If I take some liberties with orthodox psychiatric classifications, then I would say, yes, definitely, manic depression is bound up with the struggle and fluctuation between the puer and the senex. The flights of mania are very descriptive of the "positive" side of the puer, and it is a characteristic of these states that the individual feels immortal and capable of accomplishing anything. There is a sense of being the divine child, the gifted one who carries the message and can redeem humanity. But the manic dimension of manic depression is in many ways a defense against the reality of the individual's life. The mortal side of him or her—the instincts, the body, the negative feelings, the sadness and loneliness and pain of living—is anathema, because it is nothing but negative senex. Reality is experienced as only bad, and the depressive end of manic depression is like a bad caricature of a negative Saturn. It would be understandable that you would be infected by that unconscious senex in the patient, and that you would wind up carrying his depression, which he cannot face. That is what I mean by countertransference. He has escaped into the eternal world of the puer, while you and the hospital staff are left to tend to the demands of his corporeal self; and you are pushed, unwillingly, into having to experience the terrible darkness of his life as though it were your own.

Audience: But I'm not very Saturnian. I have no aspects between Saturn and my Sun or Moon or ascendant.

Liz: You don't have to be Saturnian to be infected by someone's unconscious. In fact, if you were more Saturnian, perhaps you might have understood better what you were carrying. But probably there is something of the puer strong in you, yourself, and so your patient's unconscious senex side triggers your own. The more unconscious we are of these issues within us, the more powerful the effect another person has on us. You have illustrated very nicely what I have been saying. I wish we could see the two charts together, to see how they trigger each other. What happens between two people when the dynamic of the puer and the senex is set loose is a very fraught business. Archetypes have a way of taking over, and in a person who has slipped over the edge, where the ego has been altogether swamped—what we would call psychotic—the archetypal background has become more powerful than the conscious personality. When a person walks around in such a state, the unconscious in other people is strongly constellated. It's like a nuclear chain reaction. These things begin to bounce back and forth within families, between partners, and certainly in hospital wards, where everyone, including the doctors who believe themselves to be sane and rational, is infected. And certainly as astrologers, we, too, are contaminated by these archetypal constellations in our clients.

We have an enormous amount to learn from these unconscious reactions between people. For example, the figure of the puer tends to constellate a curious reaction in many woman, which I have already alluded to. If a woman is strongly aligned with the maternal face of the feminine—and this might be reflected in the chart by, for example, many planets in Cancer and Taurus, or a dominant Moon or Neptune or Pluto—then the response to the puer is very potent and very ambivalent. On the one hand, the figure of the puer is usually very unconscious in such women, for identification with the archetypal mother usually involves a lot of self-sacrifice and living for and through others. Sometimes one sees this unconscious puer side represented by a 7th house Uranus, or by the Sun or Venus square Uranus. The puer is entirely too selfish and uncommitted and cold to be allowed expression in such a woman's life. But often he proves irresistibly attractive to her when he appears as someone else—in the guise of an actual lover or husband. Yet at the same time that he enchants, he also arouses a deep antagonism, and a desire to possess and perhaps even castrate and destroy. This emotional response is also often quite unconscious, although the man usually feels it all too clearly. The puer has extremely sensitive antennae to the smell of suppressed sulphur. The puer can invoke great anger in women, because he belongs ultimately to the realm of the father-spirit, and what a maternal woman has to offer him may be needed, but is often devalued by him. So he makes women feel innately rejected because they are women, and some women who are unaware of the dynamic in themselves—the unconscious animus who despises their instinctuality—react to this by taking revenge. They don't just clip the puer's wings, they pull them out feather by feather. If one is unconscious of all this going on, then what hope can one have of conscious choice or objective perception?

Likewise, the very maternal woman arouses strong ambivalence in the puer. If the puer is the astrologer—which is all too often the case—and a female client comes along who seems to embody this maternal principle, then the astrologer can be easily pushed into the unconscious negative side of the puer, which devalues and tries to injure what is seen as a predatory and devouring Great Mother. Yet the puer is fascinated by the figure of the archetypal mother, for she is the earth and water he needs so badly and the compassion he longs for to ease the pain of his isolation. Yet she is also Death to him.

Some clients make us quite angry for no apparent reason, and we do not always find the answers to this in a conventional synastry exploration of the two charts. Often we must look for archetypal dynamics such as puer-senex and puer-mother. If we are unaware of this level of interaction, then one day a client comes along who is very airy and boyish and infuriating, and suddenly one finds oneself thinking, "He's behaving as if my feelings don't exist." And all at once one has taken the archetypal dominant as a personal insult. That is when one is liable to slip, and come out with the really destructive remark in retaliation.

Audience: What happens if someone suppresses the puer, and lives almost entirely in the senex?

Liz: A number of things can happen. Traditional astrology phrases these things as a kind of fate—for example, the way in which difficult Uranus aspects are interpreted in the old textbooks: "You will be the victim of sudden separations, accidents, and so on." One way in which the unconscious puer forces his way into consciousness is via other people leaving us, or through sudden events such as accidents where we have unconsciously lost control. The puer also has his reflection in somatic problems, because every archetype can become an illness if it has nowhere else to live. Because the puer is in part airy, we might associate his negative somatic expression with problems connected with breathing and the lungs, such as asthma. Also, I would look at nervous problems such as twitches, tics, and stammers. One of the more interesting manifestations I have seen is vertigo, which feels very much like mountain sickness—the effects of climbing too high.

On an emotional level, the denial of the spirit, which is really what the denial of the puer is about, often ends up with quite a violent eruption in middle life. This is probably better than getting sick, although it often wreaks havoc with one's work and one's family life. It is a sad and classic tale when the puer breaks out at the age of forty. There are endless films and novels which address this theme, about the responsible family man or woman who suddenly reverts to a mad adolescent love affair that blows everything apart. Depending upon who is doing the writing, the story usually ends with a sadder but wiser senex, or a free and finally happy puer. John Fowles is a novelist who appears to be preoccupied with this theme; you meet a similar character repeatedly in novels such as *The Magus*, the apparently committed man who meets the youthful anima and enters a chaotic and enchanting world. This is a problem of the unlived puer, and there is one level on which the puer almost inevitably breaks out—the romantic level. That ultimately the puer is concerned with a spiritual quest is not immediately apparent in such cases, because the erotic feeling clouds the issue so much. In cultures which encourage early marriages and early families, I think this is a characteristic dilemma. It is very common on a certain social stratum of English life, where a man goes to public school and has little or no opportunity to get to know women, where he has been subjected to a senex system all his life which demands appropriate social behaviour, and where he marries young before he has travelled or experienced much of anything. These men, who have never been able to be irresponsible, obstreperous, idealistic, promiscuous adolescents, fall into terrible trouble in their forties. And sadly, one can understand it all too well, although the puer usually catches the label of the callous, heartless bastard.

Another characteristic explosion of the puer is a sudden religious conversion, which often has all the hallmarks of the unconscious erupting because it frequently contains a kind of blind gullibility which can exercise no discrimination over a guru or a set of spiritual or religious precepts. A spiritual search made with some consciousness is a highly individual journey, and ultimately the experience of the numinous is an inner and intensely personal confrontation. But when the unconscious puer erupts into consciousness, one joins a movement. One goes off sex because it is "lower," and decides to save humanity. And often at such times one can fall into the hands of a charismatic spiritual leader or teacher whom no senex in his or her right mind would consider as possessing any real inner authority.

Audience: This sounds like it has something to do with Uranus coming into opposition with its own place.

Liz: It does. Uranus, as we have seen, has quite a lot to do with the archetype of the puer. I think that the coincidence of Uranus opposite Uranus and Saturn opposite Saturn reflects a time when the dilemma of the puer and the senex hits some individuals very hard. Depending upon what one has been doing with it until then, it can be a devastating time when the unconscious erupts and destroys everything one has been working for. In individuals where the puer-senex polarity is a major issue in life, one or the other can be seen to rise up and begin to take over the life. But this period can also be immensely exciting and invigourating, a time when one reaps the rewards of all the efforts one has made at trying to balance the eternal youth and the old man. Although the Uranus-Uranus opposition and the Saturn-Saturn opposition do not always exactly coincide—sometimes there is a year or two in between the two—the entire period is coloured by the puer-senex polarity, and it is often a time when creative inspiration and hard work really come together and yield great fruits. But sadly, for many people it is a time of great disillusionment and heartbreak as well, because one realises one has only been living half of oneself, and many opportunities have been lost that will never be able to be reclaimed.

TWO EXAMPLE CHARTS

We can now look at an example chart which has been contributed by someone in the group. Would the person who gave me this chart care to give us a little background on it first?

Audience: This is one of my astrological clients. He is a man of forty-three. The problem he came to see me about was difficulty in

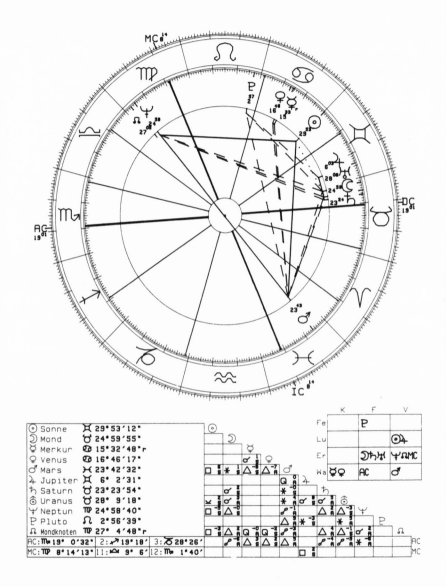

Chart 7. Puer example A. Birth data has been withheld for confidentiality. Chart calculated by Astrodienst, using the Placidus house system.

relationship. When he first arrived at my house I thought he was wearing fancy-dress. He had on a smart jockey cap and a very stylish little anorak, and ski boots and colourful hand-knitted mittens. I thought to myself, "Who is he kidding?" but then I realised that this was his normal way of dressing. He is highly intelligent, and very much stuck up in his head. He told me that he had a terrible relationship with his mother, and that from the age of three he always got into endless trouble demanding to have his own way and running away from home. He would climb through fences and ditches and hedges to get out, and was extremely rude to his mother because he hated her. He is a brilliant computer man, but had just left his umpteenth job. First he told me he had resigned, but then he forgot that he had said this, and later mentioned that he had been sacked. He kept going on about how life begins at forty-two. He can do anything he likes, and can do it in his own time. He may go to Australia, or to the south of France. He will always have enough money to do what he likes. I had several interviews with him after the initial reading, because we decided to turn the astrologer-client relationship into a counselling situation. Gradually I began to see how he was spinning a fantastic web of future fantasies. I began to realise that he didn't really wish to change at all, despite the fact that he had apparently come to me for help. I became angrier and angrier, and felt I was being manipulated. We finally ended the counselling on a very antagonistic note. Everything you were saying about the puer brought this client back to me very strongly, and I thought it might be helpful if we could look at his chart in the group.

Liz: May I first ask if any of you has any initial impressions of the chart? (See Chart 7.) Don't try to pick it apart—just look at it and see if anything leaps out and strikes you.

Audience: There is a lot of water in this chart. Scorpio is rising, Mars is in Pisces, and Mercury and Venus are in Cancer. There is also a lot of earth. The Moon, Saturn and Uranus are in Taurus and Neptune is in Virgo. That's a total of seven planets plus the ascendant and the midheaven in earth and water. It doesn't sound at all like the description you gave earlier of the puer, where earth and water are weak in the chart.

Liz: I quite agree, the chart when one first looks at it doesn't seem to describe the puer at all. So what conclusion would you draw from this? The behaviour certainly sounds rather archetypally puer.

Audience: Maybe this is what you meant by a "fake" puer. I can only think that his man has flown up into a mythic mode of behaviour because he can't cope with his own sensitivity.

Liz: Again I would agree with you. There is only one planet in fire here, and that is Pluto—so we can hardly call him a fiery type. The Sun and Jupiter are in Gemini, but they are outweighed by the rest of the chart in earth and water. Something has gone terribly wrong here. It is almost as though the figure of the puer, who might ordinarily be an important but nevertheless only partial feature of this individual's personality, has run amok and taken over the whole thing, so that aspects such as the Moon-Saturn conjunction in Taurus in the 7th house cannot express at all. This man is not expressing his whole personality; he is expressing a collective unconscious figure because I would guess that his ego is damaged and weak, and cannot cope with the challenges life might bring him. So the archetype has come in and taken over the stage entirely. What do you think he is running away from? Emotional sensitivity, yes; but I think there is more to it. We can be more specific.

Audience: I keep noticing the emphasis on the 8th house. If I were him I would run away from that too. The Sun, Venus and Mercury are all placed in the 8th.

Liz: I have observed several interesting things about people with the Sun in the 8th house. In one sense, we might interpret this placement as a statement that the individual needs to make a relationship with the hidden world, the unconscious, in order to fulfill himself or herself. The destiny or purpose in life—which I think is very bound up with the Sun's house placement—here lies in bringing light into the dark world of the Other within oneself. But as you will no doubt realise, this is much less fun than having the Sun in the 5th or the 9th. Such a life task is daunting to many people, especially since we are not socially or culturally equipped to give any value to the realm of life that the 8th house governs. A Gemini in particular is not constitutionally comfortable in this domain. Who wants to dig tunnels, unless he or she is forced to? So I have noticed that 8th house Suns often skate across the surface of life for a long time, doing everything possible to avoid confronting the compulsions and mysteries that lie underneath. Some 8th house Suns are forced to make that confrontation very early in life, and they are much healthier for it in the long run, although at the time usually everyone else thinks they are crazy. But many don't, and they seem to be cheerful, superficial extraverts, rather than deeply insightful people who have looked the unknown in the face. Usually one dose of it in early childhood is quite enough, and they have never been near it since. I have also found this characteristic in many Scorpios, and the subject of our discussion has Scorpio on the ascendant as well as the Sun in Scorpio's natural house. So it seems clear that the depths are his appointed place of journeying, and it also seems clear that he is running hard and fast to avoid having to take up the challenge of his own individuality.

Another thing which I associate with the 8th house is that the act of probing it inevitably brings one into confrontation with the family inheritance—particularly the erotic and sexual dynamics within the family. Because this is the house of the Other, the inner partner, herein lie all our incestuous dreams and fantasies, and all the sexual issues from childhood that have never come into consciousness. There is often a heavy family inheritance with a strong 8th house, as though it is the individual's task to make conscious those energies which have been suppressed by the parents and which threaten to destroy unless they are dealt with. I think emphasis in all the watery houses connotes family baggage, and the 8th is sexual family baggage in particular. So part of what this man is running from is the problem of his sexuality, his violent feelings, his incest fantasies, the issues which bind him to his mother and father, his parents' marriage, and so on. Being a Gemini, he is not comfortable in this world, because Gemini is a romantic and an idealist, and has a lot of the puer in it; even though the Sun's house placement and the sign on the ascendant demand that he explore it anyway.

Audience: I think we should talk about this mother whom he says he hates.

Liz: Yes, we will inevitably wind up with her sooner or later. All roads lead to her, as they do to Rome. This is no doubt part of the family baggage reflected by the Sun in the 8th. Also, Scorpio on the ascendant, reflecting the experience of birth itself, suggests that this man's entry into the world as a baby was met with something less than enthusiasm. I believe the ascendant reflects, among other things, the atmosphere surrounding the birth—the archetypal theme which initially represents what life is going to be about—and often the state of the mother and the mother-child bonding in the first weeks of life can be seen in the ascendant and any planets conjuncting it. Scorpio rising suggests a dark and difficult experience, as though in entering life one is confronted with death or despair on some level.

Audience: I keep looking at the Moon's aspects in relation to the mother. The Moon conjuncts both Saturn and Uranus. Even though it forms a trine to Neptune, and a sextile to Mars, I think the Saturn-Uranus conjunction suggests a very difficult experience with the mother.

Liz: I would agree. On the one hand this man needs his mother badly, and idealises her. I think that behind what he calls hatred is a very deep and mutually possessive attachment, because he has Venus in Cancer and also because the Moon trines Neptune— both of which suggest to me that he was unusually receptive to his mother's emotional needs and probably very naturally affectionate and wanting a lot of close contact with her. The presence of Neptune in the 10th also suggests an enormous idealisation, as though he saw her surrounded with light, something like the Virgin Mary, a figure of great pathos and suffering. But the Saturn-Uranus conjunction to the Moon contradicts the image of Neptune, and poses a double message. I think this mother was herself not very loving, although she may have given the impression of sacrificing herself in the name of love. It is the man's capacity for lovingness that has got him into such trouble. Moon-Saturn often reflects the experience of a very dutiful mother, especially when it is in earth as it is here—the mother who does all the right things, cares physically for her child, is responsible and reliable in the eyes of society. But there is a coldness in it, as though it were all being done by the book. And Moon-Uranus suggests a mother who might perhaps not have wanted a child at all, or found the task of mothering restrictive and stifling. The experience of the mother with Moon-Uranus contacts is one of lack of trust and reliability;

there is always the deep unconscious fear that any minute she will explode into breakdown or departure, and leave one abandoned. I think this is because on some deep level the mother really feels like that, secretly wishing she had never got trapped by having a child in the first place. I believe this man's hatred springs from a terrible feeling of rejection and abandonment which he is not really permitted to face because the Moon-Saturn tells him she did her best for him, and the 10th house Neptune in trine to the Moon reflects his idealisation of and pity for her. He cannot face the full force of his love and need for her, and the pain of being unwanted by her at the same time, so he must cut off his own feelings and hates her instead. Then he is naturally doomed to live in his head, because if he comes down to earth and begins to lift the lid of those feelings which are tucked away in the unconscious, then he must face very black and violent emotions, and a great deal of grief and sense of betrayal. Can I ask the person who worked with him, what your own reactions to him were? You saw him regularly for quite some time.

Audience: I felt extremely depressed. Occasionally I felt that he trusted me for about five minutes. I also realised that he couldn't trust any woman.

Liz: Did he express any feeling of why he didn't trust you, or what he was afraid you might do to him?

Audience: It was never verbally expressed. I don't think he knew that he couldn't trust. I picked it up on an instinctual level. The superficial relationship between us was friendly at first, and at times he was surprised at my non-judgemental attitude. He used to tell me about the dreadful things he'd done, and I could see that he was expecting me to say, "Oh, how could you have done such an awful thing?" But when I just nodded and didn't react, he was quite shaken. Maybe he expected me to be a critical mother, or maybe he projected his own guilt onto me and wanted me to give voice to it. But I felt him offering tremendous resistance to anything that might have made him look at reality. He kept trying to goad me, by saying he was leaving all the time.

Liz: I am sure you responded in the best possible way, by not responding. He was certainly trying to fit his Moon-Saturn-Uranus onto you, so that you could censure and reject him. Then he could respond by rebelling against you, as he did against his mother. But of course it is his own earth, his own senex that he rebels against, and the senex is a stronger component in his nature than the puer is. I do think that this is a puer manqué, a sort of fake puer. Gemini is one of the puer's favourite signs, and there is a bright, clever and spirited quality to him—it seems to come out in his intellectual brilliance as well as in his personal eccentricity— but it isn't strong enough to dominate the chart in the way the puer seems to dominate the man's personality. The Sun square Neptune can also suggest certain facets of the puer, because of Neptune's mystical longing and the rather Dionysian and ecstatic qualities that the planet reflects; but once again, there is too much earth in the chart which ought to be grounding that vision. If the man were able to live what he is, he might blend the creative imagination of Sun-Neptune with what is essentially a solid and sensual nature.

Audience: What about the Sun square Mars? There is a T-cross there, between the Sun, Neptune and Mars.

Liz: I think Mars is part of what the puer cannot integrate. Mars is full of anger and aggression, neither of which are comfortable in the puer's refined and spiritual world. The puer doesn't like Mars. The Scorpionic side of Mars, its "night house," is too hairy and sweaty. The Sun square Mars seems to reflect a problem of integrating aggression and anger. I am sure that this instinctual aggression is part of the stew on which he keeps the lid tightly closed, and probably it is part of what he learned very early in life was intolerable for his mother. She must have been carrying a fair pack of anger and aggression herself, and probably made it clear, subtly if not overtly, that such feelings were unbearable and unfair to inflict on her. Neptune is in many ways more favourable to the puer than Mars, because of its transcendant dimension. With any T-cross, I think you will find that two of the planets gang up on the third one, but the third one is not necessarily the one at the peg of the T-cross. This is why I am uncomfortable with the "formula" way of reading a T-cross.

Every aspect we look at seems to underline and back up why this man has such difficulty in living what he innately is. One cannot be earthy without facing the fact that one carries anger and aggression and primitive desire. Although Mars does not rule an earthy sign, he is earthy in the sense that he is instinctual. In myth, the war-god Ares was born from Hera without male seed, so he is a fatherless god; he emerges straight from the instinctual realm without a shred of spirituality in him. He is male, but chthonic. And Mars in Pisces is extremely sensual and, in a sense, very easily seduced—all the more because of its aspect to Neptune in this chart. Once again I am struck by the feeling that all his sexual and emotional needs were attached to a mother who rejected and manipulated them. The flight into the puer's realm is really his only way of escaping his pain.

Audience: I keep puzzling over the conjunction of Venus and Mercury. That pair forms no aspect with anything else in the chart. And they are in Cancer, which suggests a very sensitive and vulnerable emotional nature.

Liz: I would agree with you. Venus in Cancer potentially implies a great depth of feeling and sensitivity to the feelings of others. It also needs closeness and intimacy, and cannot bear detachment and distance. But the problem, as you say, is that they are unaspected. I think an unaspected planet is rather like a tenant in the basement of the house, whom one doesn't know about because one is so busy living upstairs. The emotional needs of Venus in Cancer—and I don't think Mercury here interferes with its habitually analytical bias, because it is in Cancer also, and I would think that Venus softens Mercury and suggests a highly imaginative and fantastic cast to the mind—are going to be largely unconscious in this man. Like the secret tenant in the basement, Venus in Cancer goes about its own business in the unconscious, so there is a trigger-point here of enormous vulnerability. If it ever erupts, then your client will be swamped by emotional needs which, because they have been unconscious for so long, are likely to be extremely infantile and regressive and dependent. I think that on some level he is absolutely petrified of becoming too attached, because then Venus in Cancer—expressing in an archaic and unsophisticated way—would land him in a situation of complete powerlessness. If one is that dependent, then one can be terribly, irrevocably hurt. I think this is what has probably happened between him and his mother. I would guess that somewhere within, he has a great capacity for devoted love—don't forget the tenacity and constancy of the crab—and once upon a time he fixed this devotion upon a mother who used it to manipulate him into good behaviour so that he would not be too much of a demand on her. He cannot risk this ever happening again, so it is completely repressed.

Of course sooner or later something is going to constellate that Venus-Mercury conjunction by progression or transit. Then the hidden tenant in the basement suddenly smashes through the floorboards and materialises in the living room. Life will eventually catch up with this man. Nothing dies that has not been lived out, and Venus in Cancer has not been lived out since childhood. Also, I suspect that the Scorpio ascendant, which is in a sense "in league" with the Venus in Cancer, is part of what he fears as well. That ascendant implies that he is a person with very powerful passions and an enormous capacity for immolating himself on the altar of the beloved. One of the ascendant rulers, Mars, is in Pisces, another watery sign, and all of these—the Venus-Mercury, Mars, and the ascendant—form a grand water trine. This adds up to the picture of a man who is tremendously vulnerable because he feels so deeply and so intensely, and the whole of his heart and his erotic feeling tends to get bound up with one person. The beloved is everything. It is not so surprising, when you look at this dimension of his personality in juxtaposition with what he has apparently experienced through his first beloved—the mother— that he would fly up into the puer's realm and live almost exclusively from his Gemini Sun. One can see how his own temperament, conjoined with his childhood, has produced a unique set of complexes. Here is someone in whom the figure of the puer is undeniably present—suggested by the Sun in Gemini—but who also has great need of relationship and also need of a stable, secure situation both in general and in partnership. This is, in potential, a lovely combination, for the warmth of the water and the solidness of the earth could provide an extremely likeable and loyal base for the brilliance and lightness of the Gemini Sun. But I think this man has suffered heartbreak in childhood, through giving so much of himself to a mother who was capable of doing nothing but using it, and who needed to feed off him to supply something she herself was lacking. So he is deeply damaged, and the chart has split in half, with the watery side slipping into the unconscious and the archetype of the puer formulating as the only possible path of salvation from pain.

I also think it is relevant that the experience of the father is shown in the chart to be a disappointment. The father is weak, or absent. Perhaps he was kindly, and charming, but unable to provide strong male support to help his son grow away from the mother. I am interpreting this from the square between the Sun and Neptune, and also because of the placement of Mars in Pisces in the 4th in opposition to Neptune. There is opposition marked here between the parents, and the man has effectively been used as a football between them.

Audience: He described his father as a kindly, generous, tolerant man.

Liz: When the father is presented in the chart as Neptunian, that is often the way he is experienced. Planets which aspect the Sun describe a good deal of what kind of psychological inheritance is culled from the father, and here Neptune is one of the significators. But the Sun is also square Mars, and Mars is in the 4th house, which relates to the experience of the father. Once again there is a double message, as there was with the mother. I would guess from the T-cross of Sun-Mars-Neptune that the man's father was saddled with exactly the same dilemma as his son. This father probably sat on a lot of repressed anger and violence, but was not sufficiently strong enough to fight the mother. I think the Scorpio ascendant in this chart would give your client a peculiarly sensitive nose for the unconscious undercurrents in the family background, and I would guess that on some level he sensed his father's buried rage and feared it. He has taken the side of the mother unconsciously, although in consciousness he hates her and thinks his father is lovely. Naturally any emotional openness to another person would mean that all the rage would come pouring out, even before the neediness and dependency. How did the work with him progress? What happened when you didn't respond to his provocation?

Audience: I just kept feeling angrier and angrier.

Liz: I think you were having to carry his anger, completely unconscious in him, but fobbed off on you, subtly and unknowingly. His anger took the form of thwarting any efforts you made to help him, so you are the one left feeling furious, manipulated and impotent, which is probably exactly the way he feels inside, and must have felt toward his mother. That is what is meant by countertransference. I think that you dealt with him in the only way possible. He was offloading all his rage against his mother on you, in that subtle and unconscious way. Not reacting is probably alien to your own nature, however, and you weren't really conscious of what he was doing to you. Non-reaction is a remarkably good analytic technique when one is up against this kind of unconscious problem. Eventually something happens, because the anger flies back home again. The more orthodox psychoanalytic methods advocate this way of working, because eventually it smokes out the complex, and the client begins to experience his or her own feelings at last. But you must be conscious of the dynamic at work, because merely pretending that you are not angry does no good. He has in fact provoked the desired response in you, even if you act as though he hasn't.

Audience: Perhaps that is where I couldn't deal with it. I did start letting my anger show in the end, because I couldn't handle my own feelings. But that orthodox analytic style is uncomfortable for me. Perhaps this man would have been better off in more structured analysis.

Liz: I don't know. I suspect he is much more deeply disturbed than at first appears, because of the strength of your reaction as well as what I would see as an almost total dissociation from huge chunks of his own psyche as represented in his horoscope. Maybe you are right, but I am not sure. This is a schizoid problem, and perhaps counselling alone is not really sufficient when someone is that dissociated, except on a practical level. But you may have given him more than you realise, because you were truly non-judgemental. That must have got through somehow, someplace.

Audience: Would it be right to say that when the puer is "genuine" as opposed to being a defense mechanism, he expresses a kind of celebration of life, a truly joyous spirit? In this man there doesn't seem to be any of the real sparkle and effervescence of the puer. He sounds very compulsive.

Liz: I think you are right. This is not a joyful puer. One often finds, when the chart is really aligned with the spirit of the puer, that whatever the person's failings, there is a lovely sparkle and infectious excitement about life. This man is not really a good vessel for the spirit of the puer, except in part. But he has too much sense of responsibility and too much emotional depth. The puer has become his unconscious defense against pain. That is why he keeps saying that life begins at forty-two. He wants very badly to believe that himself, but it sounds more like his inner experience is that it is ending. That is why there is no joy in it, despite the exotic clothes and so on. There is a lack of fire in the chart, and the intuition is not a naturally strong function.

I would also guess that, despite the potential suggested by the emphasis in earth, he has great problems with his body. He wants his sexuality back, but his mother still possesses it. She has never been a safe container for him, so he is not likely to have any real sense of safety in his own body. I think a love and harmonious acceptance of the body springs from a good sensual bond with the mother at the beginning of life. That can offset even a complete lack of earth in a horoscope. It is very difficult to care for the body in a loving, tolerant way if it has been treated with repulsion by somebody else, which is what I think has happened to him, judging by the Moon-Saturn-Uranus conjunction. So he internalises this attitude, and treats his body with the same contempt, although he no doubt would argue with this since he apparently takes care to dress interestingly and show himself off. But that is narcissism, not love of the body.

Audience: I finished working with him by my own choice. He didn't ask to finish, in spite of his threats to leave; I did. I felt a wave of despair, because we seemed to have made some headway and then he went off to do some late skiing and came back and we were at square one again. I can see from all you've been saying that I let his own unconscious despair overcome me. He must feel incurable and unhelpable.

Liz: It is sad, but I don't think the fault lies in your counselling skills at all. And maybe if you had stuck it through, you might have seen some fireworks. The transits across his chart are very interesting right now. Neptune was transiting in opposition to the 8th house Sun at the time you finished working with him. I think something was probably opening up in him, and had been for some time. Perhaps the despair you felt was the beginning of his own despair rising to the surface. I think that working with a man like this, who is really what would be called borderline—living at the edge of a psychosis—is no joke. You did extremely well with him, and very likely he would wear almost anyone down. I think he probably needs to break down, and perhaps you sensed that and knew you might not have been equipped to see him through it. We learn a lot through clients like this. Here I think we can all see very clearly how the archetypal figure of the puer becomes the only thing to which the man can cling in order to avoid slipping down into the hell of his feelings. It is a negative expression and use of the puer, but it is what a lot of people do. I suspect the transit of Neptune was activating great unconscious despair and a feeling of incipient disintegration. This is precisely what he needs to experience, but it infected you, as it would anyone with whom he worked.

It is not uncommon to begin to feel quite hopeless about a client with this kind of split. This is what they feel like inside, but they cannot dare feel it, because it is suicidal, so the therapist must carry it for a time. It's a hell of a job. That you were infected is not a reflection of your lack of skill or insight, but perhaps you were just not conscious enough of whose despair it really was, and what its emergence was signaling. On the other hand, you might not have wanted to work with him in a disintegrated, regressive state. That really needs more structured analysis, three or even four times a week. He was heading for something frightening. Probably if you had stuck it through, and been able to sit with your own depression and despair, he would have fled himself rather than face what was coming to the surface. An outer planet transiting the Sun can be very heavy indeed when there is so much unconscious in a person. And Saturn was also moving through his 12th house and approaching his ascendant, which is another indication of some deep change occurring within him. I think the Saturn transit reflects what Melanie Klein calls the depressive position—the taking back of negative projections, and the dawning realisation of one's own darkness and badness.[6] Perhaps you helped him more than you realise, because when these

---

[6]See Melanie Klein: *Love, Guilt and Reparation* (New York: Free Press, 1984; and London: Hogarth Press, 1981); *The Psycho-Analysis of Children* (New York: Free Press, 1984; and London: Hogarth Press, 1980); *Envy and Gratitude* (New York: Free Press, 1984; and London: Hogarth Press, 1980). For those who find Klein's clinical terminology daunting, try: Hanna Segal, *Introduction to the Work of Melanie Klein* (New York: Basic Books, 1980; and London: Hogarth Press, 1978), 67.

transits have finished with him I think all the work which now seems to you wasted will have built up a kernel of something inside him and perhaps helped him to cope better. It may begin to occur to him, when Saturn reaches the ascendant, that the failure of the therapy was his failure rather than yours, and that he, himself, drives people away. Saturn in his birth chart is placed in the 7th house, which means that its transit of the ascendant will raise 7th house issues. When one is trying to understand the meaning of a transit, one should always look at the house in which the transiting planet is placed natally. So Saturn over his ascendant will bring home some heavy truths about the way in which he relates to other people.

Perhaps he needed to be rejected by you, so that he can see how he makes it impossible for anyone to relate to him. That is also a 7th house Saturn; it is the person himself or herself who is the rejecting one, but it keeps coming back through others who seem to do the rejecting. Sooner or later he must face the issues behind his own lack of relatedness. You might find that he comes back into counselling eventually.

Audience: This chart reminds me of several other charts which I have done, where the character of the puer comes across very strongly, but where the placements you earlier described as belonging to the puer are not much in evidence. But there is often a strong Pluto or a lot of Scorpio in these charts.

Liz: I have seen many of them as well. It is almost as though there were two quite different manifestations of the puer—one where the chart is a true home for this archetypal figure, and one where the chart is full of deeply instinctual, sensual and turbulent qualities which are incompatible with the person's life experience and perhaps with some other isolated factor in the chart. It has occurred to me that this might also illuminate the marked difference in tone between the puer as described by von Franz and the puer as described by Hillman. The negative expression of the puer tends to be much more in evidence when he is expressed as a collective unconscious figure through a birth horoscope which is not really suited to him. One feels somehow uncomfortable with such a person, as though there were a nasty edge somewhere, something not really genuine in all that flying and fun and games. The creative dimension of the puer is much more in evidence when the chart provides a comfortable home for him, although of course then the problem of the senex immediately arises as well.

But Scorpio is a frequent factor in these—what shall we call them, pseudo-puer?—charts. There's a new piece of jargon for you. The Zurich Institute will be up at arms. I have met, as I said before, many Scorpio men who behave like fake Geminis or Sagittarians. Often they are not very fiery or airy at all, but running in terror from their own deep natures, because Scorpio belongs to the realm of the Great Mother, and it is not easy to be a man and be bound to such a myth while still maintaining one's sense of manhood and potency. The puer is a kind of replacement for a father, because often the personal father is effectively nowhere to be seen, psychologically if not physically. So the puer reaches upward toward heaven, hoping that God the Father will come and rescue him from the talons of the Dark Mother.

Audience: Do you think that a man like this example would do better working with a male therapist?

Liz: It's hard to say. Sometimes that is advisable, but it is a bit like asking whether it's better to reach Rome from Venice or Milan. Either way, one gets there. A male therapist will constellate the issue of the missing father, and can often provide a model and experience of good male relationship which strengthens the ego and helps the client to feel stronger and therefore more capable of confronting his inner chaos. A female therapist would constellate the issue of the powerful mother, and might provide a model and experience of a woman who has good mothering to offer—genuine unconditional acceptance—rather than conditional love and manipulation. But that is a generalisation too, because there are women therapists who are not motherly at all, and whose gifts lie more on the cerebral and intuitive level; and they might find it difficult to stay with the heavy atmosphere this man generates. And there are men therapists who have a strong feminine side, and who might back off from the aggressive confrontation which this man would eventually raise toward another man. We can see from the example that a woman therapist would get the client's Moon, with all its aspects, projected onto her, and if one looks at the condition of that Moon sandwiched between Saturn and Uranus, then one can get further insight into why she felt such anger and despair. That is also how the mother must have felt, burdened with a child who perpetually provoked her. Here the therapist literally acted out, and experienced, the client's Moon. We also need to consider that where the puer is a strong factor in a man's psychology, he will often avoid close relationships with other men—unless they are homosexual relationships, or father-substitutes—but will prefer the company of women. This is the boy in him, the charmer who gets on better with feminine company because he can be seductive, whereas with a man who is a peer he will feel antagonistic and inferior, and therefore contemptuous. Such a man will often choose a woman therapist anyway, thinking that on some level it will be easier to seduce her—literally or figuratively. Perhaps we can now look at another example chart.

Audience: I have a chart here which I would like to discuss. I will try to describe something of the man's background. His parents were trapped in a terrible marriage. The mother had an affair with another man for seventeen years without the husband ever knowing about it. My client was expected to support his mother in this all through his childhood, keeping the secret from his own father.

He couldn't seem to make any relationships at all with women later, and eventually decided he was happiest as a homosexual. He was a very successful estate agent for a time, and made a lot of money at it. He became successful quite early, and went on supporting and taking care of his mother, who eventually divorced the father. Then, when he was twenty-four, he had some kind of shattering peak experience. It was a religious experience, and he went to pieces. He remained more or less in pieces for several years after that, in and out of hospital, and when he came to see me he had got himself on the dole and was in a severe depression and had just attempted suicide. He came to me, not only for a chart, but also for psychotherapy. The psychiatrist who had been treating him after his suicide attempt warned me off, suggesting that I would never be able to do more than help him to live a little longer.

In fact he has done extremely well in the therapy, and it has been the spirit of the puer which has emerged. I think he had always lived out the senex: being a little old man carrying his mother's dirty secrets, then taking care of her in his father's place, becoming successful in the world, being dutiful and loyal, never really rebelling or breaking free except in his sexual preferences—

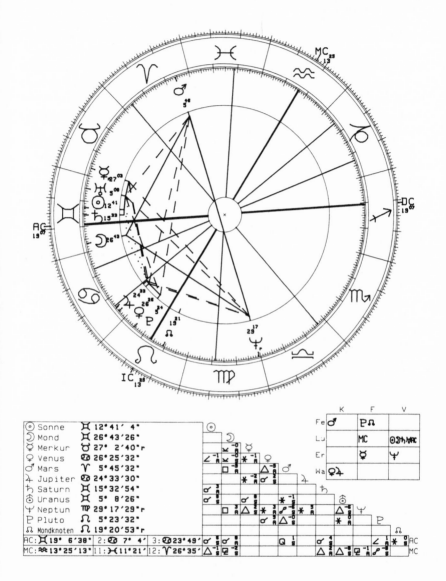

		K	F	V
Sonne	☿ 12° 41′ 4″	Fe ♂	P ☊	
Mond	☿ 26° 43′ 26″	Lu	MC	☉ ☽ ♄ ♅
Merkur	♉ 27° 2′ 40″ r	Er	☿	Ψ
Venus	♋ 26° 25′ 32″	Wa ♀ ♃		
Mars	♈ 5° 45′ 32″			
Jupiter	♋ 24° 33′ 30″			
Saturn	☿ 15° 32′ 54″			
Uranus	☿ 5° 8′ 26″			
Neptun	♍ 29° 17′ 29″ r			
Pluto	♌ 5° 23′ 32″			
Mondknoten	♌ 19° 20′ 53″ r			

AC: ☿ 19° 6′ 38″   2: ♋ 7° 4′   3: ♋ 23° 49′
MC: ♒ 13° 25′ 13″   11: ♓ 11° 21′   12: ♈ 26° 35′

Chart 8. Puer example B. Birth data has been withheld for confidentiality. Chart calculated by Astrodienst, using the Placidus house system.

the one rebellion against his mother or against women—and again in his breakdown. I think the creative spirit was completely suppressed in him, and the peak experience was a kind of pure puer breaking through from the archetypal realm. Even though it has taken him a long time to pull himself together, the religious experience has been the thing we have built on. I particularly wanted to look at the chart in relation to my own, because there are some peculiar synastry combinations. My ascendant, which is in 19 Gemini, is conjuncting his Saturn, and my Uranus is conjuncting his Moon.

Liz: Your ascendant conjuncts his Moon as well as his Saturn, and your rising Uranus also conjuncts his Moon. All right, we'll deal with the synastry shortly. I would first like to look at his chart more closely. (See Chart 8.) Also, I would be interested in what was happening in terms of transits across his chart at the time of his peak experience and subsequent breakdown. This, you say, occurred when he was twenty-four, so it would have been in 1967, when Uranus and Pluto were moving through the second decanate of Virgo. The Uranus-Pluto conjunction would have been squaring his Sun-Saturn conjunction. So the outer planets are here again constellating a profound change, and awakening what seems to be an essentially spiritual nature, repressed because of the bondage to the senex—the bondage to Saturn, which conjuncts the Sun in the birth chart.

Perhaps this man is more truly aligned with the archetypal figure of the puer than our previous example, who is also a Gemini. Here the Sun-Uranus conjunction suggests that the figure of the puer might be very powerful on an inner level, because Uranus is the primal god of heaven and the whole feeling of the planet is an upward ascent away from the instinctual world into what Plato called the world of Divine Ideas. This chart is much airier than the other. The Moon is also in Gemini, and Mars is in Aries, quite different from the Piscean Mars we saw before, because it is much freer and less subservient to feeling states and moods. Here Capricorn is rising, and the motif of the puer-senex dilemma is repeated in the juxtaposition of the signs Gemini and Capricorn, where it is also stated in the solar aspects to both Uranus and Saturn. This Saturn-Capricorn component does seem to reflect what you have been saying about him—that he became responsible at such a young age, and crushed his own spirit in order to father his mother. This is also the depression which he fights. I think this chart is much more of a true example of the archetypal youth and old man weaving their tale.

Audience: One day he came for his session dripping wet. It seems that he had saved a little boy from drowning in the Thames. Everyone else had been standing about on the bank, shouting, "Help!" but doing nothing, and he jumped straight in and brought the boy out.

Liz: What an interesting symbol. I am always awed by the way in which people act out in concrete terms what is happening inside them. I suppose in some sense his therapy has also been an act of saving the youthful spirit from drowning forever in the unconscious. I think we should look at some of the other factors in the chart, before we consider the synastry. This is a much better integrated chart than the other one, although the other at first glance seems fortuitous because of all the trines in water. Here Venus, in conjunction with Jupiter, is linked with other planets, rather than sitting isolated and unaspected. I am particularly thinking of its sextile to Mercury. The capacity for relationship is closer to consciousness, not so split off and threatening. It seems as though the aspects to the Sun, particularly the Sun-Saturn conjunction, are really a good description of what he has been struggling with. Saturn is unaspected apart from its conjunction, but the Sun is in sextile to Mars and Pluto. So once again there is better integration, because the more instinctual and aggressive side of the personality has a better possibility of being brought into the sphere of consciousness because of those sextiles. I wonder whether the unaspected Saturn says something about his inability to defend himself against his mother. If Saturn is operating unconsciously, then one lacks boundaries and a true sense of self-sufficiency. When Saturn is the secret tenant in the basement, then one is unable to make contact with one's survival capacities, one's ability to be alone and self-sufficient. In some ways we might be so bold as to suggest that this man lived much of his life as a kind of "fake" senex.

Audience: What about the Mars-Neptune opposition? This is the same as in the other chart, although here it is in Aries and Libra. He was on drugs for some time, along with everything else.

Liz: I would associate the drug problem much more with the Sun-Saturn than with the Mars-Neptune. Mars-Neptune builds fantasies, and it is vulnerable and seduceable; aggression dissipates itself through the feelings. But I don't think that in itself Mars-Neptune drives one into drugs. I know that is what the books say, but I have usually found a Sun-Saturn problem where there is a drug or alcohol problem, and I think it is because drugs or alcohol seem to ease the pain and frustration of the Sun-Saturn. Sun-Saturn can be very tough and wonderfully resilient, and your client reflects these qualities in his struggle to pull himself together. But often the early part of life is desperately lonely, and there is nowhere to go and no one to tell it to, because no one can be trusted and no one seems to be on one's side. I have found that there are Saturnian addicts and Neptunian addicts, although it takes more than Mars-Neptune to produce a true Neptunian; and their motivations for addiction are quite different. Neptune cannot cope at all with reality, and it is the puer who drinks or takes drugs to prolong the illusion of his immortality and eternal youthfulness. But Saturn sees too much of reality, often too early, and life seems a dreary and lonely place, devoid of meaning. So the senex, too, can drink and take drugs, because what is the point anyway? I think it is the latter which presses on this man, and has driven him into using drugs.

Audience: But what is it in the chart that would suggest that my client would be in such an utter mess for such a long time? The first chart seems clearly much more difficult, what with the unaspected Venus and the difficult lunar aspects. But that man is up and walking and seems to be having quite a good time.

Liz: I don't think you will find the answer to that in the chart. In many ways this is a better integrated chart from the point of view of the emotional and instinctual side of life being more accessible to consciousness. But Sun-Saturn-Uranus is no easier than the Moon-Saturn-Uranus we saw in the other chart. On the other hand, not every Sun-Saturn-Uranus breaks down and spends years in and out of psychiatric hospitals. In part, the chart has to be put in context with the environment. You saw how we considered this in relation to the first chart. But I think that these two men have reacted to their pain and difficulties in opposite ways. The first man has split off from himself, and that seems, in the eyes of society, to be more "normal," because one is not immediately aware that there is anything wrong. The second one has bled in public, had the breakdown which labels him as "sick," so we assume that he is in worse shape. I am not so sure about that.

We might also look at the childhood situation more closely. There are people with very difficult charts who have had at least a little love and support even in the midst of a problematic family; and somehow the psychic glue holds together. The environment has a powerful effect on the inherent nature reflected by the chart, just as the chart will respond to and interpret the environment in accord with its own nature. In some people the chart seems quite harmonious, but the betrayal in early life is so brutal, or so difficult for that particular nature, that a little pressure from life snaps the thread. Certainly the experience of this man, dragged into a betrayal of the father and cut off from the archetypal patriarchal principle which is so important for his Capricorn ascendant to model itself after, is one of the worst things that could have happened to him in particular. Beatings and screaming rows are kindergarten stuff compared with the subversion of love, loyalty, and reality which such a scenario generates. The environmental pressures here seem to have exacerbated the problem of the Sun-Saturn to such an extent that nothing else in the chart had a chance to develop. This places a lot of responsibility on the parents, and we all know that the perception of the parents is already embedded in the chart from the moment of birth. But I think it is possible to be too fair and psychologically sophisticated. What this mother did was not an unconscious sin of omission, as was the case with the first example. It was a sin of commission, and it is difficult to understand how a mother could not see what this might do to a child. Maybe that in part accounts for some of the difference. I don't really know. I think in the end there is a deeper factor at work. Who knows why some people are stronger than others, or have more consciousness? The first man seems better adjusted, yet he could not receive help, and runs away from his potential psychosis by driving the therapist into her own craziness. The second falls into psychosis, but because he can break, he can also heal. Which is better after all?

Perhaps we can examine the cross-chart aspects now. You say that your ascendant and Uranus conjunct his Gemini Moon and Saturn. The ascendant is in part a symbol of the presence and personality of the individual—the myth that he or she carries. In a way, you have been portraying for him what it might feel like to be a Gemini who is not burdened by Saturn. You have helped him to connect with the positive side of the puer—what he really is in essence—but what he has been unable to express because of all that Saturnian senex weight he has been carrying. Without trying, and perhaps without even realising it, you probably embody for him some of the bright spirit which he caught a glimpse of through his peak experience, but you embody it in a human form, and can therefore help him not only to validate it, but also to see how it might be part of ordinary life. It is as though you are telling him, tacitly, that it is really all right for him to be a Gemini, an irresponsible, frothy and upwardly mobile airy spirit. I think it is also important that your ascendant conjuncts his Moon as well as his Saturn, because this means that on some level you touch his inner feminine nature. He can in turn project onto you the qualities of his kind of good mother—one who does not burden him with terrible secrets and heavy responsibilities, but who can just talk to him and be his friend and allow him to breathe. Do you know what was occurring in his chart by way of transits during the time he was seeing you?

Audience: He came to me twice a week for a period of about three years. Uranus was transiting in Scorpio in opposition to his Mercury in Taurus. It also crossed his Scorpio midheaven.

Liz: The Uranus transit across the midheaven is quite interesting in context of what we have just been talking about. Since the midheaven represents, among other things, the relationship with the mother, the nature of the psychological inheritance from her, the transit of Uranus suggests that some separation from her through insight was beginning to take place. I have found that major planets moving across the midheaven often mean the untying of the umbilical cord, although often the surface effects appear in the sphere of work or vocation. One has to dig deeper to discover just how an individual's expression in society is bound up with the experience of the mother. What we meet in the mother at the beginning of life is what we meet later in the world, for mother and world are, at an archetypal level, the same. The contribution we feel compelled to make in the world is in many ways an expression, in concrete form, of that archetypal dynamic which we experienced via the mother. So something was evidentally happening inside him, freeing him from the burden of the old man which he had to be for his mother. You turned up in his life at the right time. It is a great mystery how these things work.

The psychiatrist who treated him could not help him at all, but also it seems it was not the right time for him to be helped, because he was not yet ready to lay down the burden of his mother's projection onto him. So he could allow you to reach him, your ascendant touching his Moon, at a time when the relationship with the personal mother—represented by the Scorpio midheaven with all its implied undercurrents of power and emotional possession—was undergoing a change. His mother forced him to father her, to replace what she had apparently needed both from her husband and her lover. His own father was apparently unable to rescue him, but then, what sort of man remains blind to a wife's seventeen-year-long love affair? This is what your client was forced to carry. He probably accepted the projection because he has Capricorn rising and a Sun-Saturn conjunction, and there is a deeply responsible and loyal side to him, along with the spiritually potent puer. It is not surprising that the eruption of the spiritual experience should have fragmented him, because that was the beginning of a sense of self, or Self, emerging. The separation from the mother probably began when his natal Sun was squared by the Uranus-Pluto conjunction, and completed when it transited the midheaven.

I think that in some ways these transits are very important to consider in terms of therapy, because with our first example, in a sense the therapy was premature. The movements reflected by the transit of Neptune in opposition to the Sun, and the Saturn transit approaching the ascendant, occurred only at the end of the therapy; and this may help to describe why nothing seemed to be occurring in the therapy itself. But in this case, some movement was already reflected. It started with the peak experience, when Uranus and Pluto squared the Sun, the symbol of a sense of individual selfhood. The very rigid identification with Saturn, the senex principle, started to crack at that time. A transit from Uranus or Pluto or Neptune will often release what is trapped in the unconscious, and this alters the personality in an irrevocable way. It is impossible afterward to go backward to where one has been before. This is particularly true of Pluto transits. Even though this man's development manifested first as a breakdown of a prolonged kind, this was perhaps necessary because the entire ego structure which he had built was false. It was a kind of patchwork job to become someone his mother wanted, rather than the organic development of a real self. It had to be broken down because it only allowed half his personality expression, and something more inclusive was needed. Often the unconscious will do this when the personality structure is not viable because it has been formed in a narcissistic way, to please the parent. If an entire system of defenses has been erected on a weak foundation, then the unconscious will erupt sooner or later and knock it over and start again. This kind of breakdown is really the beginning of a breakthrough, and can ultimately be immensely healing, because at last the Sun, the real identity, can struggle out from under the tyranny of Saturn. Thus you have what you described as the puer emerging— the Sun conjunct Uranus in Gemini, with its lofty spirituality and idealism and vision. The other chap will probably break, too, one day, because his adaptation to life is also false, and he has had to amputate most of his chart. But such breakdowns do not always occur at a time and on a level which are accessible. I hope that when the time comes, the man in Chart 7 has the courage to bring it back into therapy, instead of working it out through the body breaking down, or in some self-destructive fashion like falling off a mountain.

Audience: Could you comment on the relationship of the puer to homosexuality? It seems to me that in the gay world, the cult of youth and beauty suggests the dominance of the puer archetype. This man is gay.

Liz: I think there is some relationship between the archetype of the puer and male homosexuality, and it probably lies in the flight of the puer away from the instinctual world of the Great Mother. Many of the archetypal qualities of the puer are, as you say, strongly in evidence in the gay community, although they are also strongly in evidence in most spiritual movements as well, and do not necessarily imply a sexual level of meaning. The puer's flight upward toward the spirit can sometimes mean repudiation of one's biological fate—in the case of a man, to father children. It is also, on a symbolic level, a seeking of the spiritual father in concrete form—finding one's essential male self through the medium of the body of another man. And it is a way of retrieving one's masculinity from the grip of the mother. All these things may come into it, although I think there are probably a great number of varied threads behind what we call homosexuality, some of which might spring from emotional damage and fear, some from a powerful identification with an archetypal figure which is not in itself pathological. It would depend, I think, on the individual gay man. In this man's case he has found a viable alternative to the power of the mother. We can see that he is, of course, not going to be overly inclined to trust women, given the situation with his mother. And she has willfully separated him from his own masculine initiation by forcing him to betray and lose respect for his father; so he must find that initiation in some other way. The lack of a father, reflected by the Sun's conjunctions to Saturn and Uranus, might also suggest that he seeks the experience of a more loving and benign father through another man, since Saturn and Uranus imply some difficult and negative associations with the personal father. And there is also the archetypal craving for purity of spirit which Uranus embodies. In myth, Ouranos rejects his children because they are ugly and made of earth. All things of the body belong to the realm of the mother, and the beautiful male body, as the Greeks envisaged it, was pure and clean and free of those dark secret recesses in which a man might drown, or be castrated or dismembered.

We can see that the puer-senex dilemma finds a suitable home in this horoscope. The preponderance of air suggests it, along with the conjunction of the Sun and Uranus, which is certainly as strong as the Sun-Saturn; and they are in Gemini as well. Also, the house placement is suggestive. The Sun is in the 5th house, which is the house of the child, of play, and spontaneous creative expression. So his journey will lead him into the necessity of developing the childlike spirit in himself, the Leonine sense that it is sufficient for him to be himself rather than feeling, like the senex, that he must work for the air he breathes. It seems that he is beginning, with your help, to integrate these opposites, and it will be interesting to see where he directs his energy in the future.

These charts are very good examples of working with the dilemma of the puer aeternus. We can see that for the first, the puer is a kind of dissociated escape from the individual's bodily and emotional reality, while for the second, the puer is the light shining at the end of a long, dark tunnel—the promise of hope and meaning. I hope you can all see also from the discussion of these charts that it is not a simple exercise of finding the puer in the chart. I do not think one can take the great archetypal dominants such as the puer and the senex and make tight, sharply drawn equations between them and astrological factors. But one can get a feeling about certain horoscope placements, which may have a flavour of a particular archetypal dilemma or story. In a way, this is using psychological material to amplify the astrological picture so that we can see a living dynamic at work in the chart, rather than a fragmented listing of character qualities. The theme of the puer is not necessarily that relevant for everyone in the same way. For those people in whom he dominates, consciously or unconsciously, then we must understand about the archetypal figure, because we can see what the individual is doing with his or her chart—where certain placements have fallen into the unconscious, and what might be needed for a better balance and a more integrated life.

Suggested Reading

The Stages of Childhood

Erikson, Erik. *Childhood and Society*. New York: W. W. Norton, 1964; St. Albans, England: Triad Paladin, 1977.

Grof, Stanislav. *Realms of the Human Unconscious*. New York: Dutton, 1976; and London: Souvenir Press, 1979.

Houston, Jean. *The Possible Human*. Los Angeles: Jeremy Tarcher, 1982.

Janov, Arthur. *The Feeling Child*. New York: Simon & Schuster, 1975; and London: Abacus, 1973.

Klein, Melanie. *The Psycho-analysis of Children*. New York: Free Press, 1984; and London: Hogarth Press, 1980.

Sasportas, Howard. *The Twelve Houses*. Wellingborough, England: The Aquarian Press, 1985.

Whitmore, Diana. *Psychosynthesis in Education: A Guide to the Joy of Learning*. Wellingborough, England: Turnstone Press, 1982.

Wilber, Ken. *The Atman Project: A Transpersonal View of Human Development*. Wheaton, IL: The Theosophical Publishing House, 1980.

Winnicott, D. W. *Playing and Reality*. New York: Methuen, 1982; and Harmondsworth, England: Penguin, 1984.

The Parental Marriage

Jung, C. G. *The Collected Works of C. G. Jung: The Archetypes and the Collective Unconscious, No. 9, Part 1*. Princeton, NJ: Bollingen Series, Princeton University Press, 1968; and London: Routledge & Kegan Paul, 1959.

Neumann, Erich. *The Child*. New York: Hodder & Stoughton, 1973.

———. *The Great Mother: An Analysis of the Archetype*. Princeton, NJ: Bollingen Foundation, Princeton University Press, 1955; and London: Routledge & Kegan Paul, 1955.

———. *The Origins and History of Consciousness*. Princeton, NJ: Bollingen Foundation, Princeton University Press, 1954; and London: Routledge & Kegan Paul, 1954.

Wickes, Frances. *The Inner World of Childhood*. New York: Appleton-Century, 1966.

Subpersonalities and Psychological Conflicts

Ferrucci, Piero. *What We May Be*. Los Angeles: Jeremy Tarcher, 1982; and Welllingborough, England: Turnstone Press, 1982.
Greene, Liz. *Relating: An Astrological Guide to Living with Others*. York Beach, ME: Samuel Weiser, 1978; and Wellingborough, England: The Aquarian Press, 1985.
Marks, Tracy. *The Astrology of Self-Discovery*. Reno: CRCS Publications, 1985.

Puer and Senex

Greene, Liz. *Saturn: A New Look at an Old Devil*. York Beach, ME: Samuel Weiser, 1976.
Hillman, James. *Puer Papers*. Dallas: Spring Publications, 1979.
Kiley, Dan. *The Peter Pan Syndrome: Men Who Have Never Grown Up*. New York: Dodd Mead, 1983; and London: Corgi Books, 1984.
Samuels, Andrew. *The Father*. London: Free Association Books, 1985.
Stroud, Joanne and Thomas, Gail. *Images of the Untouched*. Dallas: Spring Publications, 1982.
Von Franz, Marie-Louise. *Puer Aeternus*. Boston: Sigo Press, 1981.

ABOUT THE CENTRE
FOR PSYCHOLOGICAL ASTROLOGY

The Centre for Psychological Astrology provides a unique work-shop and professional training programme designed to foster the cross-fertilisation of the fields of astrology and depth, humanistic and transpersonal psychology. The programme includes two aspects. One is a series of seminars and classes, ranging from beginners' courses in astrology to advanced seminars in psycho-logical interpretation of the horoscope. The seminars included in this volume are representative of the latter, although the same seminar is never given verbatim more than once because the con-tent changes according to the nature of the participating group and the new research and development which is constantly occurring within the field of psychological astrology. All these seminars and classes, both beginners' and advanced, are open to the public. The second aspect of the programme is a structured, in-depth, three-year professional training which awards a Diploma in Psychologi-cal Astrology upon successful completion of the course. The main aims and objectives of the three-year professional training are:

- To provide students with a solid and broad base of knowl-edge both within the realm of traditional astrological symbol-ism and techniques, and also in the field of psychology, so that the astrological chart can be sensitively understood and interpreted in the light of modern psychological thought.

- To make available to students psychologically qualified case supervision along with training in counselling skills and tech-niques which would raise the standard and effectiveness of astrological consultation.

- To encourage investigation and research into the links between astrology, psychological models and therapeutic tech-niques, thereby contributing to and advancing the already existing body of astrological and psychological knowledge.

The in-depth professional training programme cannot be done by correspondence, as case supervision work is an integral part of the course. It will normally take three years to complete, although it is possible for the trainee to extend this period if necessary. The training includes approximately fifty seminars (either one-day or short, ongoing weekly evening classes) as well as fifty hours of case supervision groups. The classes and seminars fall broadly into two main categories: astrological symbolism and technique (history of astrology, psychological understanding of signs, planets, houses, aspects, transits, progressions, synastry, etc.), and psychological theory (history of psychology, psychological maps and dynamics, survey of counselling skills and techniques, psychopathology, mythological and archetypal symbolism, etc.). Case supervision groups meet on weekday evenings and consist of no more than twelve people in each group. All the supervisors are both trained psychotherapists and astrologers. Each student has the opportunity of presenting for discussion case material from the charts he or she is working on. At the end of the third year, a 15,000-20,000 word paper is required. This may be on any chosen subject—case material, research, etc.—under the general umbrella of psychological astrology. Many of these papers may be of publishable quality, and the Centre will undertake facilitating such material being disseminated in the astrological field.

Completion of the in-depth professional training course entitles the trainee to the Centre's Diploma in Psychological Astrology. The successful graduate will be able to apply the principles and techniques learned during the course to his or her professional activities, either as a consultant astrologer or as a useful adjunct to other forms of psychological counselling. Career prospects are good as there is an ever-increasing demand for the services of capable astrologers and astrologically oriented therapists. In order to complete the professional training, the Centre asks that all students, for a minimum of one year, be involved in a recognized form of psychotherapy with a therapist, analyst or counsellor of his or her choice. The rationale behind this requirement is that we believe no responsible counsellor of any persuasion can hope to deal sensitively and wisely with another person's psyche unless one has some experience of his or her own.

The seminars included in this book are part of the fifty or so workshops offered by the Centre. Previous volumes in the Seminars in Psychological Astrology Series are *The Development of the Personality*, Volume 1, *The Dynamics of the Unconscious*, Volume 2, and *The Luminaries*, Volume 3. Volume 5, *Through the Looking Glass*, edited by Howard Sasportas, was transcribed from lectures given by Richard Idemon at a conference he gave with Liz Greene in Vermont in August 1985. The Centre's seminars are never repeated in precisely the same way, as the contributions and case material from each individual group vary, and as there are constant new developments and insights occurring through the ongoing work of the seminar leaders and others in the field.

Liz Greene co-founded the Centre with Howard Sasportas in 1982. Together they successfully ran the programme for ten years. The tragic death of Howard Sasportas in May 1992 has been a great blow to the whole astrological world. However, due in large part to Howard's work and effort, the structure and purpose of the Centre have over the last decade proven themselves to be sound. The school will continue to offer its unique contribution to modern astrology, now under the co-directorship of Liz Greene, a Jungian analyst, and Charles Harvey, a full-time consultant astrologer, who has taught for the Faculty of Astrological Studies since 1967 and has been President of the Astrological Association of Great Britain since 1973.

If the reader is interested in finding out more about either the public seminars or the in-depth professional training offered by the Centre, please write to:

Centre for Psychological Astrology
BCM Box 1815
London WC1N 3XX
England

Your request for information should include a stamped, self-addressed envelope (for United Kingdom residents only) or an International Postal coupon to cover postage abroad.